THE CANNONS ROAR

[THE] CANNONS ROAR

FORT SUMTER AND THE START OF THE CIVIL WAR

AN ORAL HISTORY

BRUCE CHADWICK

PEGASUS BOOKS
NEW YORK LONDON

THE CANNONS ROAR

Pegasus Books, Ltd.
148 West 37th Street, 13th Floor
New York, NY 10018

First Pegasus Books cloth edition April 2023

Interior design by Maria Fernandez

Library of Congress Cataloging-in-Publication Data is available.

ISBN: 978-1-63936-339-1

10 9 8 7 6 5 4 3 2 1

Printed in the United States of America
Distributed by Simon & Schuster
www.pegasusbooks.com

For my late wife Marjorie

and for all the veterans of America's wars

CONTENTS

Main Characters

Political: North

Abraham Lincoln, President
James Buchanan, former President
William Seward, Secretary of State
Joseph Holt, Secretary of War, then Judge Advocate General
Simon Cameron, Secretary of War
Edward Bates, Attorney General
Montgomery Blair, Postmaster General
Gideon Welles, Secretary of the Navy
Salmon Chase, Secretary of the Treasury
Lyman Trumbull, Illinois Senator, longtime Lincoln friend
Ward Lamon, Lincoln envoy
Stephen Hurlbut, Lincoln envoy

Political: South

Jefferson Davis, President
Varina Davis, wife of Jefferson Davis
Alexander Stephens, Vice President
L. P. Walker, Secretary of War
Robert Toombs, Secretary of State
Francis Pickens, South Carolina Governor
William Gist, former South Carolina Governor
John Manning, former South Carolina Governor

Judge Campbell, Peace Commissioner
Martin Crawford, Peace Commissioner
Samuel Nelson, Peace Commissioner
Laurence Keitt, South Carolina Congressman
Louis Wigfall, Texas Senator
Robert Bunch, Great Britain Consul to Charleston
Edmund Ruffin, Virginia State Senator

Military: North
General Winfield Scott
Major Robert Anderson
Captain Abner Doubleday
Mary Doubleday, Abner Doubleday's wife
Wylie Crawford, Fort Sumter surgeon
Captain John Foster, at Fort Sumter
Sergeant James Chester, at Fort Sumter

Military: South
General P. G. T. Beauregard
David Jamison, South Carolina Secretary of War
Colonel Charles Simonton

Press: North
Horace Greeley, *New York Tribune*
Murat Halstead, diarist and author
Henry Villard, *New York Herald*

Press: South
Edward Pollard, *Richmond Examiner*
Robert Rhett Jr., *Charleston Mercury*

Foreign Press

William Russell, *London Times*

Civilians: North

Billy Herndon, Lincoln's former law partner

George Templeton Strong, New York lawyer and diarist

Charles Francis Adams Jr., grandson of President John Quincy Adams

Fanny Seward, daughter of Secretary of State William Seward

Helen Nicolay, daughter of Lincoln's secretary, John Nicolay

Wendell Phillips, abolitionist

Ralph Waldo Emerson, philosopher

Carl Schurz, Lincoln friend

Edmund and Joseph Halsey, New Jersey brothers who would later fight on opposite sides

Samuel Halsey, Edmund and Joseph Halsey's father

Katie Skillen, daughter of officer at Fort Sumter, age sixteen

Joshua Speed, Lincoln friend from Springfield

Civilians: South

Mary Chestnut, South Carolina socialite

Henry Ravenel, planter and botanist

Sarah Lowndes, wife of Charles Lowndes

Elizabeth Van Lew, Richmond

Reverend John Bachman

Robert E. Lee, Virginia planter and later head of the Army of Northern Virginia

Catherine Edmondson, wife of North Carolina planter

William Porcher Miles, Charleston politician and later Confederate general

Robert Gourdin, Charleston merchant

James Pettigrew, Charleston, Union sympathizer

Eliza Browne, Montgomery socialite

Catherine Thompson, wife of Jacob Thompson, US Secretary of the Interior, who resigned to join the Confederacy

Evelyn Ward, teenager from Tappahannock, Virginia

Emma Holmes, Charleston socialite

Mrs. A. M. Vanderhorst, Charleston socialite

Senator James Chestnut, husband of Mary Chestnut

William Haskell, one of the South Carolina Haskell brothers who wanted to enlist in the Confederate Army

PRELUDE

Blaming Major Anderson

March 4, 1861

Major Robert Anderson stood on the top of one of the walls at Fort Sumter, the unfinished federal military installation in Charleston Harbor, on the morning of March 4, 1861, and adjusted his spyglass. Once in focus, he found the moving figure of General P. G. T. Beauregard, his old student and close friend at West Point (Beauregard graduated second in his class in 1838), directing hundreds of Confederate troops. They were hauling heavy black cannons over roadways and winding dirt paths that cut through groves of palmetto trees to sites on the two islands across the harbor on either side of the island on which Sumter sat. Every day there were more troops. The dashing, well-dressed, handsome General Beauregard, with his neatly trimmed moustache and elegant goatee, the scion of a wealthy New Orleans French Creole family, had made a good impression on Charlestonians as soon as he had arrived in the city earlier that week. Beauregard had seen action in the Mexican War, serving as an engineer, and was a former superintendent of West Point. He was a colorful figure and adored by Charlestonians. "He is the hero of the hour," gushed one woman.

Beauregard commanded six thousand busy Confederate and South Carolina state soldiers, and more of all shapes and sizes walked into his camp each day from all over the South. Anderson, from his elevated perch over the calm blue waters of the harbor, watched Beauregard's every movement as he prepared his army for a possible bombardment of Fort Sumter. The Union major and his rival believed they soon might face off in the very first battle of the Civil War.

The road to Fort Sumter began with the election of Republican Abraham Lincoln as the nation's sixteenth president in November 1860. Southerners were certain that Lincoln, who took office with a Republican-controlled Senate and House of Representatives, would eradicate slavery, and wanted no part of him and his government. South Carolina seceded from the Union on December 20, 1860, and six more states soon followed. South Carolina demanded that the federal government turn over Fort Sumter. Negotiations to do so had failed with President James Buchanan and had started anew with Lincoln, who took office nine weeks after South Carolina seceded. The South threatened to take the fort by force and had begun to surround it with troops from the new Confederate government's hastily formed army. In Washington, D.C., Lincoln and his Cabinet would soon debate what to do about the fort. Tensions grew.

Unlike the flamboyant Beauregard, Anderson was conservative. He was a by-the-book officer and did little without guidance from Washington. He was highly conflicted, too, because he was from Kentucky, a slave state, and believed in slavery, and was here at Fort Sumter supporting a new anti-slavery president's army. Torn between North and South, Anderson, father of five (and great-grandfather of actor Montgomery Clift), admitted "that my heart was never in this war." He brought his spyglass down to his waist but kept staring. He knew from the number and size of the cannons, including a substantial number of large, powerful Columbiads nestled into thick green groves of palmetto trees, that the fort could be taken in a day or two of heavy bombardment. He scoffed at Northern newspaper reports that said it would take six months to level the fort (the *New York Herald* even called Sumter "the strongest fort of its size in the world"). Anderson shivered in the chilly early morning March air.

On the day Abraham Lincoln was sworn in as president, Fort Sumter was an unfinished, odd-looking facility occupied by eighty-four officers and enlisted men, nineteen of them musicians, under Major Anderson. Ironically, one of the Unions lieutenants was Jefferson Davis—no relation to the new Confederate president. The men had fled Fort Moultrie, across the harbor from Sumter, undetected, on the night of December 26, 1860, six days after South Carolina seceded. Anderson thought the unfinished Sumter offered better protection for his garrison than Moultrie.

Sumter was a pentagonal facility that sat on a flat artificial island two and a half acres in size. It had been under construction since 1829. It had room for 135 cannons, but so far only forty-eight had been installed, and twenty-five of them were not pointed at the Confederates, but at Fort Moultrie. Anderson went to Sumter because of its guns and because its twelve-foot-thick red brick walls were an impressive sixty feet high. It was well out into the water and could be reached by any Union supply or troop ship arriving from the Atlantic Ocean.

Anderson had taken down his flag from the flagpole at Fort Moultrie and carried it with him to Sumter. Early the following morning, when the men were safely settled, he raised it to the top of a flagpole there. When Charlestonians awoke that morning and saw it, they were stunned.

The men, who were running out of supplies, worked at Sumter as the Confederate Army went about its business on shore. The Confederate general was under orders to prevent any Union reinforcements from arriving by sea and, if necessary, to bombard the fort. Every day his men stockpiled more and more cannonballs; they had hundreds already.

One of the Confederate officers preparing to fire on the fort, if need be, was Colonel Chanson, who helped to build Sumter. He told friends he was now worried that he had done too good a job and that the South would be unable to take the fort. A man who had toured Sumter before Anderson occupied it, Edward Ruffin, told friends that "it would be extremely difficult to be taken."

The Union soldiers who were stationed there in the winter of 1860–1861 remembered living conditions in the fort as very unpleasant. In addition to the lack of food, there was no mail, no lights, no real mess hall, the nights were windy, and the temperatures varied. "The fort . . . was a deep, dark, damp gloomy looking place, where sunlight rarely penetrated," said Captain Abner Doubleday, Anderson's second-in-command.

Inside the walls of Fort Sumter on that brisk March morning, Major Anderson found himself in a precarious situation. He had been forbidden to fire on the Confederate troops for any reason, and also to just give up if Confederate forces fired on him. "It is neither expected or desired that you should expose your own life, or that of your men in a hopeless conflict in defense of these forts. . . . It will be your duty to yield to necessity," wrote former Secretary of War John Floyd. That communiqué was one of the few anyone in Washington sent Anderson, and he had taken it upon himself to move to Sumter—something he did not want to do—in preparation for a possible attack.

Anderson started to mount more cannon, raising them to the tops of the walls with block and tackle and a derrick. The men bricked up open cannon embrasures that would not be used to hold guns, as well as all the windows in the brick walls. The fort had few cartridge bags, so the men's flannel shirts and socks were used for that purpose. The fort's main gate was repaired and buttressed with large sheets of black iron. A three-foot-thick wall was built in front of it. Sharpshooters in their blue uniforms were stationed atop the walls. To improve the defenses, Captain Doubleday cleverly strung together huge dry goods boxes at the top of the walls that stretched for a hundred yards.

The large Columbiad cannons presented the greatest problem because of their excessive weight. To lift them up to the third level of the fort, Anderson had their carriages cut away and used for blocks in the rather creaky block and tackle lifting process. Dozens of men hoisted two cannons up to the third level, where they were rolled into firing position to loud cheers from the troops. Each night after dinner, the troops took turns picking up and carrying the huge, heavy cannonballs to the third tier, step by slow step up the stairs, under the moonlight.

A trench was built outside the fort and several cannons were placed there, aimed at the Confederate artillery clusters. Anderson had several mines buried under the wharf—any soldiers who might charge over the roadway to attack would trigger an enormous explosion. More mines were placed under pyramids of stone on the esplanade, a promenade that was built outside Sumter's walls. Howitzers were then placed on each end of the esplanade so any invaders running on it could be fired upon. Ammunition was moved much closer to the guns for immediate use. Finally, there were the homemade hand grenades. Anderson had his men take all the shells they could find, no matter what their size, stuff them with gunpowder, and attach handles to them. In an attack, the men would then attach ropes to the handles and hurl the grenades at the enemy. He had no mortars so he strung four large Columbiad cannons together as a substitute. He filled one cannon with paving stones and prepared to blow it up, firing the stones all over the grounds to kill any invaders. A traverse was constructed in front of the south gate to block shells, and several rooms were converted into a hospital to care for the wounded in case of an attack.

Anderson used well the eighty-four men he had, and continually sent letters—unanswered—to the War Department suggesting they send him 10,000 to 20,000 troops to battle the enemy and defend Sumter properly.

The major was careful to avoid any dangerous or provocative situations. That had happened in mid-January when a United States Army supply ship, the *Star of the West*, had sailed into the harbor. There was a mix-up in signals. The Confederates fired on her, and Anderson, ever the cautious commander, did not fire back. The ship was forced to sail out of the harbor and disappeared. He did not want another questionable encounter like that one. As a result, one of the problems Anderson had at the fort was a very limited amount of food that he would have to ration if supplies did not arrive soon.

On shore, General Beauregard was keeping an eye on Major Anderson, his former professor at West Point, for whom he had great respect. Beauregard wrote of the Sumter commander, "In my opinion, a most gallant officer, incapable of any act that might tarnish his reputation as a soldier."

The Sumter drama was watched carefully from downtown Charleston, four miles away, by Mary Chestnut, the wife of former United States Senator James Chestnut, who resigned that post when South Carolina seceded. Chestnut had held numerous public offices in the state, and from 1858 until 1860 served as its senator. His father was one of the wealthiest men in America. He owned several plantations and 448 slaves. Chestnut Sr. did not permit James to run any of his businesses and never gave him or loaned him any money. Chestnut Jr. scraped by on a law office salary. His father lived to be ninety, long after the end of the war, and when hostilities ceased in 1865, James and Mary found themselves practically penniless.

She kept a thick, detailed diary filled with scenes that she described with great color and tension. She had mixed emotions whenever she peered out across the harbor to Sumter from her Charleston rooftop. She wrote of South Carolina's secession, "I felt a nervous dread and horror of this break with so great a power as the United States but I was ready and willing."

She was not alone. All Charlestonians talked about in the winter and spring of 1861 was if and when the Yankees would clear out of Sumter and very gracefully go home. The residents of the city wanted the Union soldiers, their horses, their luggage, their bugles, and, most of all, their damned flag, out of their city and out of the South.

They wondered—all of America wondered—if the dispute over Fort Sumter would end up in a battle and whether that fierce, fiery confrontation would set off a Civil War.

ONE

Washington, D.C., The White House

March 5, 1861

Shortly after 9, the newly sworn in President Abraham Lincoln arrived at his second-floor office in the White House to find Joseph Holt, the holdover Secretary of War from James Buchanan's administration, waiting. Holt looked nervous. He told Lincoln that Major Robert Anderson, the commandant at Fort Sumter, had just sent a dispatch saying he had only six weeks of food and supplies left and feared the worst from Confederate troops who now surrounded the fort on two nearby peninsulas. Anderson also told Holt he would need an army of 20,000 soldiers to hold the fort.

The first thing the new president did was get in touch with General Winfield Scott, the Commander of the United States Army—a huge, six-foot-five, portly man with stringy, curly white hair, the father of seven children—to see what he thought about this supply dilemma at Fort Sumter. Lincoln knew so little about Sumter that he constantly misspelled and mispronounced it, as he did in this letter to General Scott.

Abraham Lincoln

To what point of time can Major Anderson maintain his position at Fort Sumpter without supplies or reinforcements? Can you, now with all the means in your control, supply or reinforce Fort Sumpter within that time?

If not, what amount of means and of what description in addition to that already within your control, would enable you to supply and re-enforce the fortress within that time?

He did not receive a clear answer from General Scott.

General Winfield Scott, Commander of the United States Army
Major Anderson has hard bread, flour and rice for about . . . 26 days . . . and salt meat for about 48 . . . how long he could hold out cannot be answered with absolute accuracy.

Then Scott wrote another note to the president.

General Winfield Scott
I now see no alternative but a surrender . . . as . . . we cannot send the third of the men in several months necessary to give them relief. Evacuation seems almost inevitable . . . the worn out garrison [might] be assaulted & carried in the present week. . . .

As a practical military question, the time for succoring Sumter with any means at hand had passed away nearly a month ago. Since then, a surrender under assault or from starvation has been merely a question of time.

General Scott was seventy-four, sometimes fell asleep at meetings, and was a man whose prodigious dining was a source of great humor in Washington, D.C. Scott was having dinner at Wormsley's Hotel, a five-story hotel in Washington, as the Fort Sumter crisis started. The proprietor described Scott to a friend.

James Wormsley
The General looks worried in his mind. He doesn't talk as usual, but he eats, does the General. He eats powerful!

Four days later, on March 9, Lincoln summoned his Cabinet to his office in the White House to address the Fort Sumter crisis. Each of them, in one way or another, had been promised their Cabinet positions in exchange for their support of Lincoln at the 1860 Republican Convention in Chicago. The brand new president wanted their opinions on the Sumter issue before making up his mind on what to do. He went around the table, soliciting the view of each Cabinet member.

This was their second meeting on the Fort Sumter crisis. On March 6, they all met with General Winfield Scott, head of the Army, who had given them very secret and distressing news.

Gideon Welles, Secretary of the Navy

[Scott] told us he had taken the responsibility to order a small military force to Washington for the protection of the government and the public property and archives and that other troops were on their way from the West.

He [described the] perilous condition of the country, and of the difficulties and embarrassments he had experienced for months past, related the measures and precautions he had taken for the public safety, the advice and admonitions he had given President Buchanan, which, however, had been disregarded, and, finally, the apprehensions, perhaps convictions, that hostilities were imminent, and, he feared, inevitable. His statement was full, clear in its details, and of absorbing interest to those of us who were to meet and provide for the conflict now at hand.

Scott told the Cabinet members about Anderson's food and supplies shortage.

Gideon Welles

It became a question of what action should be taken and for that purpose, as well as to advise us of the condition of affairs he had convened the gentlemen present. The information was to most of us unexpected and there was on the part of such of us who had no intimation of the condition of things in Sumter, an earnest determination to take immediate and efficient measures to relieve and reinforce the garrison. But General Scott without opposing this resolution, related the difficulties which had already taken place and stated the formidable obstacles which were to be encountered. . . .

Any attempt to reinforce or relieve the garrison by sea, Welles opposed as impracticable. (There was a naval officer, Commander West, willing to try it, though.)

Gideon Welles

Many of the naval officers then in Washington and about the Naval Department, were of questionable fidelity. A number had already resigned and most of those who were tainted [by secession] had left the service.

A land attack with Anderson's requested 20,000 men was deemed impracticable by Scott, too. Mr. Seward, who made many suggestions or inquiries, had doubts and was evidently wholly opposed to any attempt at relief. The President, until decisive steps were finally taken, was averse to offensive measures and anxious to avoid them.

Lincoln listened long and hard to the opinions of all.

Gideon Welles

[President Lincoln] was satisfied that it was impossible to relieve and reinforce the garrison, the attempt would provoke immediate hostilities.

The President, though much distressed with the conclusions of the military officers, and the decisive concurrence of the Secretary of State in this conclusion, appeared to acquiesce in what seemed to be a military necessity but was not disposed to yield until the last moment, and when there was no hope of accomplishing the work if attempted.

Edward Bates, US Attorney General

I was astonished to be informed that Fort Sumter, in Charleston harbor, may be evacuated, that General Scott, General Totten and Major Anderson concur in the opinion that as the place has but 28 days provisions, it must be relieved, if at all, in that time, and that it will take a force of 20,000 men at least, and a bloody battle, to relieve it. For several days after this, consultations were held as to the feasibility of relieving Fort Sumter, at which were present, explaining and aiding, General Scott, General Totten, Commodore Stringham and Mr. G. V. Fox, who seems to be *au fait* in all matters in both nautical and military. The army officers and navy officers differ widely about the degree of danger to rapid moving vessels passing under the fire of land batteries. The army officers think destruction almost inevitable where the navy officers think the danger but slight. The one believes that Sumter cannot be relieved, even provisioned, without an army of 20,000 men and a bloody battle. The other (navy) believes that with light, rapid vessels they can cross the bar at a high tide of a dark night, run the enemy's forts and reach Sumter with little risk.

Gideon Welles

General Scott related the difficulties which had already taken place and stated the formidable objects which were to be encountered from the numerous and well-manned batteries that were erected in Charleston Harbor.

Some would later disagree with the military advice they received, but at the time, the Cabinet saw it as the only information they had.

Gideon Welles

It was a duty to defer to these military gentlemen whose profession and study made them experts, who had by long and faithful service justly acquired the positions they held, and who possessed the confidence of the country. [Lincoln was satisfied that] it was impossible to relieve and re-enforce the garrison. The attempt would provoke immediate hostilities and, if hostilities could not be avoided, he deemed it important that the Administration should not strike the first blow.

William Seward, Secretary of State

Assuming it to be possible to now provision Fort Sumter, under all the circumstances, is it wise to attempt it? It would be both unwise and inhuman not to attempt it. But the facts of the case are known to be that the attempt must be made with the employment of military and marine which would provoke combat and possibly initiate a civil war.

Seward reminded the Cabinet that history had shown that there is no one best policy that governs all circumstances—and that he had been telling Congress this for more than a decade.

William Seward

I learned early from Jefferson that in political affairs we cannot always do what seems to be absolutely best. . . . It seems to me that we will have inaugurated a Civil War by our own act, without an adequate object after which reunion will be hopeless.

When confronted by angry Southerners, Lincoln had backed off, telling them what they wanted to hear. Around this time Seward and Lincoln were trying to get the Virginia Secession Convention to abandon their idea of following South Carolina. Seward had a newspaper friend assure the convention chairman, George Summers, that if they stayed in the Union, Lincoln would agree to evacuate Fort Sumter.

Lincoln had a private meeting with several delegates from the Virginia Secession Convention while it was in session in late February. Its spokesperson, William Rives, told him bluntly that if he used force in any capacity at Fort Sumter, Virginia would secede from the Union, too.

Abraham Lincoln, walking directly in front of Rives

Mr. Rives! Mr. Rives! If Virginia will stay in, I will withdraw the troops from Fort Sumter.

After he left, Lincoln met with his secretary, John Hay, and told him what they had discussed.

John Hay, Lincoln's secretary

He promised to evacuate Sumter if they would break up their convention, without any row or nonsense. They demurred. Subsequently, he renewed the proposition to Summers, but without any result. The President was most anxious to avoid bloodshed.

Abraham Lincoln

A state for a fort is no bad business.

Lincoln had been courting Virginia since before his inauguration, with mixed results. The Force Bill, which would give Lincoln unprecedented powers if there was a Civil War, was stridently opposed by Congressman A. R. Boteler of Virginia.

Representative A. R. Boteler, Virginia

It served to deepen the impression that Mr. Lincoln was a kind hearted man, that he was . . . by no means disposed to interfere, directly or indirectly, with the institutions of slavery in any of the states, or to yield to the clamorous demand of those bloody-minded extremists, who were then so very keen to cry "havoc" and "let slip the dogs of war."

The president persisted with the Virginia politicians. On April 4, he asked Summers to send a representative of the state legislature to the White House for a peace conference. Summers sent John Baldwin.

John Baldwin
Mr. Lincoln received me very cordially, and said he desired to have some private conversation with me. He started through to a back room, opening into another room, but we found two gentlemen there engaged in writing, he seemed to think that would not do and we passed across the hall into a small room opposite. And through that into a large front room. He had locked the door and . . . drew up two chairs and asked me to take a seat.

Lincoln reiterated his offer to evacuate Sumter if Virginia remained in the Union.

John Baldwin
That will never do under heaven . . . Mr. President, I did not come here to argue with you. . . . I tell you before God and man that if there is a gun fired at Sumter, war is inevitable.

As early as March 21, some Southern leaders were telling friends that there would be a war.

William Browne, future Confederate Secretary of State
I am still confident we shall have a collision.

Judah Benjamin, future Confederate Secretary of the Treasury
We have almost certain intelligence of an intention to reinforce Fort Pickens [in Florida], and that is of course war, and must be treated by us at all hazards.

Seward then sent Lincoln an astounding note.

William Seward, to Abraham Lincoln
What do you think of George Summers for Justice of the Supreme Court?

Abraham Lincoln, to William Seward
No!

From the start, there were squabbles in the Cabinet over Fort Sumter and Seward.

Gideon Welles
Mr. Seward, who from the first had viewed with no favor any attempt to relieve Sumter, soon became a very decisive and emphatic opponent of any proposition that was made; said he had entertained doubts and the opinions and arguments of Major Anderson and his officers, confirmed by the distinguished military officers who were consulted had fully convinced him that it would be abortive and useless.

The President, though much distressed with the conclusions of the military officers, and the decisive concurrence of the Secretary of State in those conclusions, appeared to acquiesce in what seemed to be a military necessity but was not disposed to yield until the last moment.

Edward Bates
[Welles's] earnestness and indignation aroused and electrified the President that the abandonment of Sumter would be justly considered by the people, by the world, by history, as treason.

It annoyed many members of the Cabinet that the President held Seward, his Secretary of State, in such high regard. Lincoln thought Seward an experienced lawmaker, popular with the people, and so did not want to offend him. An example of this popularity was displayed in the recent presidential campaign. When Seward arrived in Chicago to give a speech for Lincoln, a long parade formed for his carriage that was attended by tens of thousands, and soon the crowd surged across the street, halting Seward's travel.

Reporter, *Chicago Daily Democrat*

It was only after a severe struggle that the police were finally able to clear a passage for Gov. Seward, accompanied by General Nye and Mayor Wentworth, for the carriage to the hotel entrance. . . . The vast assemblage broke into a shout of welcome, which echoed like the voice of many waters through the streets.

Seward's campaign tour for Lincoln became legendary. He began in Michigan and the welcome received there was matched elsewhere.

Michigan reporter

[He was greeted with] cannons, brass bands, and processions of torch bearing "Wide Awakes" (young Lincoln supporters). . . . They created a circus atmosphere at Republican rallies, surrounding the perimeters of crowds and marching in meandering, illuminated processions.

Charles Francis Adams Jr., grandson of President John Quincy Adams, accompanied Seward on the tour and admired the way the parades were set up, with bands, marchers, and carriages carrying candidates for every office, and then Seward in his carriage.

Charles Francis Adams Jr.

All of this reminded me of a menagerie where each of the beasts, beginning with the lion, is passed in review before a gaping crowd.

Seward's speeches were not only memorable, but each, in every city, was different—unlike the standard stump speeches of the day. The mercurial Seward thrived on the noise of the crowd and appeared at home.

Charles Francis Adams Jr.

The early morning sun shone on Seward, wrapped in a strange and indescribable Syrian cashmere cloak, and my humble self, puffing on our morning cigars.

Seward, in fact, never appeared so well as at home. He walked the streets exchanging greetings with everyone. [He created] an impression of individuality approaching greatness.

Reporter, *Chicago Press and Tribune*

[Seward's arrival was] a day ever memorable in the political history of our state . . . [streets] alive with people, the pioneer, the back woodsman, the trapper, the hunter, the trader from the Red River.

Eyewitnesses to the parades wrote laudatory letters to Seward's wife, Frances.

Richard Blatchford, friend of the Sewards

I am sure you must be most happy. He has shown throughout a depth of power, eloquence and resonance of thought and mind, which we here who know him so well, are not a little taken aback by.

After Lincoln's election, the London journalist who found the president so ugly saw Seward as an American king.

William Russell, *London Times*

A subtle, quick man, rejoicing in power . . . fond of badinage, bursting with the importance of state mysteries.

Seward was acting like he, and not Lincoln, had been elected President. He seemed to be everywhere in the White House, shaking hands with all, and gave rousing speeches to visiting state delegations, such as Lincoln's home state of Illinois.

William Seward, to the Illinois Delegation

I implore you to remember that the battle for freedom has been fought and won. Henceforth, forget that freedom was ever in danger and exert your best influence now to save the Union.

Despite Seward's insistence on evacuating Fort Sumter, the other Cabinet members continued this discussion with the president.

Salmon Chase, Secretary of the Treasury

The attempt to provision is to include an attempt to reinforce for it seems to be generally agreed that provisioning without reinforcements notwithstanding hostile resistance, will accomplish no beneficial purpose. If the attempt will so inflame civil war as to involve an immediate necessity for the enlistment of armies, I cannot advise it. . . .

Simon Cameron, Secretary of War

It would be unwise now to make such an attempt. . . . I am greatly influenced by the opinions of the army officers who have expressed themselves on the subject and who seem to concur that it is perhaps now impossible to [help] the fort substantially if at all.

Montgomery Blair, Postmaster General

[I am] in favor of provisioning that fort. To the connivance of the late administration it is due alone that this rebellion has been enabled to attain the present proportions. We must look to the people in these states for the overthrow of the rebellion, [but] I am willing to evacuate Fort Sumter rather than be an active party in the beginning of civil war.

Blair, who spoke slowly and cautiously, was a man who always made his presence known in a room. One reason Lincoln admired him was that Blair was one of the lawyers who represented Dred Scott and his wife before the Supreme Court. In that landmark 1857 case, the court ruled that no one of African ancestry could claim American citizenship. Blair told friends that the Army and Navy were split.

Montgomery Blair

The army officers think destruction almost inevitable where the Navy officers think the danger but slight. . . . They think the greatest danger will be in landing at Sumter.

[Giving up] Sumter strengthens their [the rebels'] hand at home and their claim to recognition as an independent people abroad. . . . It [resupply] will in any event indicate the hearty courage of the North and the determination of the people and their President to maintain the authority of the government.

Fortunately, Lincoln's legendary mental depression had not set in that first week of his administration, as many had expected, and many thanked his wife, Mary, for that.

Lincoln friend

She was the only one who had the skill and tact to shorten their duration.

Ward Lamon, a huge man who had served as Lincoln's bodyguard, was another friend for peace who was worried. He expressed his concern to a Southerner.

Ward Lamon

Our countries not being at war and wishing as far as it lies in my power to avoid the latter calamity, no such condition will be expected of you unless brought about as the natural result of hostilities.

One thing Lincoln did not want to do was make the Union the aggressor in any confrontation over Fort Sumter. Illinois politician Orville Browning was among his many friends who agreed.

Orville Browning
In any conflict which may ensue between the government and the seceding states, it is very important that the traitors shall be the aggressors and that they be kept constantly and palpably in the wrong.

Attorney General Bates did not see the Cabinet secretaries as a united advisory board, and was very worried about the disagreements.

Edward Bates
There is no quarrel among us but an absolute want of continuity of intelligence, purpose and action. In truth, it is not an administration but the separate and disjointed action of seven independent officers, each one ignorant of what his colleagues are doing. . . . The President is an excellent man and in the main is wise, but he lacks will and purpose and I generally fear he has not the power to command.

The press was fed up with cabinet feuds.

Reporter, *New York Herald*
The Cabinet will not hold together two months.

◆

By March of 1861, Fort Sumter had become a national issue. Many Republicans did want to give the South anything, much less a valuable fort. The day after Lincoln's first Cabinet meeting on Sumter, the New York Herald *weighed in.*

Reporter, *New York Herald*

The gloom and mortification of Republican politicians at the humiliation involved in the impending withdrawal of Major Anderson is indescribable.

Northerners sensed that Fort Sumter was a problem, but few understood the full ramifications of what might or might not happen there. One New York newspaper editor did, though.

Editor, *New York Illustrated News*

While we do accept . . . the alarm that this movement [secession] is calculated to generate, we cannot overlook the fact that immense mischief may too soon ensue to the commercial interests of the whole country. The South is unquestionably in a fever of indignation be the cause well founded or not. The North looks complacently on the calmness deep felt or not. That we have reached a crisis in our country's history there is no need of assurance from any political sage . . . [over] the vested interests of the South in the peculiar institution [slavery] which [it] is bound to protect in all its forms.

It was a dangerous time in Washington, D.C.

Gideon Welles

A strange state of things existed at that time in Washington. The atmosphere was thick with treason. Party spirit and old party differences prevailed, however, amid accumulating dangers. Secession was considered by most persons as a political party question and not as rebellion. The Democrats, to a large extent. sympathized with the Rebels more than with the administration, which they opposed. . . . They hoped that President Lincoln and the Republicans would be overwhelmed by obstacles and embarrassments . . . [and] prove failures. The Republicans, on the other hand, were scarcely less partisan and unreasonable. . . .

Neither party [realized] the gathering storm. There was a general belief, indulged in by most persons, that adjustment would in some way be brought without an extensive resort to extreme measures.

It seemed probable that there might be some outbreak in South Carolina, and perhaps, in one or two other places, but such would, it was believed, be soon and easily suppressed. . . . [Southern] threats [were] considered as the harmless bulletins of excited demagogues.

Despite its disagreements, the Lincoln Cabinet would last almost completely intact for the entire war and be very successful. Lincoln mastered all of them in subtle ways; he was not worried.

When the Fort Sumter crisis began, one of the president's secretaries, awed by the fame, reputations, and power of his fellow Cabinet members, said to Lincoln, "They'll eat you up." Lincoln smiled at him and replied, "They'll eat each other up."

Abraham Lincoln

I must myself be the judge how long to retain, and when to remove, any of you from his position. It would greatly pain me to discover any of you endeavoring to procure another's removal or in any way to prejudice before the public. Such endeavor would be a wrong to the country. My wish is that on this subject no remark be made, or question asked, by any of you, here or elsewhere, now or hereafter.

Lincoln wanted the members of his Cabinet to help him become a good president. The political ambition that always burned in him, he transformed into a burning desire to be a successful chief executive. And Lincoln had always been ambitious. His skill was to mask that ambition from all. By 1832 he had already mastered that. Back then, when he was asked about his personal ambition, he shrugged.

Abraham Lincoln

Every man is said to have his peculiar ambition. Whether it be true or not, I can say for one that I have no other so great as that of being truly esteemed of my fellow men, by rendering myself worthy of their esteem. How far I should succeed in gratifying this ambition is yet to be developed. I am young and unknown to many of you. I was born and have ever remained in the most humble walks of life.

Lincoln's former law partner in Illinois, Billy Herndon, knew better.

Billy Herndon

In Abraham Lincoln, ambition burns like a little engine that knows no rest.

Lincoln grew up in an era between the Revolution and the Civil War, an era when the nation was moving westward. The population was exploding and the development of the railroad moved millions of people much faster. It was an era when more people had opportunity—and took it.

Alexis de Toqueville, French philosopher who traveled throughout the United States

When both the privileges and the disqualification of class have been abolished and men have shattered the bonds which once held them immobile, the idea of progress comes naturally into each man's mind; the desire to rise swells in every heart at once, and all men want to quit their former special position. Ambition becomes a universal feeling.

There was much talk that if there was a war, the conflict would be fought in the North, not the South.

Editor, *Detroit Free Press*
That war will be fought at the North.

Editor, *Chicago Tribune*, to Illinois Senator Lyman Trumbull
I believe upon my soul that if the Union is divided on the line of the Ohio, we shall be compelled to struggle to maintain the territorial integrity of the state.

Samuel Medary, publisher of the Columbus, Ohio, Crisis, *agreed and feared that the Northern half of the nation would be destroyed.*

Samuel Medary
Cincinnati will be converted into a camp of soldiers instead of a busy mart of peace and prosperous commerce. With the Ohio River only dividing her from a hostile foe, she will be exposed to the shell and the ball from the overlooking hills beyond. Fear and absolute safety would compel others to remove to a more distant point and give the city to camp life and all the ills that follow. And for what are we to be driven to this desolate condition? Can any one answer?

Most believed that a Civil War, regardless of where it was fought, would destroy the country.

Editor, *New York Express*
If the people of one section madly propose to itself the task of trying to whip the other, the hope of reconciliation is extinguished forever. . . . There is a chance that fraternal relations, though temporarily ruptured, may one day be restored, if peace [now] is preserved.

Many Southerners sneered at Northern hopes for peace. One was William Tecumseh Sherman, the recently retired superintendent of the Louisiana Seminary of Learning and Military Academy [later Louisiana State University] and a former soldier—a man who would later become one of Lincoln's top generals. He thought Lincoln did not understand Southern anger at all. He met the president in the White House just after the inauguration, along with his younger brother John, a Congressman from Ohio. Lincoln asked them how Southerners were "getting along."

William Tecumseh Sherman
They are getting along swimmingly—they are preparing for war.

Sherman was upset with Lincoln after he left the White House meeting.

William Tecumseh Sherman
You have got things in a hell of a fix and you may get them out as you best can. . . . The country is sleeping on a volcano that might burst at any minute.

Sherman wrote to his brother a few days later.

William Tecumseh Sherman
Lincoln has an awful task, and if he succeeds in avoiding strife and allaying fears he will be entitled to the admiration of the world; but a time has occurred in all governments, and has occurred in this, when force must back the laws and the longer the postponement, the more severe must be the application.

Ironically, the former military man had visited Charleston several times as a young soldier and was unimpressed with Sumter and Fort Moultrie. In 1846 he wrote about them.

William Tecumseh Sherman

There would be no difficulty in taking Charleston—our fort [Moultrie] is weak and has only about 100 men—it is not ditched or strengthened in such a way as to defy an assault. A new fort is being built in the channel [Sumter] which, when done, will be very strong, but its walls are yet hardly out of the water.

Sherman was spoiling for a fight that day at the White House, if war came. He had always been ready to go to war. Back in 1846, he was so despondent at the lack of action he saw in the Army that he wrote to his bosses asking them to put him in the line of fire.

William Tecumseh Sherman

[I felt] compelled by a feeling of shame at leading so quiet a life while my comrades were at war. I wrote to the Adjutant General, requesting him to order me upon any expedition—the more hazardous the more to my liking. [It will be dangerous] but I trust to fortune.

TWO

The Coming Storm

Lincoln did not think a crisis over Fort Sumter, and the smaller but similar problem of Fort Pickens in Pensacola, Florida, would come this early in his presidency. It seemed that everybody, North and South, wanted the new president to do something, and wanted members of his Cabinet to do something, too.

Charleston Mercury

The bewilderment of the Lincoln administration is not lessened today. The outside pressure both for and against . . . a war policy is tremendous. Meantime, it is said that the Southerner Commissioners, like other people, are getting heartily sick of Seward's do-nothing tactics.

However, the United States president-elect had a sense of foreboding about secession and slavery from the moment he departed Springfield, Illinois, his hometown, for the journey to Washington, D.C. He spoke of it to an early morning gathering of his neighbors and friends who came to see him off at the train station.

Abraham Lincoln

I now leave not knowing when or ever I may return with a task before me greater than that which rested upon Washington. Without the assistance of that Divine being who ever attended him, I cannot succeed. With that assistance, I cannot fail. Trusting in him who can go with me, and remain with you and be everywhere for good, let me confidently hope that all will yet be well. To his care commending you, as I hope in your prayers you will commend me, I bid you an affectionate farewell.

Illinois Journal

Full of simple and touching eloquence, so exactly adapted to the occasion, so worthy of the man and the hour. Although it was raining fast when he began to speak, every hat was lifted and every head bent forward to catch the last words of the departing chief. When he said, with the earnestness of a sudden inspiration of feeling that "with God's help he should not fail," there was an incontrollable burst of applause. . . .

At precisely eight o'clock, city time, the train moved off, bearing our honored townsman, our noble chief Abraham Lincoln, to the scenes of his future labors and, as we firmly believe, of his glorious triumph. God bless honest Abraham Lincoln.

The president-elect stayed overnight at the Bates House hotel in Indianapolis. There, a crowd pressed him for a few words. He walked out onto the balcony to loud applause. In his remarks, he said of secessionists:

Abraham Lincoln

When men wrangle by the mouth with no certainty that they mean the same thing while using the same words, it perhaps would be as well if they would keep silence.

The Republican press applauded this speech, but the Democratic press hated it.

Editor, *Baltimore Sun*

He is a clown.

Cincinnati Daily Enquirer

Old Abe is a failure as a President. By the time he gets through his tour, his friends will wish they had boxed him up and sent him home.

There were mixed feelings about Fort Sumter and a Civil War in the various towns the president-elect stopped at on his railroad journey to the nation's capital for his inauguration. The Fort Sumter crisis heated up as Lincoln headed east. One Cincinnati reporter spoke to a South Carolina newspaper about Lincoln's visit to Ohio.

Charleston Mercury

I do not think that many battalions from this state, however, are likely to volunteer to make a "foray upon the South" in carrying out the "irrepressible conflict." They will prefer to stay at home, as Old Kentucky may have something to say about such a demonstration.

When Lincoln's train stopped in Columbus, Ohio, he assured the crowd that despite all the secession hoopla, no harm had come to anyone.

Abraham Lincoln

I have not maintained silence [on issues] from any want of real anxiety. It is a good thing that there is no more than anxiety, for there is nothing going wrong. It is a consoling circumstance that when we look out there is nothing that really hurts anybody.

Despite the rising concerns and the opinions of the Democratic press, Lincoln's train trip was a triumph. One paper described the reaction when he reached Dunkirk, New York.

New York World

The arches of the depot echoed and re-echoed with the ring of countless cheers. Men swung their hats wildly, women waved their handkerchiefs and, as the train moved on, the crowd, animated by a common impulse, followed as if they intended to keep it company to the next station. It is impossible to describe the applause and acclamation.

At Dunkirk, Lincoln met a man as tall as he—always an oddity considering Lincoln's height—and kept measuring himself against the other man, something he had done, and would do, all of his life.

When the train stopped at the town of Girard, Pennsylvania, standing on the platform, surprisingly, was Republican Party leader Horace Greeley, editor of the nation's largest newspaper, the New York Tribune. *The eccentric Greeley would unsuccessfully run for president in 1872. Clad in his signature long white coat and carrying a duffel bag with his name printed on it in huge yellow letters, Greeley thought the Lincoln train was the regular train he wanted to catch and was mystified.*

New York World

[Greeley] at first made an incursion into the reporters' car, where he was captured, and marched in triumph by Mr. Secretary Nicolay to the President's car. Here he was introduced for the first time to Mrs. Lincoln. At the next stopping place, Greeley suddenly disappeared. His arrival and departure were altogether so unexpected, so mysterious, so comical, that they supplied an amusing topic of conversation during the rest of the journey.

Lincoln made many speeches along the route. He told members of the Pennsylvania Assembly, in very careful language, that any possible war would not be his doing.

Abraham Lincoln

I promise that in so far as I may have wisdom to direct, that if so painful a result [bloodshed] shall in any way be brought about, it shall be through no fault of mine.

He had told a crowd in Indianapolis the same thing, aiming his remarks at Southerners.

Abraham Lincoln

The maintenance of this government is your business and not mine. I wish you to remember, now and forever, that if the Union of these states and the liberties of this people shall be lost it is but little to any one man of fifty-two years of age but a great deal to the thirty millions of people who inhabit these United States and to their prosperity in all coming time. It is your business to rise up and preserve the Union and liberty for yourselves, and not for me.

Lincoln did fear trouble of some kind and was, he told the people, ready for it. He told the New Jersey General Assembly about possible problems over Sumter and slavery. After vocally whipping his crowd into a frenzy, he stunned them when he lamented that, because of the Fort Sumter crisis, he might be the last president of the United States.

Abraham Lincoln

The man does not live who is more devoted to peace than I am. None who would do more to preserve it. But it may be necessary to put the foot down firmly. And if I do my duty, and do right, you will sustain me, will you not? Received as I am by the members of a legislature the majority of whom do not agree with me in political sentiments, I trust that I may have their assistance in piloting the ship of state in this voyage surrounded by perils as it is; for, if it should suffer attack now, there will be no pilot ever needed for another voyage.

When his train stopped in Pittsburgh, Lincoln told the crowd that they had to keep calm about the nation and Sumter.

Abraham Lincoln

There is really no crisis except an artificial one. . . . If the great American people will only keep their temper, on both sides of the line, the troubles will come to an end.

On a speaking stop at Independence Hall in Philadelphia on George Washington's birthday, he repeated that message.

Abraham Lincoln

If this country cannot be saved without giving up that principle [slavery]—I was about to say I would rather be assassinated on this spot than to surrender it. Now, in my view of the present aspect of affairs, there is no need of bloodshed and war. There is no necessity for it. I am not in favor of such a course, and I may say in advance, there will be no blood shed unless it be forced upon the Government.

Later, his train stopped at tiny Westfield, New York. Lincoln had received a letter from a little girl, Grace Bedell, who lived there, in which she suggested he grow "whiskers" and that they would make him look better. He did, on her suggestion. He probably thought the beard would make him look older and wiser and perhaps cover up some of the ungainliness of his face. The little girl went up to the train platform to meet a smiling Lincoln, who gently kissed her on the cheek. The encounter became part of American lore.

Abraham Lincoln

You see, I let these whiskers grow for you, Grace.

Detective Alan J. Pinkerton and a personal friend, Ward Lamon, accompanied Lincoln on his railroad trip because death threats had been made against the president-elect. They kept an eye on his visitors and the crowds. In Baltimore, Pinkerton heard of a credible assassination plot against Lincoln and secretly ushered him off the train, in disguise, and sneaked him into Washington unnoticed on another train.

New York Tribune

It is the only instance recorded in history in which the recognized head of a nation—head whether by choice or inheritance—has been compelled, for fear of his life, to enter the capital in disguise. Tyrants have fled from palaces under false names and assumed characters when the exasperated people have compelled them to abdicate their thrones, dethroned monarchs have escaped in the garb of common men, at the approach of a foreign enemy pretenders to royal seats to which they had no right have sought from secret hiding places and with feigned names and purposes to rally the discontented into open rebellion, but never before among civilized people has a king or President been reduced by the circumstances of the times to such an extremity for protection. . . . One section of this country [the South] is only semi-civilized.

The talk about Lincoln's assassination, and the Baltimore plot, alarmed Pinkerton, in whose care Lincoln had placed himself. He thought the hatred of Southerners for Lincoln could push some to go too far.

Alan Pinkerton

The proposed plan to get rid of Mr. Lincoln, whatever it was, and of whatever expense of the lives of others, even of women and children, are merely new developments of Southern and slaveholder barbarism. The only way that innate ruffians can meet the new contingencies of the moment. And these will be followed by acts with uncertain results, unless, in the meantime, the supremacy of the law shall be asserted in obedience to Northern civilization and by other means than persuasive words.

Lincoln remained nervous, as his former law partner recounted.

Billy Herndon
During the anxious moments that intervened between the general election and the assembling of the legislature, he slept, like Napoleon, with one eye open.

In fact, just after his election as president, Lincoln had expressed his fear of assassination to Herndon.

Abraham Lincoln
If I live, I'm coming back [to Springfield] sometime and then we'll go right on practicing law as if nothing had ever happened.

Despite the threats, no one was happier to see Lincoln in the White House, despite the simmering Fort Sumter issue, than his wife, Mary, who had pushed him considerably in his political career. John Stuart, a law partner and friend of the Lincolns, once described Mary this way.

John Stuart
She had the fire, will and ambition.

Mary Lincoln wrote to a friend who had married an older, wealthy husband:

Mary Lincoln

I would rather marry a good man, a man of mind, with a hope and bright prospects ahead for position—fame and power—than to marry all the houses of gold and bones in the world.

One man who was surprised to see Lincoln take the oath of office was his old Springfield friend and rival, Senator Stephen Douglas, long expected to be president someday by just about everybody. It was Douglas who, in 1854, sponsored the Kansas–Nebraska Act, which permitted residents of territories to determine whether they wanted slavery—an issue that led to the Fort Sumter crisis. Lincoln himself thought that Douglas, not he, would become president.

Abraham Lincoln

Twenty two years ago, Judge Douglas and I first became acquainted. We were both young then, he a trifle younger than I. Even then, we were both ambitious; I perhaps, quite as much so as he. With me, the race of ambition has been a failure—a flat failure. With him it has been one of splendid success. His name fills the nation; and he is not unknown, even in foreign lands. I effect no contempt for the high eminence he has reached. So reached, that the oppressed of my species, might have shared with me in the elevation. I would rather stand on that eminence, than wear the richest crown that ever pressed a monarch's brow.

Many were relieved—possibly even surprised—that the United States had not already dissolved over the Fort Sumter crisis. Some had predicted that the United States would be redrawn into two, or three, or four countries, all due to the intransigent stance taken by slaveholders. Congressman John Sherman made a prediction two months before Lincoln took office.

Representative John Sherman, Ohio

The people, alarmed, excited, yet true to the Union, and the Constitution, are watching with eager fear, lest the noble government, baptized in the blood of the Revolution, shall be broken into fragments before the President-elect shall assume the functions of his office.

Lincoln had always dismissed the secessionists who stood so firm on Fort Sumter and was surprised that they took seven states out of the Union. He had lectured some of them prior to his election.

Abraham Lincoln

Will you make war upon us and kill us all? Why gentlemen, I think you are as gallant and brave men as ere (ever) lived that you can fight as bravely, in a good cause, man for man, as any other people living, that you have shown yourselves capable of this on various occasions, but men for men, you are not better than we are, and there are not so many of you as there are of us. You will never make much of a hand at whipping us. Were we fewer in number than you, I think you could whip us; if we were equal it would likely be a drawn battle, but being inferior in numbers, you will make nothing attempting to master us?

Lincoln argued that "states' rights," the doctrine upon which the South upheld slavery, was a historical fabrication.

Abraham Lincoln

The Union is older than any of the states. And, in fact, it created them as states. Having never been states, either in substance or in name outside the Union, whence this magical omnipotence of "states' rights," asserting a claim of power to lawfully destroy the Union itself?

The new president never did understand the hatred in the Southern states for him.

Editor, *Georgia Star*
Any Southerner who worked for Lincoln should be outlawed and killed.

Editor, *Charleston Mercury*
Lincoln is a bloodthirsty tyrant.

Chairman, Alabama Young Man's Club
Resistance to Lincoln is obedience to God.

Lincoln had always been clear in his position on slavery, but did not identify himself as an abolitionist. He said he did not want slavery ended right away, as the abolitionists did. Most Southerners did not believe him. And indeed, in an 1858 debate with Stephen Douglas, Lincoln argued that slavery needed to be on the national agenda.

Abraham Lincoln
Do you not constantly argue that this is not the right place to oppose it? You say it must not be opposed in the free states, because slavery is not here; it must not be opposed in the slave states because it is there; You say it must not be opposed in politics because that will make a fuss. It must not be opposed in the pulpit because it is not religion. Then where is the place to oppose it? There is no suitable place to oppose it.

[There are two principles.] The one is the common right of humanity and the other the divine right of kings. It's the same principle in whatever shape it develops itself. It is the same spirit that says "you work and toil and earn bread, and I'll eat it." No matter what shape it comes whether from the mouth of a King who seeks to bestride the people of his own nation and lives by the fruit of their labor or from one race of men as an apology for enslaving another race, it is the same tyrannical principle.

On his way to the inauguration, Lincoln told Southerners they could avoid extreme action over slavery by just waiting until the next election.

Abraham Lincoln

You have another chance [election] in four years. No great harm can be done by us in that time—in that time there can be nobody hurt. If anything goes wrong, however, and you find you have made a mistake, elect a better man next time.

But most Southerners believed nothing Lincoln said about slavery—or about Fort Sumter—and were convinced that great harm could, indeed, be done. The grumbling started as soon as Lincoln was elected.

Governor William H. Gist, South Carolina

The election to the Presidency of a sectional candidate [Lincoln] by a party committed to the support of measures which, if carried out, shall inevitably destroy our equality in the Union . . . [so] the only alternative left, in my judgment, is the secession of South Carolina from the Federal Union.

H. Pinckney Walker, Illinois lawyer

Lincoln's government will be bent on the destruction of southern institutions.

Southerners argued that when the new president had spoken of slavery in the past, it was always in strong opposition. In 1854, for example, Lincoln said that ending slavery would not only right a wrong but purify the United States.

Abraham Lincoln

Our Republican robe is soiled, and trailed in the dust. Let us re-purify it. Let us turn and wash it white in the spirit, if not the blood, of the

Revolution. Let us turn slavery from its claim of "moral right" back upon its existing "legal rights" and its argument of "necessity." Let us return it to the position our fathers gave it and there let it rest in peace. Let us readopt the Declaration of Independence and with it the practices and policy which harmonize with it. Let North and South—let all Americans—let all lovers of liberty everywhere—join in the great and good work. If we do this, we shall not only have saved the Union, but so have so saved it as to make and to keep it, forever worthy of the saving. We shall have so saved it that the succeeding millions of free happy people, the world over, shall rise up, and call us blessed to the latest generations.

In 1855 he had written to a friend about the prospect of ending slavery in America.

Abraham Lincoln

There is no peaceful extinction of slavery in prospect for us . . . so far as peaceful voluntary emancipation is concerned, the condition of the Negro slave in America . . . is now fixed and hopeless.

And in 1856 at the Republication State Convention in Bloomington, Illinois, he said this:

Abraham Lincoln

Let us draw a cordon so to speak, around the slave states and the hateful institution, [that is] like a reptile poisoning itself, [and] will perish of its own infamy. We shall be in a majority after a while and then the revolution which we shall accomplish will be none the less radical. . . . [S]lavery is a violation of eternal right . . . a detestable crime and ruinous to the nation. Those who deny freedom to others deserve it not for themselves and, under the rule of a just God, cannot long retain it.

Lincoln always scoffed at Southerners' claims that Negro slaves were property, like hogs and pigs.

Abraham Lincoln

Judge [Douglas] has no very vivid impression that the Negro is a human and consequently has no idea that there can be any moral question in legislating about him. In his view, the question of whether a new country shall be slave or be free, is a matter of utter indifference as it is whether his neighbor shall plant his farm with tobacco, or stock it with horned cattle.

He had likewise expressed disgust at Southerners' claims that there was nothing wrong with owning slaves.

Abraham Lincoln

[I hate it] because of the monstrosity of slavery itself . . . [which deprived] our Republican example of its just influence in the world.

The practice, he said, had offended God, and they would be punished for it.

Abraham Lincoln

Pharaoh's country was cursed with plagues and his hosts were drowned in the Red Sea for striving to retain a captive people who had already served them more than four hundred years. May like disasters ever befall us!

Lincoln often quoted and paraphrased the Bible, as he did in his defiant "house divided" speech in 1858.

Abraham Lincoln

A house divided against itself cannot stand. I believe this government cannot endure permanently half slave and half free. I do not expect the Union to be dissolved—I do not expect the house to fall—but I do expect it will cease to be divided.

He argued, too, that all men were indeed created equal.

Abraham Lincoln

If the Negro is a man, why then my ancient faith teaches me that all men are created equal and that there can be no moral right in connection of one man making a slave of another. Slavery, in sum, is a total violation of the sacred right of a man to govern himself which was guaranteed by the Declaration [of Independence] and was the sheet anchor of American Republicanism.

Lincoln always embraced the Declaration of Independence. On his trip to Washington to be sworn in as president, he told a crowd in Philadelphia:

Abraham Lincoln

I have never had a feeling politically that did not spring from the sentiments embodied in the Declaration of Independence. It was that which gave promise that in due time the weights should be lifted from the shoulders of all men and that all men should have an equal chance.

He reminded them of their heritage and guaranteed that he would preserve it.

Abraham Lincoln

It was not the mere matter of the separation of the colonies from the motherland, but that something in the Declaration giving liberty, not alone to the people of this land, but hope to the world for all time. It was that which gave promise that in due time the weights should be lifted from the shoulders of all men and that all should have an equal chance.

When a longtime friend, Joshua Speed, wrote to him that slavery was acceptable if a state wanted it, Lincoln replied tersely.

Abraham Lincoln

I confess that I hate to see the poor creatures hunted down, and caught, and carried back to their stripes, and unrewarded toils, but I bite my lip and keep quiet.

Lincoln also disputed the South's argument that since most of the world had slaves, it was not wrong in America, either.

Abraham Lincoln

[Mankind] considers slavery a great moral wrong. And their feeling against it is not evanescent, but eternal. It lies at the very foundation of their sense of justice, and it cannot be trifled with. It is a great and durable element of popular action and, I think, no statesman can safely disregard it.

Numerous Southerners saw all abolitionists in the face of Lincoln and themselves as eternal victims in all discussions about slavery.

Editor, *Richmond Whig*

He would at once unite the whole Southern people in resistance and produce a universal conflagration.

Editor, *West Baton Rouge Sugar Planter*

If the administration of Mr. Lincoln in any manner interferes with those states [that secede] can the others who may not agree with them, stand idly by and witness the outrage? Certainly not. Every southern sword will leap from its scabbard to avenge an insult to a southern state, be he in the right or wrong.

Montgomery (Alabama) Daily Mail

The South is infested with scores and hundreds of abolition agents, whose business here, it is, to prepare our people for the rule of Lincoln.

Letter to the Editor, *Charleston Courier*

It is well known that our city is at the present overrun with Abolition emissaries disseminating incendiary principles among our Negroes, deluding these credulous people with the belief that the election of Lincoln will be their millennium. . . . Our safety lies in extreme measures.

Keziah Brevard, plantation mistress

It is time for us to show the rabble of the North we are not to be murdered in cold blood because we own slaves.

Emma Holmes, Charleston

We have truth, justice and religion on our side and our homes to battle for.

Soon after she arrived in Charleston, Mary Chestnut explained Southern distaste for abolitionists simply.

Mary Chestnut

We are separated because of incompatibility of temper. We are divorced, North from South, because we hate each other.

The North and South both saw connections between the South's love, and the North's hatred, of slavery and the South's insistence that a state had the right to license slavery. If that right was threatened by the federal Union, the Southern states reasoned, each of those states then had a right to secede. And to completely secede they needed all the federal forts within their borders—which led to the crisis over Fort Sumter. That belief was held by numerous Southern politicians, but also by planters, shipbuilders, merchants, newspaper editors, and even soldiers.

One of those soldiers was Virginia's Robert E. Lee, on furlough from the Army in 1860. He backed states' rights but did not want a war, and had no idea what would happen to him if hostilities broke out over Fort Sumter. He expressed his thoughts in an 1860 letter to his son.

Robert E. Lee

The South, in my opinion, has been aggrieved by the acts of the North, as you say. I feel the aggression and am willing to take every proper step for redress. It is the principle I contend for, not individual or private benefit. As an American citizen, I take great pride in my country, her prosperity and institutions, and would defend any state if her rights were invaded. But I anticipate no greater calamity for the country than a dissolution of the Union. It would be an accumulation of all the evils we complain of and I am willing to sacrifice everything but honor for its preservation. I hope, therefore, that all Constitutional means will be exhausted before there is a resort to force. Secession is nothing but revolution. The framers of our Constitution never exhausted so much labor, wisdom and forbearance in its formation and surrounded it with so many guards and securities, if it was intended to be broken by every member of the Confederacy at will.

In the face of all these opposing views, many sought the wisdom of descendants of the founders, such as John Jay, a radical and an emotional speaker and grandson of the first Chief Justice of the Supreme Court.

John Jay

No surer political destruction ever awaited a northern representative than that which awaits every man in the Senate or the House who devotes to slavery the territory of the American people, in the wretched hope of conciliating rebels who have gained a temporary advantages by the meanest treachery & theft.

Many Southerners dismissed those ideas, with one Southern congressman making a comparison to the French Revolution.

Representative Laurence Keitt, South Carolina

The concentration of absolute power in the hands of the North will develop the wildest democracy ever seen on this earth—unless it should have been matched in Paris in 1789. What of conservatism? What of order? What of social security or financial prosperity can withstand northern license? I see no alternative but the sword.

Abraham Lincoln had to ponder how Fort Sumter came to be a tinderbox for the troubles of an entire nation. Millions discussed it. In his diary, prominent New York lawyer George Templeton Strong perhaps best analyzed the debate.

George Templeton Strong

Why do the people so furiously rage together just now? What has created our unquestionable irritation against the South? What has created the Republican Party?

Its nucleus was the abolition handful that had been vaporing for thirty years. And which, until about 1850, was the most insignificant of our time. Our feeling at the North until that time was not hostility to slavery, but indifference to it and reluctance to discuss it. It was a disagreeable subject with which we had nothing to do. . . . The clamor of the South about the admission of California ten years ago introduced the question of slavery to the North as one in which it had an interest adverse to the South. That controversy taught us that the two systems could not co-exist in the same territory. It opened our eyes to the fact that there were two hostile elements in the country and that if we allowed slaves to enter any territorial acquisition our own free labor must be excluded from it. The question was unfortunate for our peace. The Missouri Compromise was the fatal blow. Then came . . . war in Kansas . . . [the] fugitive slave law . . . other issues.

Another civilian who gave the issue a lot of thought was William Tecumseh Sherman. He wrote to his brother in December, 1860.

William Tecumseh Sherman

The quiet which I thought the usual acquiescence of the people was merely the prelude to the storm of opinion that by now seems irresistible—politicians have, by hearing the prejudices of the people, and moving with the current, succeeded in destroying the Government—it cannot be stopped now I fear—I was in Alexandria [Louisiana] all day yesterday and had a full and unreserved conversation with Dr. S. A. Smith, State Senator, who is a man of education, property, influence and qualified to judge—he was during the canvas a Breckenridge man, but though a Southerner in opinion is really opposed to a dissolution of our government. He has returned from New Orleans, where he says he was amazed to see evidence of public sentiment which could not be mistaken. . . . The calling of [a secession] convention forthwith is to be unanimous, the bill for arming the state ditto. The Convention will meet in January and only two questions will be agitated—immediate dissolution, a declaration of state independence, a General convention of Southern states with instructions to demand of the Northern states to repeal all laws hostile to slavery and pledges of future good behavior.

And now all of that was coalescing around Fort Sumter.

Abraham Lincoln

The Fort in the present condition of affairs is of inconsiderable military value. For it is not necessary for the Federal Government to hold it in order to protect the city of Charleston from foreign invasion nor is it available under existing circumstances. . . . It is difficult to see how possession of the fort by the Secessionists can be rendered a means of annoyance to the federal government.

The Republicans in the new administration were just as worried about a war over Fort Sumter in March of 1861 as James Buchanan's Democratic administration had been earlier. Lincoln had to decide whether to evacuate Fort Sumter or resupply it and risk an attack by Confederate troops and a Civil War.

George Templeton Strong

The progress of events has startled and staggered some of our notables who were laughing secession to scorn a fortnight ago. I think, from all indications, that Republican leaders are frightened and ready to concede everything, to restore the Missouri Compromise line and satisfy the fugitive slave remedies of the South. A movement that way has certainly begun. But it may be too soon for the North and too late for the South.

Many maintained faith in the president's leadership in the midst of the conflict.

Senator Charles Sumner, Massachusetts

Abraham Lincoln has those elements of character needed to carry us through. . . . He is calm, prudent, wise and also brave. . . . The Union shall be preserved and made more precious by consecration to human rights.

This kind of admiration reminded longtime Lincoln supporters of a toast made to him at a Whig Party dinner in Illinois in 1837.

Sangamon Journal

[The toaster said] to A. Lincoln: He has fulfilled the expectations of his friends and disappointed the hopes of his enemies.

In fact, all of the Republicans and most of the Northern Democrats stood with Lincoln in the Fort Sumter crisis and against slavery, too, but warned that his radical views might help the South in the long run. Over the years, the Republicans had never tied themselves to violent abolitionists. Some saw firebrands such as John Brown as a sign of a coming war. Brown and some of his followers, determined to eliminate slavery, had staged a military raid on Harper's Ferry in Virginia just eighteen months earlier that caused a political firestorm, North and South. The angry editor of one Rhode Island newspaper had this to say:

Editor, *Providence Post*

The Republicans would stand as a wall of fire against the admission of any more slave states. . . . They would change the Supreme Court. They would, in short, pursue such a course as would instantly unite the South against the general government and make a separation of the states the only remedy.

Abraham Lincoln

John Brown was no Republican and you have failed to implicate a single Republican in the Harper's Ferry enterprise. John Brown's effort was peculiar. It was not a slave insurrection. It was an attempt by white men to get up a small revolt among slaves in which the slaves refused to participate. In fact, it was so absurd that the slaves, with all their ignorance, saw plainly enough it could not succeed.

Jefferson Davis, President of the Confederate States of America

It was not the passage of personal liberty laws. It was not the circulation of incendiary documents. It was not the raid of John Brown. It was not the operation of unjust tariff laws, not all combined, that constituted the intolerable grievances, but it was the systematic and persistent struggle to deprive the Southern states of equality in the Union.

Many Southerners agreed with Davis, and pointed to the American Revolution as their precedent. The concept was exactly the same, they argued. One of the key proponents of that argument was William Yancey of Alabama, a champion of slavery who was dubbed "the prince of fire-eaters" by the Northern press. One journalist described Yancey this way:

Murat Halstead

He is a compact, middle sized man, straight limbed, with a square built head and face, and an eye full of expression. He is mild and bland in manner . . . and has an air of perfect sincerity. No one would be likely to point him out in a crowd of gentlemen as the redoubtable Yancey, who proposes, according to common report, to precipitate the cotton states into a revolution, dissolve the Union and build up a southern empire.

Many Northerners, even anti-slavery crusaders, agreed with Yancey. including Wylie Crawford of Pennsylvania, assistant surgeon at Fort Sumter.

Wylie Crawford
The South in her position stands by the Constitution, which in spirit and in letter has been violated by the aggressive power now in power.

James Freeman Clarke, theologian and abolitionist
According to the fundamental principles of our government, the secessionists are right in their main principle. [Withdrawal] is in accordance with the principles of self-government, which are asserted in the Declaration of Independence.

Others said that was not so, and that the comparison was a weak one.

George Frederickson, philosopher
What the abolishionists [sic] were really saying was . . . that there are two kinds of revolutions "good revolutions" and "bad revolutions."

Still others charged that the South had twisted the meaning of the Declaration of Independence.

Wendell Phillips, abolitionist
The people south of the Mason-Dixon line have re-modeled their government to suit themselves—and our function is merely to recognize it.

Many secessionists ignored those views and put their fate in God's hands. Just after his resignation, Howell Cobb of Georgia, the Secretary of the U.S. Treasury, made such a statement.

Howell Cobb

The evil has now passed beyond control and must be met by each and all of us, under our responsibility to God and our country.

Northerners also turned to God, even if God's will meant Civil War.

William Lloyd Garrison, Editor, *The Liberator*

Stand still and see the salvation of God. [Lincoln's party] is an instrument in the hand of God.

Henry James Sr., philosopher

[American liberty] is identical to the God made constitution of the human mind itself and which consists in the inalienable right of every man to believe according to the unbridled inspiration of his own heart, and to act according to the unperverted dictates of his own understanding.

Former Congressman Martin Conway, Kansas

This is a holy war!

The Sumter issue united Southerners, and some wanted war right away, such as John Saunders, a member of a Washington, D.C., light artillery company. On the night of Lincoln's inauguration, on his way to one of the inaugural balls, he passed some Virginians he knew on a Washington street.

John Saunders

You fellows are off! I wish I were with you. But today [Lincoln's inauguration] settled it and my resignation goes in tonight. I don't wait for Virginia. If I have to shoot at Americans, I'll do it from the other side of the Potomac.

◆

As the debate raged on a national level, South Carolina was already bracing for war. A frustrated President Buchanan, in his last days in office, had just wanted to keep the country together.

James Buchanan

The framers of the national government never intended to implant in its bosom the seeds of its own destruction nor were they guilty of the absurdity of providing for its own dissolution. . . . [If secession is legitimate] our Constitution is a rope of sand . . . our thirty-three states may resolve themselves into as many petty, jarring and hostile republics. . . . The hopes of the friends of freedom throughout the world would be destroyed.

In his last days in office, Buchanan had been tough with the seceders and all the officials of Charleston, South Carolina. Several peace commissioners had been sent to see the president in December and tried to bully him into evacuating Fort Sumter. Buchanan, furious, instead told them he would keep the fort and that he would send a man-of-war naval vessel to Charleston, with troops, and reseize all the forts the South had taken, shell the city and take it, and might arrest the commissioners on charges of treason.

He did not do any of these things, which disheartened many—Abner Doubleday, the second-in-command at Fort Sumter, among them.

Captain Abner Doubleday

He might indeed have arrested the commissioners for high treason, but his Unionism was of a very mild type and far from aggressive.

One of those commissioners, scared, wired officials in Charleston and told them to get ready for an attack on Sumter.

Captain Abner Doubleday

This dispatch caused a great uproar and excitement in Charleston. The banks at once suspended specie payments. It was expected that a fleet would bombard the city and land troops. All was terror and confusion.

New South Carolina Governor Francis Pickens was so scared that he rushed to Fort Moultrie to prepare it for an anticipated shelling. Laborers were kept at work night and day piling up sandbags to shield Confederate troops from a naval shelling.

Captain Abner Doubleday

The Governor was in a very angry mood. He stopped our mail for a time and cut off all communications with us. We were, of course, prevented from purchasing fresh provisions and were reduced to pork, and hard-tack. Anderson was quite indignant at this proceeding.

Life at Fort Sumter became exceedingly grim.

W. T. Early, Union enlisted soldier

If there are no guarantees on slavery, the whole South will be bullied into a measure which will result in our own union . . . destruction of our government . . . [and] the Negroes would be put to the sword.

Not only were there no guarantees on slavery, but visitors to Lincoln in his first days in office said he was vehemently against it and hated putting up with it where it existed.

Abraham Lincoln

I will suffer death before I will consent or will advise my friends to consent to any concession or compromise [on slavery]. I should regard any concession in the face of menace the destruction of the government itself.

All of this led to the crisis over Fort Sumter and made it the nation's tinderbox, needing only a small spark to explode.

B. L. Hodge

The fate of the Union is sealed. It must be dissolved.

Many Southerners, including Robert Rhett Jr., believed Lincoln was the head of a massive cabal determined to destroy the South, and that this cabal, after the election, included just about all the powerful men in the North. As editor of the Charleston Mercury, *Robert Rhett Jr. had a public platform to share his views.*

Robert Rhett Jr.

The satanic churches of . . . Stowe, Greeley, Seward, Webb, etc. are even now loading the Sharpe rifles and whetting the Bowie knives and buckling on the revolver for the purpose of gratifying that demonic frenzy, which nothing short of diabolical tragedies of the midnight torch, the poisoned fountain, and daily assassination in Virginia, the Carolinas and Texas [will satisfy]. . . . Emancipation or revolution is now upon us!

Rhett was so angry that neither the Confederate Army nor the South Carolina militia would attack Fort Sumter that he offered to lead the local militia in an assault himself. That tumbled him into a Punch and Judy type of comedy with the governor of South Carolina.

Governor Francis Pickens

Certainly, Mr. Rhett. I have no objections. I will furnish you with some men and you can storm the work yourself.

Robert Rhett Jr.
But sir, I am not a military man.

Governor Francis Pickens
Nor I, either, and therefore I take the advice of those that are.

The powerful Rhett family was disliked by many Southerners as well as Northerners because they had too much money, too much influence, and a cavalier attitude towards Charlestonians.

The Charlestonian
The world, you know, is composed of men, women and Rhetts.

◆

Lincoln had held his stand against slavery all of his life. He never wavered. It had cost him a seat in the US Senate. At the 1856 Illinois Republican Caucus for the Senate nomination, supported by the anti-slavery coalition, he had forty-seven votes and Governor Joel Matteson had forty-eight. Lincoln's friend Lyman Trumbull, also against slavery, had just five. No one gave in and so Lincoln, to help the anti-slavery cause, dropped out of the race and ordered all his votes switched to Trumbull, who took the nomination and won the seat in the fall election. At the time, Lincoln's friends told one another he was finished.

Anonymous Lincoln adviser
[It was] perhaps his last chance for that high position.

Ironically, his allegiance to the anti-slavery cause, and friend Trumbull, would help him win the presidential nomination in Chicago four years later—something no one anticipated. Many of Lincoln's friends realized how heated the national atmosphere was and how incensed Southerners were about Fort Sumter.

Francis Blair, Lincoln friend
They are ready now even to apply the torch which will light the fire of civil discord.

And yet, many Northern newspaper editors sneered at suggestions that the South would secede after Lincoln's election.

Horace Greeley, *New York Tribune*
The South could no more unite upon a scheme of secession than a company of lunatics could conspire to break out of bedlam.

Cincinnati Daily Commercial
The doctrine of secession is anarchy. If any minority have the right to break up the government at pleasure because they have not had their way, there is an end of all government.

There was no need for eyeball-to-eyeball confrontation, many felt, if diplomacy could overcome the cannons at Fort Sumter.

Judge Henry Binney, Pennsylvania
[The secession crisis is] a universal demoralization such as we witnessed in the French Revolution. [Government] must decide firmly and calmly to deny and resist [secession] to assert the obligation of the Supreme law and to enforce it, by every means at command, which can reasonably promise success.

Many Republicans feared Lincoln's indecision about Sumter would destroy their party.

Ohio Republican

If Fort Sumter is evacuated, the new administration is done forever, the Republican Party is done.

As Lincoln departed for Washington, Republican politicians from coast to coast assured the South that Lincoln would not interfere with slavery in their states, as the president-elect had continually promised.

Senator John Sherman, Ohio

The Republican Party is not likely to interfere with slavery directly or indirectly in the states or with the laws relating to slavery; that, so far as the slavery question the contest was for the possession of Kansas and perhaps, New Mexico, and that the chief virtue of the Republican success was in its condemnation of the narrow sectionalism of Buchanan's administration and the corruption by which he attempted to sustain his policy.

I rejoice in the result, for in my judgment the administration of Lincoln will do much to dissipate the feeling in the South against the North by showing what are the real purposes of the Republican Party. . . . If [the South] will hold on for a little while they will see that no injury can come to them unless by their repeated misrepresentations of us they stir up their slaves to insurrection. I still hope that no state will follow in the wake of South Carolina. If so, the weakness of her position will soon bring her back again or subject her to ridicule and insignificance.

As the urgency of the Sumter crisis grew, Lincoln urged his Republican colleagues to support his stand on slavery. The President told them again and again, as he told the South, that he would honor slavery where it already existed; he only opposed it in the territories. It was an important aspect of his feelings on slavery, and he thought the reinforcement of his stand would calm the troubles at Fort Sumter.

Abraham Lincoln
I think differently and as this subject is no other part and parcel of the larger general question of domestic slavery, I wish to make and to keep this distinction between the existing institution and the extension of it so broad and so clear that no honest man can misunderstand me and no dishonest one successfully misrepresent me.

A young man in Ohio, James Garfield, who would be president later, went several steps further in crusading against slavery and predicting its spread to the West if unchecked in the 1860s. He applauded the majority against slavery in the North, too.

James Garfield
The center of national power is moving with the sun—and in the West will be the final arbitrament of the question. When civilization has linked the seas and filled up the wilderness between there will have been added to our own present union 40 states as large as Ohio—or 200 as large as Massachusetts. . . . Upon what system of labor shall these new states be erected? What shall be the genius and spirit of their institutions?

When Garfield heard that Lincoln was elected:

James Garfield
God be praised!

Many agreed with Garfield.

Henry David Thoreau, philosopher
When were the good and brave ever in a majority?

Wendell Phillips, philosopher
In God's world there are no majorities, no minorities; one, on God's side, is a majority.

Public figures and Constitutional scholars had argued for years that majority rule was essential in both democracy and capitalism.

James Madison, fourth President of the United States
See the law of Virginia restricting foreign vessels to certain ports—of Maryland in favor of vessels belonging to her own citizens of N. York in favor of the same.

Southerners disagreed.

Jefferson Davis
Neither current events or history show that the majority rule, or ever did rule.

The rule of an anti-slavery, Northern majority in both houses of Congress both comforted and worried some Northerners—who predicted an arrogant Northern political majority would further antagonize the South.

William Tecumseh Sherman
For many years, the Southern politicians have struggled to maintain that equal representation in the Senate, long since lost in the House, and when, as now also, a majority is obtained in the Senate beyond chance of alteration, the question is settled and all angry controversy

might and ought to cease. The South, with a minority of representation in both branches, and with the presence of three millions of slaves in their midst, are weak and in the power of the North, so it seems to me that the Northern representation can afford to lay low and let events develop the solution of the dangerous political problem. If Congress does admit Kansas as a slave state her people will forthwith abolish it and the South will never again attempt to coerce their southern ideas upon any new territory so ill-adapted to their slave labor. . . .

William Tecumseh Sherman

Now, so certain and inevitable that the physical and political power of this nation must pass into the hands of the free states that I think you can all afford to take things easy, bear the buffets of a sinking dynasty and even smile at their impotent threats. You ought not to expect the Southern politicians to rest easy when they see and feel this crisis so long approaching and so certain to come, absolutely, at hand.

The abolitionists, of course, loved the new president and anyone who wanted to hold Sumter. This veneration, here and abroad, would persist. Years later, in 1909, Russian novelist Leo Tolstoy shared his thoughts with a reporter from the New York World *about President Lincoln.*

Leo Tolstoy

The greatness of Napoleon, Caesar or Washington . . . is only moonlight by the sun of Lincoln. His example is universal and will last thousands of years. . . . He was bigger than his country—bigger than all the Presidents together . . . and as a great character he will live as long as the world lives.

But in 1861, people no doubt wondered if the world as they knew it would survive. Politicians from both parties, and many newspapers, urged Lincoln to find a way—any way—to avert a war. He replied to all of them that he had to save the Union, no matter what the cost.

Abraham Lincoln
The Constitution will not be preserved and defended unless it is enforced and obeyed in every part of every one of the United States. It must be respected, obeyed, enforced and defended. Let the grass grow where it may.

Lincoln would later tell a friend, Orville Browning, that the stress of the Sumter crisis was enormous.

Abraham Lincoln
Browning, of all the trials I have had since I came here, none begin to compare with those I had between the inauguration and the fall of Fort Sumter. They were so great that could I have anticipated them, I would not have believed it possible to survive them.

Meanwhile, at Fort Sumter on March 4, just a few days before the inauguration, Major Robert Anderson seems to have been certain about what was coming for him and his men within the walls of the old, unfinished brick fort.

Captain Abner Doubleday
On the first of March, Anderson informed the general government that we would soon be attacked. The communication, however, led to no comment and no immediate action.

THREE

Washington, D.C. Lincoln's Inaugural Address to a Nation Holding Its Breath

Abraham Lincoln's inaugural address on March 4, 1861, was the most awaited speech in American history to that point. The crisis at Fort Sumter loomed. The biggest crowd ever to hear a speech, more than 25,000 people, massed in the streets in front of the Capitol. General Winfield Scott had ordered dozens of U.S. Army sharpshooters to stand on the rooftops of buildings nearby to provide security for the new president.

Lincoln consulted his new Secretary of State, William Seward, a gifted orator, who added some lyrical lines to the speech, and some other Republican leaders. He did not write the first draft in Washington, though. He wrote it in a nondescript little room in Springfield, Illinois, before he traveled by train to the nation's capital to be sworn in as chief executive.

Billy Herndon

He locked himself in a room upstairs over a store across the street from the state house and there, cut off from all communication and intrusion, he prepared the address.

It was in Springfield, too, that Lincoln had written to William Seward in February 1861.

Abraham Lincoln

I say now, however, as I have said all the while, that on the territorial question—that is, the question of extending slavery under the national auspices—I am inflexible. I am for no compromise which assists or permits the extension of the institution on soil owned by the nation. And any trick by which the nation is to acquire territory, and then allow some local authority to spread slavery over it, is as obnoxious as any other.

President-elect Lincoln had attended the swearing in of Vice President Hannibal Hamlin, of Maine, in the Senate chamber earlier and then accompanied others to the Capitol steps for his own inauguration. It was a cold day and the sky was overcast. He looked out on a massive sea of Americans, all very worried about the near and far future and Fort Sumter. He warned them in his inaugural address that secession would not work.

Abraham Lincoln

The union of these states is perpetual. . . . No state, upon its own mere motion, can lawfully get out of the Union. . . . Ordinances to that effect are legally void. . . . Acts of violence within any state or states, against the authority of the United States, are insurrectionary or revolutionary, according to circumstances.

The Union is unbroken, and, to the extent of my ability, I shall take care, as the Constitution expressly enjoins upon me, that the laws of the Union shall be faithfully executed in all the states. . . .

Physically speaking, we cannot separate. We cannot remove our respective sections from each other, nor build an impossible wall between them. A husband and wife may be divorced, but the different parts of our country cannot do that.

In your hands, my dissatisfied fellow countrymen, and not in mine, is the momentous issue of civil war. The government will not assail you. You can have no conflict without yourselves being the aggressor.

You have no oath registered in heaven to destroy the government while I shall have the most solemn one to protect and defend it.

We are not enemies, but friends . . . the mystic chords of memory stretching from every battlefield and patriot grave to every living heart and hearthstone, all over this broad land will yet swell the chorus of the union when again touched, as surely, they will be, by the better angels of our nature.

The pro-Lincoln crowd gathered for the speech cheered and roared at its finish. Lincoln may have captured just 39 percent of the popular vote in the four-man election of 1860, but his supporters were fanatical. A reporter on one of the trains returning delegates home from the summer 1860 convention in Chicago described the scene.

Murat Halstead, independent journalist

I left the city on the night train on the Fort Wayne and Chicago road. The train consisted of eleven cars, every seat full and people standing in the aisles and corners. I never before saw a company of persons so prostrated by continued excitement. The Lincoln men were not able to respond to the cheers which went up along the road for "old Abe." They had not only done their duty in that respect, but had exhausted their capacity. At every station where there was a village, until after two o'clock, there were tar barrels burning, drums beating, boys carrying rails; and guns, great and small, banging away. The weary passengers were allowed no rest, but plagued by the thundering jar of cannons, the clamor of drums, the glare of bonfires, and the whooping of the boys who were delighted with the idea of a candidate for the Presidency who thirty years ago on the Sangamon River, whose neighbors named him "honest."

Lincoln knew what was going on in those train cars in the summer of 1860—and out in the streets of Washington on the day of his inauguration.

Billy Herndon

The truth is Lincoln was as vigilant as he was ambitious, and there is no denying the fact that he understood the situation perfectly from the start.

Lincoln's goal as president was to serve all the people, North and South. That goal had not changed in all his years in public life. He had said the same thing, simply and forcefully, in an 1836 letter to the Sangamon Journal *about his state legislature race.*

Abraham Lincoln

If elected, I shall consider the whole people of Sangamon as my constituents, as well those that oppose, as those that support me.

While acting as their representative, I shall be governed by their will on all subjects upon which I have the means of knowing what their will is; and upon all others, I shall do what my own judgment teaches me will best advance their interests.

Lincoln's unique oration style, which made his inaugural address so powerful, featured a slow start and a powerful finish. This had not changed throughout his life. A man who heard him speak in 1836 gave this description to the Sangamon Journal. (*His reference was to Martin Van Buren, one of the founders of the Democratic Party.)*

Letter to the Editor, *Sangamon Journal*

His speech became more fluent, and his manner more easy as he progressed. In these degenerate days, it seems to be the fashion of the day for all parties to admire even the frailties of the administration. The Van Buren men, in particular, are even taking shelter like ghosts under the rotten bones and tombstones of the dead acts of the administration. Mr. Lincoln, however, lifted the lid and exposed to the eye the wretched condition of some of the acts of the Van Buren party.

A girl might be born and become a mother before the Van Buren men will forget Mr. Lincoln. From beginning to end, Mr. Lincoln was frequently interrupted by loud bursts of applause from a generous people.

Lincoln's speaking style from that long-ago speech was the same, and even better, when he was sworn in as president on March 4, 1861. Most Northern newspaper editors loved Lincoln's inaugural address.

Horace Greeley, *New York Tribune*
Every word of it has the ring of true metal.

Editor, *Illinois State Journal*
It electrified the whole country.

Senator Charles Sumner, Massachusetts
He has a hand of iron and a velvet glove.

Southern newspaper editors, of course, hated it.

Edwin Pollard, *Richmond Examiner*
It was a declaration of war.

Richmond Enquirer
The cool, unimpassioned deliberate language of the fanatic. . . . [S]ectional war awaits only the signal gun. The question "Where shall Virginia go?" is answered by Lincoln. She must go to war.

Editor, *Montgomery Weekly Advertiser*
War, war, war and nothing less than war will satisfy the Abolition chief.

Another critic was Robert Rhett Jr., who took over as editor of the Charleston Mercury, *perhaps the most influential newspaper in the South, in 1857.*

Robert Rhett Jr.
It was a lamentable display of feeble inability.

Many Southerners working in Washington detested Lincoln. One was Supreme Court Justice John Campbell, who had previously worked in Georgia and Alabama and was an ardent champion of slavery.

Supreme Court Justice John Campbell
A stump speech, not an inaugural message . . . incendiary.

One of the most severe critics of Lincoln's address was Louis Wigfall, a hot-headed politician from South Carolina who had moved to Texas and was elected to the US Senate there. The temperamental Wigfall was, in just a three-month period in South Carolina, shot in a duel, involved in three near-duels, and participated in a savage fist fight. Texans loved the hard-drinking politician who was also, when sober, a gifted orator.

Senator Louis Wigfall, Texas
The inaugural means war.

Wigfall went on to elaborate why the South had no need of the Union.

Senator Louis Wigfall

We are an agricultural people; we are a primitive but civilized people. We have no cities—we don't want them. We have no literature—we don't need any yet. We have no press—we are glad of it. We do not require a press because we go out and discuss all public questions from the stump with our people. We have no commercial marine—no navy—and don't want them. We are better without them. Your ships carry our produce, and you can protect your own vessels. We want no manufacture; we desire no reading, no mechanical or manufacturing classes. As long as we have our rice, sugar and tobacco, and our cotton, we can command wealth to purchase all we want from those nations with whom we are in amity.

While Lincoln made no reference to Fort Sumter in his inaugural address, the editors of many Southern newspapers said that when Lincoln said he intended to "hold occupy and possess the property and places belonging to the government and to collect the duties and imposts," he was speaking of Sumter.

Editor, *Richmond Whig*

We desire to repeat what he said yesterday [about holding properties] that the coercive policy foreshadowed in Lincoln's Inaugural towards the seceding states will meet with the stern and unyielding resistance of a united South. . . . [It] necessarily involves war and war, as remarked by Mr. Durma in his speech [the Virginia secession convention] yesterday involves a total and permanent disruption of the Union. Let Lincoln carry out the policy indicated in his Inaugural and Civil War will be inaugurated forthwith throughout the length and breadth of the land.

He added that Lincoln's goal should be to let the seceding states leave the Union to avoid warfare.

Editor, *Richmond Whig*

[Holding properties] is inadmissible—it is utterly absurd and ridiculous and if Lincoln and his advisers wish to avoid serious trouble, and save the peace of the country, they will abandon their coercion policy and take their stand on the broad platform of common sense and common justice . . . [and] the Union may yet be restored in all its pristine dimensions. Strength and glory.

Editor, *Richmond Dispatch*

The Inaugural address of Abraham Lincoln inaugurates a civil war. The Demon of Coercion stands unmasked.

Charleston Mercury

It is a declaration of war. . . . Abraham still staggers to and fro like a drunken man under the intoxication of his new position and the pressure of opposing forces. Such has been the strain upon the poor creature's nerves by his partisans Chase and Cameron that a day or two ago he burst into tears and oaths and cried "My God! Gentlemen, what shall I do? How can I decide?" Unhappy being.

Many Southerners saw Lincoln's inaugural address, and his anti-slavery sentiments, as a direct attack on their way of life. To them, it once again underscored the growing attacks on the slavery system by Lincoln and his "Black Republicans." One plantation overseer in Louisiana was especially fuming.

Overseer

I pray sincerely to God that every Black Republican, in the whole combined world, every man woman and child, that is opposed to Negro slavery as it existed in the southern confederacy be troubled with pestilence & calamity of all kinds and drag out the balance of their existence in misery and degradation and scarcely food and payment enough to keep soul and body together and, oh God, I pray to direct a bullet or a bayonet to pierce the heart of every northern soldier that invades the South.

Southern women especially castigated Lincoln. When she heard of Lincoln's election, plantation mistress Keziah Brevard, a widowed plantation owner, offered a chilling response.

Keziah Brevard
Oh my God!!! This morning I heard that Lincoln was elected. . . . I do pray that if there is to be a crisis, we all lay down our lives sooner than free our slaves in our midst. No soul on earth is more willing for justice than I am, but the idea of being mixed up with free blacks is horrid!

Southerners had seen slaves as essential for more than two hundred years. Back in the days of George Washington, the prominent South Carolinian planter Charles Cotesworth Pinckney explained the place of blacks in the South.

Charles Pinckney
Negroes are to this country what raw materials are to another country.

And at an 1850 Nashville convention, delegate Langdon Cheves was asked his opinion of what to do if Congress banned slavery.

Langdon Cheves
Unite, and you shall form one of the most splendid empires on which the sun ever shone.

Before the Fort Sumter crisis, some Northerners also saw slavery as necessary in the farm economy of the South. One was future Union General

William Tecumseh Sherman, who wrote to his congressman brother, John, in 1859.

William Tecumseh Sherman
I go South among gentlemen who have always owned slaves, and probably always will and must, and whose feeling may pervert every public expression of yours, putting me in a false position to them as my patrons, friends and associates, and you as my brother. I would like to see you take the highest ground consistent with your party creed.

But that was certainly not the only view. Lincoln friend and US Senator James Harlan had this to say to Southerners.

Senator James Harlan, Iowa
You offensively thrust slavery on us as a great good to be desired and extended and perpetuated by all the powers of a national government.

John Dix served as Secretary of the Treasury under President James Buchanan from January to March 1861, after other Southerners deserted Buchanan's Cabinet. Lincoln would soon appoint him a major general in the Union Army. Dix wrote to Lincoln about the Sumter crisis.

John Dix
I can hardy realize that I am living in the age in which I was born and educated. In the . . . face of the humiliating spectacle of base intrigue to overthrow the government by those who are living upon its bounty, and of a pusillanimous or perfidious surrender of the trusts confided to them, the country turns with a feeling of relief . . . to the noble example of fidelity and courage presented by you and your gallant associates [at Sumter].

Lincoln saw the inaugural addresses of Republican governors as another way to strengthen his own position. With an eye on the crisis brewing at Fort Sumter, he told newly elected Pennsylvania Governor Andrew Curtin to stick with Washington's policy.

Abraham Lincoln

I think you would do well to express, without passion, threat or appearance of boasting, but nevertheless with firmness, the purpose of yourself and your state, to maintain the Union at all hazards.

Slaves all over the South who listened carefully to their masters' conversations got the news of Lincoln's election, too, and were elated.

Captain Abner Doubleday

The Negroes [in Charleston] overheard a great deal that was said by their masters and in consequence became excited and troublesome, for the news flew like wild fire among them that "Massa Linkum" was going to set them free.

Would he though?

Chapter 4

Washington, D.C., The White House

Ugly Abe Lincoln

There was another discussion in the nation in early March 1861 that was just as vociferous as the one about Fort Sumter, and that was the ungainly physical appearance of the new president. Many, North and South, criticized the appearance of their new president from the frontiers of Illinois. He may have regaled the nation with his delightful humor and his soaring oratory, but Abraham Lincoln did not look like a president at all.

Even foreigners were aghast at his looks when they met him. One was the famous war correspondent from the London Times, *William Howard Russell. The journalist had built an impressive reputation during the years he had covered the Crimean War and an uprising in India. Well-dressed and well-spoken, he had met hundreds of dignitaries. He was stunned by the appearance of President Lincoln, whom he met at a White House reception in March 1861.*

William Howard Russell

He had a shambling loose, irregular almost unsteady gait, a tall, lanky, lean man considerably over six feet in height with stooping shoulders, long, pendulous arms, terminating in hands of extraordinary dimensions, which, however, were far exceeded in proportions by his feet. He was dressed in an ill-fitting, wrinkled suit of black, which put one in mind of an undertaker's uniform at a funeral. 'Round his neck a rope of black silk was knotted in a large bulb . . . his turn down shirt collar disclosed a sinewy, muscular neck and above that, nested in a great black mass of hair . . . [then] rose the strange quaint face and head covered with its thatch of Republican hair. The nose itself—a prominent organ—stands out from the face with an inquiring, anxious air as though it were sniffing for some good thing in the wind. The eyes, dark, full and deeply set, are penetrating and full of expression which almost amounts to tenderness . . . a person who met Mr. Lincoln in the street would not take him to be a gentleman.

Russell was equally appalled by Mary Lincoln.

William Russell

[She is] plain, her nose and mouth of an ordinary type, and her manners and appearance homely, stiffened, however, by the consciousness that her position requires her to be something more than plain Mrs. Lincoln, the wife of the Illinois lawyer. She is profuse in the introduction of the word "sir" in every sentence.

Most Southerners agreed with Russell's assessment of the new president. So did many soldiers at Fort Sumter, including Wylie Crawford, the garrison's assistant surgeon. Crawford had graduated from the University of Pennsylvania and was now celebrating his tenth year in the Army. He was an ambitious, confident man with long black sideburns at the edges of his face. A skilled artist, he sold sketches of Fort Sumter to Harper's Weekly *(for the goodly sum of $25 each). He accepted his job as surgeon, but told friends he would rather be a field commander. He did not like the president.*

Wylie Crawford

Lincoln is a vulgar, third rate politician, a man without anything to entitle him to the position which he holds, an uncouth Western Hoosier.

One high society woman, Mrs. Scott, just shook her head from side to side when talking about Lincoln.

Mrs. Scott
He was awfully ugly, even grotesque in appearance, the kind who is always at the corner stores, sitting on boxes, whittling sticks and telling stories as funny as they are vulgar.

Her husband saw Lincoln as an amusing country bumpkin.

Mr. Scott
Lincoln is an utter American specimen—course, rough, and strong; a good natured and kind creature as pleasant tempered as he is clever and if this country can be joked and laughed out of its rights, he is the kind hearted fellow to do it.

George Harding, lawyer
[He is] a tall, rawly boned, ungainly back woodsman, with coarse, ill-fitting clothing, his trousers hardly reaching his ankles, holding in his hands a blue cotton umbrella.

Why did you bring that damned, long armed ape here . . . he does not know anything and can do you no good.

Back in Illinois, Lincoln had been badly disrespected at a trial by several well-dressed, powerful East Coast lawyers who saw him as a frontier barrister. Lincoln was not intimidated.

Abraham Lincoln
For any rough and tumble case, I am enough for any we have out in that country, but these college trained men are coming West. They have all

the advantages of a life-long training in the law, plenty of time to study and everything, perhaps, to fit them. Soon they will be in Illinois . . . and when they appear, I will be ready.

Many said he was just uncouth.

New Yorker, overheard in a hotel lobby
Could he, with any honor, fill the Presidential chair? Would his midwestern gaucherie disgrace the nation?

Emma Holmes, a Charleston socialite whose Uncle Edward was a well-connected Washingtonian, was quite certain Lincoln could not fill that chair.

Emma Holmes
[He is] stupid, ambiguous, vulgar and insolent.

Most of the Southern newspaper editors agreed with her—and even some of the Northern ones. Some said the whole country would become bad real estate under Lincoln.

Editor, *New York Evening Day Book*
The great Black Republican "Wigwam," in which Abe Lincoln was nominated for President, was to have been sold at auction on Saturday, last. The country, under his administration, is rapidly going the same way.

Even Lincoln's friends and admirers agreed that he was not a handsome man.

George Templeton Strong
[Lincoln was] lank and hard featured, among the ugliest white men I have seen.

Joshua Speed, Illinois friend of Lincoln

[Abe was] a long, gawky, ugly, shapeless man.

Anna Gentry, Illinois friend of Lincoln

Abe was a long, thin, leggy, gawky boy.

Robert Rhett Jr., the editor of the Charleston Mercury, *just hated Lincoln, and described him as simian.*

Robert Rhett Jr.

The "ourang outang" at the White House has not issued his orders yet . . . for the reinforcements of the forts. . . . [He is] vain, ignorant, a low fellow, a blatant old ass and a preposterous buffoon.

In an 1860 editorial, Rhett blasted Lincoln as an abolitionist's dream and went so low as to compare him to William Seward, the most hated man in the South. A senator who sat within a few feet of Lincoln while he was in the Senate chamber on the day of the inauguration went even further.

Anonymous US Senator

His face is enough of its own to hang him; if he happened to be in a California mining district while any stealing was going on and the thief was not known, but only suspected . . . a horrid looking wretch he is . . . sooty and scoundrelly in aspect, a cross between the nutmeg dealer, the horse swapper and the night man.

State Representative Robert Wilson, Illinois

[Lincoln's] hands were large and bony . . . when standing straight, and letting his arms fall down his sides, the points of his fingers would touch a point lower on his legs by more than three inches than was usual with other persons [and his feet were large, too].

Lincoln had been a poor dresser all his life. A merchant who knew him in his early twenties in New Salem, Illinois, attested to it.

Abner Ellis

Frequently he had but one suspender, no vest or coat.

Washingtonians called him all sorts of names, but they had been harsh with his predecessors, too, especially James Buchanan. Maria Lydia Daly was the wife of a New York judge and a frequent visitor to Washington, where she partied with the rich and influential and had met President Buchanan.

Maria Lydia Daly

I never saw so incapable a face as Buchanan's. Surely, no woman would have been crazy enough had he been in the profession of medicine, to entrust him with the health of her favorite poodle.

Buchanan relaxed when he could, dressed as casual as anyone could be. Julia Taft wrote that he would sit in the library at night, clothed sparingly.

Julia Taft

[In his] long skirted, faded dressing gown, belted around his waist, Bible next to him . . . [he liked to read] in his big chair by the window in his stocking feet with one leg crossed over the other, the unshod foot slowly waving back and forth, as if in time to some inaudible music.

Compared to Lincoln, though, Buchanan was the Best Dressed Man of the Year.

Nathaniel Grigsby, Indiana friend of Lincoln

Between the shoe and sock and his britches—made of buckskin—there was barc and naked six or more inches of Abe Lincoln's shinbone.

Lincoln was aware of, and understood, his detractors.

Abraham Lincoln

Nobody has ever expected me to be President. In my poor, lean, lank face nobody has ever seen that any cabbage was sprouting out. . . . A party of plain people began to comment on my appearance saying he was a very common-looking man. The Lord prefers common-looking people. That is the reason he makes so many of them.

Lincoln was once startled by a portrait of himself.

Helen Nicolay

He said it was "horribly like me."

Nicolay was the daughter of Lincoln's secretary, John Nicolay, and an artist as well as a writer. In her memories of the president, she sized him up well.

Helen Nicolay

He was fully aware of the worst aspect of his personal appearance and regretted it. . . . He was a huge spare man, slightly stooping, who walked with the peculiar slow woods-and-field movement of the western pioneer and who sat as tall people have to sit, in chairs made for shorter folk. Not erect, but disposing of their long limbs as best they may. . . . A sad and sallow man upon whom clothes hung loosely.

Southern writers liked to compare Lincoln to other men they despised. The Washington Constitution's *favorite whipping boy was Joshua Giddings, the abolitionist Congressman from Ohio.*

Editor, *Washington Constitution*

Lincoln appears to be a man after Joshua R. Giddings own heart—vile and brutal abolitionist as he is. The old fanatic has made a speech at Oberlin warmly recommending Lincoln to the support of the Abolitionists of that neighborhood and has also written a letter to the nominee.

Southerners, after all, had their own good-looking, fire-eating men, such as William Tennent Jr., the young writer. Tennent, twenty-two, wrote dozens of pro-South political pamphlets. He had newspapers print thousands of these "incendiary" pamphlets that he would hand out promoting secession. He was, people said, as handsome as Lincoln was ugly.

William Tennent Jr.

Stir the sleeping South out of the lethargy fostered by the poison called love of Union.

Merchant Robert Gourdin, head of Charleston's 1860 Association and a Charleston alderman, also loved using pamphlets to get his message across. He took arguments written by different authors, printed about 200,000 of each, and distributed them to every home in Charleston and to other cities across the South. The pamphlets lambasted everything about Lincoln, not just his ungainly physical appearance.

"The South Alone Should Govern the South"

[Time is] hurrying the question to your hearthstones. . . . How then do you decide? Is it for manly RESISTANCE, to be followed with security and a prosperous end? Or is it for SUBMISSION, and a short inglorious ease, to be followed with certain ruin? Say!

People all over the South applauded the pamphlets and their authors.

Editor, *Montgomery (Alabama) Daily Mail*
Circulate the documents. The people take it and read it with avidity. We could distribute thousands of copies instead of hundreds. We call upon our States' Rights friends, in every county of the state, to collect funds and forward them to the *Mercury* or *Courier* offices in Charleston for this and other pamphlets.

John Townsend himself became a literary hero in the Southern states. Others wrote to Townsend urging him to run for governor of South Carolina.

"Palmetto," pamphlet reader
John Townsend . . . his cultivated intellect, his high practical sense, fixed and approved political opinions.

Many people who formed a poor opinion of Lincoln at first, heavily influenced by the way he looked and dressed, or the way his home was appointed, changed their minds as they got to know him.

Cooper Union audience member, New York, 1860
When Lincoln rose to speak, I was greatly disappointed. He was tall, tall, oh, how tall, and so angular and awkward that I had, for an instant, a feeling of pity for him for so ungainly a man. [After a few minutes, the man went on]: His face lighted up as with an inward fire. The whole man was transfigured. I forgot his clothes, his personal appearance and his individual peculiarities. Presently, forgetting myself, I was on my feet like the rest yelling like a wild Indian cheering this wonderful man.

New York Tribune *editor Horace Greeley also thought Lincoln's Cooper Union speech was superb.*

Horace Greeley

One of the happiest and most convincing political arguments ever made in this city. The vast assemblage frequently rang with cheers and shouts of applause, which were prolonged and intensified at the close. No man ever before made such an impression on his first appeal to a New York audience.

A. K. McClure, a politician from Pennsylvania, befriended Lincoln after McClure bolted from the side of fellow Pennsylvanian Simon Cameron and led the Pennsylvania delegates to the Republican Convention to vote for Lincoln—an important move that helped Lincoln win the Republican nomination for president. He visited Lincoln at his home in Springfield after the 1860 presidential election. He was startled when the president-elect himself answered the door.

A. K. McClure

I doubt whether I wholly concealed my disappointment at meeting him. Tall, gaunt, ungainly ill-clad with a homeliness of manner that was unique in itself. I confess that my heart sank within me as I remembered that this was the man chosen by a great nation to be its ruler in the gravest period in its history. I remember his dress as if it were yesterday—snuff colored and slouchy pantaloons, open black vest held by a few brass buttons, straight or evening dress coat, with tightly fitting sleeves to exaggerate his long, bony arms, and all supplemented by an awkwardness that was uncommon among men of intelligence. Such was the picture I met in the person of Abraham Lincoln. We sat down in his plainly furnished parlor and were uninterrupted during the nearly four hours that I remained with him, and, little by little, as his earnestness, sincerity and candor were developed in conversation,

I forgot all the grotesque qualities which confounded me when I first greeted him. Before half an hour had passed I learned not only to respect but, indeed, to reverence the man.

Lincoln's sincerity and lack of artifice impressed everyone who met him. Senator Stephen Douglas met Lincoln when both men were in their twenties.

Senator Stephen Douglas, Illinois

I was never more quickly or completely put at ease at the presence of a great man than that of Abraham Lincoln.

Albert Beveridge, historian

It cannot be too often stated that friendliness was the most striking feature of his personality—so striking that it is noted with emphasis in all accounts given by acquaintances and observers of Abraham Lincoln in those days.

Lincoln impressed even newspaper editors who did not like him.

Cincinnati Daily Commercial

He is not guilty of any diplomacy, and does not understand why he should not in his own plain way tell the plain truth as it appears to him. . . . [This contrasts with] the courtly graces and diplomacy of the whited sepulcher who is the present occupant of the White House [Buchanan].

Criticism of Lincoln never ended.

FIVE

Washington, D.C., Lincoln's Humor

Abraham Lincoln's wit was legendary. One could not get through a meeting with him without hearing one of his funny stories. After the inauguration, his humor began to be as appreciated in Washington, D.C., as it had been in his native Illinois.

Helen Nicolay

Some men, born with the gift of wit, lack judgment, or persistent energy. Others, endowed with unusual sagacity, are hampered by a cold earnestness which repels confidence. Still others, afflicted with blind, unreasoning energy, blunder perpetually into destructive acts of courage and daring. Lincoln had these qualities in happy combination: wit to attract and hold men, logical sense and clear vision to plan methodical action; and, best of all, that high courage which, when the golden moment came inspired him to bold and fearless action, regardless of what others thought and careless of consequences to himself.

Lincoln used a lot of humor during the Fort Sumter crisis to calm his listeners—and himself.

Helen Nicolay

[People] could not see that, tortured almost beyond endurance by the responsibility and the horror of war, he was telling stories for a purposes—reaching out instinctively for something to turn the current of his thoughts even for a moment in order that he might get a firmer grip again and a saner outlook upon life.

Abraham Lincoln
If it were not for this occasional vent, I should die.

Alexander Stephens, Vice President of the Confederacy
Mr. Lincoln was careful as to his manners, awkward in his speech, but was possessed of a very strong clear, vigorous mind. He always attracted and riveted the attention of the House when he spoke. He had no model. He was a man of strong convictions and what Carlyle would have called an earnest man in anecdote and socially he always kept his company in a roar of laughter.

One of Lincoln's closest friends was Springfield General Store owner Joshua Speed, one of the first people he met when he moved to that city. The two became roommates and best friends. Later, Lincoln offered Speed several jobs in his administration, but Speed turned them all down.

Joshua Speed
His world-wide reputation for telling anecdotes—and telling them so well—was in my judgment necessary to his existence.

Some understood his witty approach, some did not, and some were just dumbfounded by his style, such as this listener at an 1839 speech.

Illinois State Register
Mr. Lincoln's argument was truly ingenious. He has, however, a sort of assumed clownishness in his manner which does not become him and which does not truly belong to him. It is assumed—assumed for

effect. Mr. Lincoln will sometime make his language correspond with his clownishness, and he can thus frequently raise a loud laugh among his Whig hearers but this entire game of buffoonery convinces the mind of no man and is utterly lost on the majority of his audience. We seriously advise Mr. Lincoln to correct this clownish fault before it grows upon him.

Lincoln never did take the advice. His humor worked too well. He loved to repeat stories he had heard from someone else, and went so far as to officially stand in the Illinois State Legislature to ask permission to tell a funny story he had just heard. Permission granted, he told the story and the House convulsed with laughter.

◆

Lincoln was also a virtuous man. None of his friends had a bad thing to say about him, and could think of no Lincoln vices.

E. R. Thayer, Springfield merchant

When [William Henry] Harrison defeated Van Buren, there was a great frolic in Springfield. I do not believe there has ever been such a jollification since then. The center of the celebration was a high saloon, and there champagne flowed like water. It was a favorite trick to knock off the head of a bottle by striking it on the stove. Lincoln was present and made a great deal of sport with his speeches, witty sayings and stories. He even played leap frog, but he did not drink a thing.

Abner Y. Ellis, New Salem merchant

He did not in those days either smoke or chew tobacco. . . . Springfield in those days was a hard place for a temperate young man and I have often wondered how he could be so extremely popular and not drink and carouse with them. He used to run footraces and jump and play ball. . . . He was good at telling stories and anecdotes and I think that was the one great reason of his being so popular.

Row Herndon, Lincoln cousin

He never used bad language. I never remembered him drinking or playing cards or even cursing.

The Clary's Grove Boys lived in a settlement near New Salem, Illinois, where Lincoln moved in 1831. They were a loud, reckless group of local toughs who enjoyed fighting and drinking—and befriended Lincoln as a young man.

Henry McHenry, one of the Clary's Grove Boys

During all the time—during all those years—I never knew Mr. Lincoln to run a horse race—then being common if not universal, over the whole county. I never knew him . . . to gamble or play cards.

McHenry added that Lincoln was also free from the vice of running after women.

A Kentuckian who met Lincoln on a stagecoach repeatedly offered him a drink or some tobacco, and was repeatedly refused.

Kentucky stagecoach passenger to Lincoln

See here stranger, you're a clever, but strange, companion. I may never see you again, and I don't want to offend you, but my experience has taught me that a man who has no vices has damned few virtues.

One thing that all who met him, or heard of him, agreed on was that he had considerable physical strength, which he had often displayed as a young man.

Springfield resident
I think it is safe to say he was never thrown in a wrestle.

Albert Beveridge, historian
Lincoln had great physical strength. So great that tales of his performances are well-nigh unbelievable.

A Springfield militiaman who served under Lincoln's command in the Black Hawk War commended him.

Springfield militiaman
The Genial Captain jumped, ran, boxed and wrestled better than any man in the expedition.

Lincoln was also resolute in his beliefs. He never wavered in his opinions, whether about local New Salem politics as a young man or about slavery throughout his adult life. This impressed everyone who knew him. And it was never exemplified more than in Congress during the winter of 1860–1861.

After the 1860 election, a senator stared at Stephen Douglas and told him he had spent his life changing his opinions on slavery in order to gain higher office. Lincoln, the man said, had always been steady in his opposition to slavery, even though it had hurt him politically.

Senator
Now, look where you are and look where he is.

To what did Lincoln himself attribute his success in life?

Abraham Lincoln
Work, work, work.

SIX

Charleston, South Carolina

What to Do About Fort Sumter?

By the time Abraham Lincoln sat down with his Cabinet to discuss Fort Sumter several days after his inaugural address, the Northern press had seemingly made up its mind about the South Carolina fort. When the Southern states started to secede, major Northern newspapers told them to go. Their editors assumed that they would stay out of the Union for few months, realize they had made a mistake, and come crawling back on their knees to beg for forgiveness and rejoin the United States.

Horace Greeley, Editor, *New York Tribune*

We hold, with (Thomas) Jefferson, of the inalienable right of communities to alter or abolish forms of government that have become oppressive or injurious and, if the cotton states should decide that they can do better out of the Union than in it, we insist on letting them go in peace. The right to secede might be a revolutionary right but it exists nonetheless and we do not see how one party can have a right to do what another party has a right to prevent. We must ever resist the assertive right of any state to remain in the Union and to nullify or defy the laws thereof: To withdraw from the Union is quite another matter. And, whenever a considerable section of our Union shall deliberately resolve to go out, we shall resist all coercive measures designed to keep her in. We hope never to live in a republic whereof one section is pinned to the residue by bayonets.

Other newspaper editors disagreed. They believed that two nations could not exist on one continent.

Henry Raymond, Editor, *New York Times*

If the two sections can no longer live together, they can no longer live apart in quiet till it is determined which is master. No two civilizations ever did, or can, come into contact as they North and South threaten to do without a trial of strength in which the weaker goes to the wall. . . . We must remain master of the occasion and dominant power on this continent.

At first, most Northerners believed Southerners would quickly come back.

Charles Eliot Norton, philosopher

I am inclined to believe that they will not try violence, and that their course as an independent Confederacy is nearly at an end.

Charles Francis Adams Jr.

The experiment will ignominiously fail.

William Tecumseh Sherman believed a national economy in the Southern states would not work very well.

William Tecumseh Sherman

If the South had free trade, how can you collect revenues in the eastern cities? Freight from New Orleans to St. Louis, Chicago, Louisville, Cincinnati, and even Pittsburgh would be about the same as by rail from New York and importers at New Orleans, having no duties to pay, would undersell the East if they had duties to pay. Therefore, if the South makes good their confederation and their plan, the Northern

Confederacy must do likewise or blockade. Then comes the question of foreign nations. So, look on it in any view, I see no result but war and consequent changes in the form of government.

Horace Greeley told his readers that the new president had his hands full and agreed that if the South wanted to secede, they should be allowed to.

Horace Greeley, *New York Tribune*

The new President must fulfill the obligations assumed in his inaugural oath no matter how shamefully his predecessor may have defied them. . . . [If states say] "We want to get out of the union" we shall feel constrained by our devotion to human liberty to say "Let them go!"

Harry Carey, Philadelphia economist

So, I say to let them go peacefully as fast as they see fit to go. It would be a fitting exit for the wildest men the world has yet seen.

Editor, *Albany (New York) Argus*

We sympathize with and justify the South as far as this—their rights have been invaded to the extreme limit possible within the Constitution and, beyond this limit, their feelings have been insulted and their interest and honor assailed by almost every possible form of denunciation and invective and, if we deemed it certain that the real amicus of the Republican party could be carried into the administration of the federal government, and become the permanent policy of the nation, we should think that all the instincts of self-preservation and manhood rightfully impelled them to a resort to revolution and a separation from the Union and we would applaud them and wish them Godspeed in the adoption of such a remedy.

Editor, *New York Herald*
Each state is organized as a complete government holding the purse and wielding the sword, possessing the right to break the tie of a confederation as a nation might break a treaty, and to repel coercion as a nation might repel invasion. . . . Coercion, if it were possible, is out of the question.

The editor also asked the South to acknowledge that Lincoln was now in charge, however unhappy that made Southerners. In short, he told them to stop being sore losers.

Editor, *New York Herald*
What's the use? They are beaten now and may triumph next time; in fact, they have generally had their own way had they been subjected to the discipline of adversity as often as we have, they would probably bear it with more philosophy; and deport themselves more befittingly.

Editor, *Bangor (Maine) Union*
The difficulties between the North and the South must be compromised or the separation of the states shall not be peaceable. If the Republican Party refuses to go the full length of the Crittenden [Compromise] Amendment, which is the very least the South can or ought to take—then here in Maine, not a Democrat will be found who will raise his arms against his brethren of the South. From one end of the state to the other, let the cry of the Democracy be, Compromise or peaceable separation!

The Crittenden Compromise, introduced in the Senate in December 1860, attempted to permanently enshrine slavery on the Constitution. It was defeated.

No one in the North hated slavery more than William Lloyd Garrison, the editor of the abolitionist newspaper The Liberator. *But he, too, preferred to see the Southern states secede.*

William Lloyd Garrison

What is the true course of the people of the North? Is it to vindicate sovereignty by the sword until the treason is quelled and allegiance restored? Constitutionally, the sword may be wielded to this extent, and must be, by . . . President Lincoln, if the Union is to be preserved. The Federalist government must not pretend to be in actual operation, embracing thirty-four states and then allow the seceding states to trample upon its flag, steal its property, defy its authority with impunity; for it would then be a mockery and a laughing stock.

Whipping the South into subjugation and extorting allegiance from millions of people in the cannon's mouth is utterly [un]American. It is in the power of the North to deluge her soil with blood but not to conquer her spirit. Depart in peace.

Surprisingly, Garrison did not want to force the abolitionist view down the throats of Southerners, but simply wanted to let them go to start their own country. Thank God we're rid of them! *he believed.*

William Lloyd Garrison

The people of the North should recognize the fact that the Union is dissolved, and act accordingly. They should see, in the madness of the South, the hand of God, liberating them from a covenant with death and an agreement with hell, made in time of terrible peril, and without a conception of the inevitable consequences, and which has corrupted their morals poisoned their religion, petrified their humanity as towards the millions in bondage, tarnished their character, harassed their peace, hardened them with taxation, shackled their prosperity and brought them into abject vassalage.

New Orleans, which had never really regarded itself as a part of the traditional South, saw disaster looming in secession.

Editor, *New Orleans True Delta*

The odds and ends of every faction which have combined themselves together to precipitate the cotton states to revolution have shown an audacity which Marat, Danton or Robespierre [French Revolution leaders] might have envied. Special privileges, a rag money aristocracy and favored classes will now be fastened upon unfortunate Louisiana, and in return the people will have the consolation derivable from the reflection that one of her greatest domestic interests is destroyed and her importance as a state of the Union dwarfed into a pigmy association with decaying, retrograding and penniless confederates. The depth of our own degradation for the time distracts the attention of the people from the progress of oligarchical usurpation and tyranny in our sister states, which are made participants with us in a humiliating calamity.

Some Northerners stunned the nation by suggesting that sections of the North secede, too. New York City Mayor Fernando Wood was one of them. He wanted his city to quit the Union just as quickly as the Southern states were quitting. Politicians in New Jersey and California entertained the same idea.

Mayor Fernando Wood, New York

When disunion has become a fixed and certain fact, why may not New York disrupt the bands which bond her to a venal and corrupt master—to a people and a party that have plundered her revenues, attempted to ruin her commerce, taken away the powers of self-government and destroyed the Confederacy of which she was the proud Empire City?

Soldiers at Fort Sumter raised their eyebrows at Wood and others like him, as well as their idea of leaving the Union.

Captain Abner Doubleday

At the time, the seeming indifference of the politicians to our fate made us feel like orphan children of the Republic, deserted by both the state and federal administrations.

Most Northerners scoffed at Wood. They castigated the South and warned of trouble up ahead.

The Illinois State Journal, *Lincoln's mouthpiece newspaper, repeatedly threatened Charlestonians that a single shot fired by one of them could cause a war. Back in December 20, 1860, the day secession was passed in South Carolina, the newspaper fired off a warning.*

Editor, *Illinois State Journal*

Disunion, by armed force, is treason and treason must and will be put down at all costs.

Many newspaper editors waffled on the issue, though.

Mary Chestnut

Today the papers say peace again. Yesterday the *Telegraph & the Herald* were warlike to a frightful degree.

Some Northern and Western politicians were not bothered by secession, either, and said the law indicated that the federal government did not own property, such as Fort Sumter, in Charleston, or in any state.

Senator Joseph Lane, Oregon

If there is, as I contend, the right of secession, then whenever a state exercises that right this government has no laws in that state to execute nor has it any such property in that state that can be protected by the power of this government. By attempting, however, to substitute the smooth phrase "execute the laws" and "protecting public property" for coercion, for a civil war, we have an important concession: that is, this government dare not go before the people with a plain avowal of its real purposes and of their consequences; no sir, the policy is to inveigle the people of the North into civil war, by masking the designs in smooth and ambiguous terms.

What constituted public property became a large issue. Was the entire fort a piece of property within the South Carolina state lines that therefore belonged to the state, or was the fort federal property that happened to sit within the state lines of South Carolina?

....

Captain Abner Doubleday

Even if the state had a right to secede, it does not follow that the public property within her limits properly belonged to her. . . . [T]o seize it at once, and without a declaration of war and while the subject was still pending, was a violation of all rights and precedent.

Confederate President Jefferson Davis agreed with them all and rattled his sword once or twice.

....

Jefferson Davis

Ten thousand swords that would have leaped from their scabbards—as the English statesman thought—to avenge even a look of insult to a lovely queen hung idly in their places when she was led to the scaffold in the midst of the vilest taunts and execrations. The case that we have been considering was, perhaps, only an illustration of the general truth that in times of revolutionary excitement the higher and better elements are crushed and silenced by the lower and baser—not so much on account of their greater extent as of their greater violence.

There were Northerners who did not want a war but saw one coming as Congressional negotiations between North and South broke down. The Committee of Thirty-Three was a select committee of the House of Representatives established on December 4, 1860, to explore possibilities for resolving the secession crisis. Congressman Thomas Corwin was a member of the committee.

Representative Thomas Corwin, Ohio

If the states are no more harmonious in their feelings and opinions than these 33 representative men then appalling as the idea is, we must dissolve and a long and bloody Civil War must follow. I cannot comprehend the madness of the times. Southern men are theoretically crazy. Extreme northern men are practical fools. The latter are really quite as bad as the former. Treason is in the air around us everywhere and goes by the cause of Patriotism. Men in Congress boldly grow it and the public offices are full of acknowledged secessionists. God alone I fear can help us. Four or five states are gone, others are driving before the gate. I have looked on this horrid picture till I have been able to gaze on it with perfect calmness.

Northerners said the South's problem was that it injected the slave question into every single discussion with Northerners. William Tecumseh Sherman wrote this to his brother John, the Congressman from Ohio.

William Tecumseh Sherman

If Southern representatives will thrust slavery into every local question they must expect the consequences and be outvoted; but the Union of states and general union of sentiment throughout all our nation are so important to the honor and glory of the confederacy [nation] that I would like to see your position yet more moderate.

At that time, Jefferson Davis argued that leaving the Union was not a rebellion and did not require a war on either side.

Jefferson Davis

The withdrawal of a State from a league has no revolutionary or insurrectionary characteristic. The government of the State remains unchanged as to all internal affairs. It is only its external relations that are altered. To them this action of a Sovereign "rebellion" is a gross abuse of language.

Many in the business community kept insisting, over all these months, that there was a way out so that both Northern and Southern businesses could continue to make money. One was James Thayer, a former Whig from New York.

James Thayer

We can at least . . . arrive at the basis of a peaceable separation. We can at least by discussion enlighten, settle and concentrate the public sentiment in the state of New York upon this question, and save it from that fearful current that circuitously, but certainly, sweeps madly on, through the narrow gorge of "the enforcement of the laws" to the shoreless ocean of Civil War. Against this, under all circumstances, in every place and form, we must now and at all times oppose a resolute resistance.

As the Fort Sumter crisis expanded, Lincoln's close friends urged him not to be so concerned about secession and focus on Fort Sumter. But the fort came to symbolize secession and just about all North versus South troubles.

Senator Lyman Trumbull, Illinois, longtime Lincoln friend

Be bold and protect public property [Sumter].

James I. Hill, Lincoln friend from Springfield, Illinois

We hear with pain and regret that you are debating evacuating Sumter, lowering our glorious old flag that Washington through so many trials and privations unfurled and sustained to be trampled on by traitors and to be made the hiss and scoll of the world. Do you know that Gen. Washington or Jackson never said "I can't. . . ." Say the word and by the eternal Fort Sumter SHALL by reinforced and that glorious old flag sustained and my word for it 100,000 good and true men, with Jim Hill among them, shall at once respond to the call.

◆

Mary Chestnut had arrived in Charleston on March 26, 1861, amid a surprise snowfall throughout the region. She had just spent two weeks witnessing the Confederate government's creation in Montgomery, Alabama, where the new President, Jefferson Davis, was sworn in amid much hoopla.

Charleston was full of wealthy women, residents, and visitors. Mary Chestnut was one of them. The well-dressed plantation woman, thirty-eight, was the wife of James Chestnut, who had been a US Senator from South Carolina. He resigned from the Senate after secession and joined the Confederate Army. He was a general's aide in Charleston and his wife was staying there with wealthy friends to be near him. The Chestnuts owned a large plantation 145 miles from Charleston. They were in town with the Army and had brought several domestic slaves with them.

Socialite Mary, the instant queen of the Charleston social scene, was opposed to slavery because of the sexual relations between white owners and slave girls, which she thought were immoral. Mary kept a detailed diary of the events of the day, wherever they carried her. In Charleston,

Mary listened to all her husband's complaints and wrote continually about the social life in the city, the strife, the worries, and the lives of her friends and new neighbors, all of whom always kept an eye on Fort Sumter far out in the harbor.

She listened to all the politically connected people in Charleston discuss local politics in the state and city as heatedly as they discussed secession. Then she made her own judgment.

Mary Chestnut

The old story. The outs want to be in.

But she felt a great sense of tension and even doom in the lovely port city, perhaps exacerbated by dental problems and recent arguments with her husband.

Mary Chestnut

Something's wrong in the atmosphere here for me. It enervates & destroys me.

SEVEN

Fort Sumter

Peace, Not War

At Fort Sumter, Major Anderson was ready for war but, based on his experiences in the Black Hawk and Mexican wars, did not want one.

Major Robert Anderson

I think that killing people is a very poor way of settling national grievances. In [the Black Hawk conflict] I saw misery exceeding any I ever expected to see in our happy land. Dead bodies, males & females, strewn along the road, left unburied, exposed—poor, emaciated beings. . . .

It really goes to my heart to be compelled to do my duty when I know that every shot either seriously injures or distresses the poor, inoffensive women and children who have neither part of lot in the war.

His men greatly admired Anderson.

Captain Abner Doubleday

[Major Anderson] wins the esteem and regard of all who know him. I consider him an honorable and brave man and as much as we differ in the propriety in some of his acts, I have a high respect for him as a man and as an officer.

Lieutenant Richard Meade
He is a strong and true Southern man.

Meade, a Southerner whose father was US Minister to Brazil, was very conflicted. At the end of January, he received a telegram urging him come home to visit old friends.

Captain Abner Doubleday
[It was] a strategic move to force poor Meade into the ranks of the Confederacy by detaching him temporarily from us and taking him where tremendous political and social influence could be brought to bear upon him. He had previously been overwhelmed with letters on the subject. He was already much troubled and some months after the bombardment of Fort Sumter the pressure of family ties induced him, very reluctantly, to join the disunionists. It was stated that he never was a happy man afterwards.

Meade was killed in combat one year later.

Captain Abner Doubleday
Unfortunately, he desired not only to save the union but to save slavery with it. . . . In this spirit he submitted to everything and delayed all action in the expectation that Congress would make some new and more binding compromise which would restore peace to the country. He could not read the signs of the times and see that the consciences of the nation and the progress of civilization had already doomed slavery by destruction.

Jefferson Davis had a very different opinion of Major Anderson at Sumter.

Jefferson Davis

Fort Sumter was still occupied by the garrison under the command of Major Anderson, with no material change in the circumstances. . . . This standing menace at the gates of the chief harbor of South Carolina had been tolerated by the government and the people of that state, and afterward by the Confederate authorities in the abiding hope that it would be removed without compelling a collision of forces. . . . The condition of affairs at [this fort] was a subject of anxiety of the friends of peace and the hopes of settling by negotiation the questions involved in [its] occupation had been one of the most urgent motives for the prompt dispatch of [peace] commissioners to Washington.

Back in January of 1860, William T. Sherman became one of the first to fear that a Civil War was brewing. He wrote to his brother.

William Tecumseh Sherman

The rampant Southern feeling is not so strong in Louisiana as in Mississippi and Carolina. Still, holding many slaves, they naturally feel the intense anxiety all must whose property and existence depend on the safety of their property and labor. I do hope that Congress may organize and that all things may move along smoothly. It would be the height of folly to drive the South to desperation, and I hope after the fact is admitted that the North has the majority and right to control national matters and interests, that they will so use their power to reassure the South that there is no intention to disturb the actual existence of slavery.

The Union soldiers at Sumter hoped Sherman was right. Meanwhile, Anderson had no orders from Washington and needed them quickly, because the situation at Charleston was growing tense. Anderson believed that he and his men would soon be fired upon. His only previous orders were under the Buchanan administration and had been harsh.

Assistant Adjutant General of the Army Don Carlos Buell

You are to hold possession of the forts in this harbor and if attacked you are to defend yourself to the last extremity. . . . [A]n attack on or attempt to take possession of any of them will be regarded as an act of hostility, and you may then put your command into either of them.

Everyone at Fort Sumter was indignant at how the government had left the soldiers without express orders.

Major Robert Anderson

I trust in God that wisdom and forbearance may be given by Him to our rulers and that this severance may not be cemented in blood.

The days would grow long for the fort's surgeon, and he would come to hate the fortress.

Wylie Crawford

Sumter is impressed upon my life. I have lived years in the events that have transpired here.

Crawford was one of the many men at Sumter who feared losing their Union Army friends to the Confederate forces—a process that had started already as dozens of cadets left West Point to join the Confederate Army.

Wylie Crawford

We cannot repress the sadness that comes over us when we see one by one of our old comrades dropping away, men with whom we have shared many a bivouac in the far distant frontier. How are we to regard them as our enemies now?

Anderson was just about out of supplies and food, but he had one last card to play: a threat to blow up the entire fort to keep it out of the hands of the enemy.

Major Robert Anderson
I am opposed to the shedding of blood. But if the strife be forced upon me, and we are overcome by numbers, not a soul will probably be found alive in the ruins of the work.

Anderson may have gotten the idea from his wife. She wrote to him:

Eliza Anderson
I would never be found in the same Confederacy with South Carolina. For the first time in my life, I was ashamed of being a Southerner. I, for one, will not be satisfied if you are made to leave . . . Fort Sumter or the Carolinians. . . . I would make it a special request—to let you blow it up—sky-high on leaving it.

Tensions at Fort Sumter grew every day.

Captain Abner Doubleday
The Charlestonians are surrounding us with batteries on every point of land in the vicinity This is done with the hope of preventing any vessels from coming to our assistance with a view to force us ultimately to surrender the fort.

Residents of Charleston understood Doubleday's fear of an attack and Crawford's worries. Charleston newspaper editors and South Carolina politicians had been warning of an assault for more than four months. Robert Rhett Sr., father of the Mercury's *editor, even wrote President Buchanan of the coming attack.*

Robert Rhett Sr.

South Carolina, I have no doubt, will go out of the Union. It is in your power to make the event peaceful or bloody. If you send any more troops into Charleston Bay, it will be bloody. . . . [B]elieve me.

The necessity of shedding blood in a breakup of the states had been talked about for more than a generation. In the 1840s Henry Clay had warned of it.

Henry Clay

I am for ascertaining whether we have a government or not—practical, efficient, capable of maintaining its authority. . . . Nor, sir, am I to be alarmed or dissuaded from any such course of intimations of the spilling of blood. If blood is to be spilt, whose fault is it?

In that same era, Senator Thomas Hart Benton railed that no Northerner would give away anything to anybody.

Senator Thomas Hart Benton, Missouri

No party in the North will ever consent to a division of the national territory, national armaments, the national archive, or the national treasury.

There was tension everywhere in Charleston.

Mary Chestnut

One's heart is in one's mouth all the time. Any minute the cannon may open on us.

Throughout the nation, Fort Sumter was all anyone talked about. It was discussed at taverns, town meetings, and dinner parties. Even the clergy got involved, adding their opinion about the Sumter standoff in their sermons on Sundays.

Woman at a party in Baltimore

The state of the country was, of course, the chief subject of discussion. All were sure that if there was a Civil War, Maryland would remain with the Union.

The Charlestonians were indignant about the continued presence of the Union Army.

James Orr, South Carolina Legislator

No Black Republican President . . . should ever execute any law within our borders unless at the point of a bayonet and over the dead bodies of our state sons.

David Jamison, South Carolina Secretary of War

There are 20,000 men from South Carolina just spoiling to come down from the hills and tear the fort to pieces with their fingers. The waters of the harbor will be stained with their blood.

The Mercury's editor, *Robert Rhett Jr., kept pushing the Southern soldiers and Charlestonians of all stripes toward an attack on the fort—and a war.*

Robert Rhett Jr.

Will South Carolina sit quietly and with folded arms, and see a fort garrisoned by our enemies and in their possession, armed with power to forbid ingress and egress to vessels into and out of the harbor? Never!

Roger Pryor, a visiting Virginian and fire-eating orator, agreed. Speaking about Sumter, he told a Charleston crowd:

Roger Pryor
Strike a blow!

Nobody was more enraged at the North than newly elected South Carolina Governor Francis Pickens, in office for just a month, a surprise winner in the election. He did not care what anyone thought of him. Pickens, "Pick" to his friends, was one of the wealthiest men in the South and one of the region's staunchest slavery advocates. He owned 417 slaves on his South Carolina plantations and in other states. He came from a wealthy family and was well educated. He owned numerous horses and carriages. He was a fine dresser, a good speaker, and was interested in the affairs of his state all his life.

Pickens had been aided tremendously by the fact that he was John C. Calhoun's cousin. He married a beautiful woman, Charleston's Lucy Holcombe, twenty-nine. (She was his third wife; his first two had died.) Personally, he was intensely disliked by many. He was said to be overbearing, egomaniacal, vindictive, and a rather cold man to all who were not in his inner circle. Many felt that he was ill equipped to be governor.

His political career had been topsy-turvy. He was elected to Congress in 1834 and served until 1843. His career stalled with the death of Calhoun in 1850 and he was defeated rather badly in a Senate run in 1851. He lost another race for a House seat in 1853, and was defeated in another Senate run in 1857, the year he married Lucy.

The battered Pickens was named Minister to Russia in 1858 but quit after two years because his wife hated the country. He returned home and found himself at the state Democratic Convention. He was given the gubernatorial nomination (and subsequent election victory) because the convention could not settle on a candidate. He was sworn in as governor just two hours after the secession convention opened in Charleston. Francis Pickens, then, after so many defeats, found himself as governor of his state just as it was ready to explode and blow him into history.

Governor Pickens's outrageous actions made him the enemy of Southerners as well as Northerners. He regarded himself as the mayor of Charleston, the governor of South Carolina, the president of the Confederacy, and the emperor of a new world. His behavior infuriated all.

At the start of the Fort Sumter crisis, he was annoyed that merchant vessel captains refused to obey his rash orders. They replied that they were in the marine service and not residents of the city, so their ships were outside his jurisdiction. The governor immediately sent soldiers to the ships, where they rounded up several dozen sailors and officers, arrested them, and threw them into a Charleston jail. His authority for doing that?

Governor Francis Pickens
[I am] the head of an independent nation.

Pickens not only believed that, but gloried in it. He was also quite proud of his order to the state militia to prepare for a forty-eight-hour bombardment of Sumter and another order to prepare to storm the fort.

Governor Francis Pickens
If I know the pulse of South Carolina, I know the pulse of Southern men. The great heart of the South is beating steadily in the march of Southern independence—independence now and forever.

The governor was disliked by the Union soldiers out in the water as much as he was disliked by Charlestonians on land. Pickens's moves angered Doubleday.

Captain Abner Doubleday

He had taken forcible possession of two United States forts, of the money in the customs house, of the customs house itself, and other national property in Charleston. He had closed the harbor by destroying the most prismatic lenses in the light houses, and by withdrawing the warning light ship from Rattlesnake Shoal. He had cut off all communications between us and the city and had seized United States mails. His steamboats, laden with war material to be used in erecting batteries against us, were allowed to pass.

◆

Charleston would soon become the target of Lincoln's "innovative" naval blockade, but Southern military leaders had thought of that months before, when Buchanan was still in office, as a way the North might try to disrupt the profitable cotton trade, and had plans to counter it.

Major W. H. Chase, of Florida, in *De Bow's Review*

The first demonstration of a blockade of southern ports would be swept away by English fleets of observation hovering on the Southern coasts, to protect English commerce and especially the free flow of southern cotton to English and French factories. The flow of cotton must not cease for a day because the enormous sum of $150,000,000 is devoted to the elaboration of raw cotton and because five millions of people daily and annually derive their daily and immediate support therefrom. In England alone, every interest in the kingdom is connected therewith. Nor must the cotton states be invaded by land, because it would interrupt the cultivation of the great staple.

He was not alone in his belief that the whole world venerated cotton and its Southern American producers of it. Robert Rhett Jr. knew about

Southern–British relations from his years living in Charleston, and wrote in mid-December of 1860:

Robert Rhett Jr.

The President will surrender [the forts] upon receiving official word that the state has left the Union. Under these circumstances, foreign nations would be at perfect liberty to consider the secession as an accomplished fact and to use their own discretion as to recognizing or making treaties with the new state.

The wishes and hopes of the southern states centered on England; that they would prefer an alliance to her to one with any other power; that they would be her best customer; that free trade would form an integrated portion of this scheme of government with import duties of nominal amount . . . [facilitating] direct communication by steam between the Southern and British ports. I hope that with Great Britain dependent upon the South and the South upon her for manufactured goods and shipping, an interchange of commodities would lead to an unrestricted intercourse of the most friendly character.

He was wrong about British sentiment, though. A British friend of Henry Gourdin, a Charleston merchant, wrote to him from Manchester, England.

British friend of Henry Gourdin

I dare say that you are well aware that English sympathies are not much with you in the South. Public opinion here thinks you South Carolinians are unreasonable in not giving Lincoln a trial, that you are pre-judging the question, and that you are altogether wrong in not waiting to see what the new government will propose.

In fact, many believed that the British were the South's enemy. Fifteen years earlier, William T. Sherman, stationed in the Charleston area with the Army, wrote that he expected the British to persuade all the slaves in the South, and in Charleston in particular, to rise up against Southerners during the war with Mexico from 1846 to 1848.

William Tecumseh Sherman

The English, in case of war, would doubtless do all they could to make the slaves rise and would supply them with the necessary arms and ammunition to make them really formidable.

He also warned Southerners that their belief that the slaves would never rise against their masters was wrong.

William Tecumseh Sherman

I have never seen the least sign of disaffection on the part of the Negroes and have seen them in the cotton fields and the rice ditches. I met them hunting at all hours of the day and on the road at night without anything but [pleasantries]. However, it is easy, no doubt to make them believe they can own the fields and houses they now see and to excite them to resort to means that would even astonish their provokers.

Southerners saw trade with Great Britain, especially the cotton trade, as their salvation. It would bring in money, establish the trade of other commodities, and perhaps bring Britain into the war on the Southern side. The only possible problem was slavery. A tremendous number of people in Britain were opposed to the slave trade in the United States, and earlier the trade had been outlawed throughout their empire. Now, though, British business friends of Southern merchants were pushing hard to establish trade with the South while, at the same time, turning a blind eye to slavery. One of them was diplomat Robert Bunch, a friend of Rhett's and Her Majesty's Consul in Charleston.

Robert Rhett Jr.

Now, I'm not obscuring the fact that that the feeling of the British public is against the system of slavery. But I don't see any reason at all why this sentiment should stand in the way of commercial advantages. Great Britain trades with Brazil, which is a slave holding country and Great Britain is, moreover, the largest customer of the Southern states for the production of slave labor.

....

Robert Bunch

I have no authority to speak on behalf of Her Majesty's government, so any remarks I might make here would be strictly my own. We're talking about this as friends, you and I, and nothing more. But, as far as I can judge, there seems to be no reason why your ideas shouldn't be carried into practice. Great Britain has a great interest in the success of free trade and is a firm believer in its benefits. If the South wants to carry out this idea and perhaps open its coastal trade to British shops, I think that such a movement would be perfectly acceptable to the British people.

And slavery?

....

Robert Bunch

I am talking about the African slave trade which Great Britain views with horror and which, as far as I have been informed, is likely to be tolerated, if not encouraged, by the new Confederation. In my personal opinion, Great Britain would require from that body some very distinct assurance of a satisfactory nature on this subject before she could be brought to enter cordially into communication with this Confederation.

This opinion, presented most cordially by the British consul, infuriated Rhett.

Robert Rhett Jr.
No Southern state or Confederacy will ever be brought to negotiate upon such a subject. To prohibit the slave trade would be virtually to admit that the institution of slavery is an evil and a wrong instead of, as the South believes, a blessing to the African race and a system of labor appointed of God.

But Bunch was not convinced.

Robert Bunch
Other nations, especially those enlightened and more old-fashioned in their notions, rebel, fight and die for liberty, while [South Carolina] is prepared to do the same for slavery.

On December 26, 1860, the day after Christmas, in a stunning move that took the country by surprise, Major Anderson sneaked out of Fort Moultrie in the middle of the night and took his eighty-five men across the harbor to Fort Sumter. The departure was abrupt. He met with his second-in-command, Abner Doubleday, and gave him direct orders to move the troops.

Major Robert Anderson
I have determined to evacuate this post immediately for the purpose of occupying Fort Sumter. I can allow you 90 minutes to form your company and be ready to start.

Before the men left for Sumter, Anderson tied up all of his and his men's business with Charleston shopkeepers.

Captain Abner Doubleday

The Major took great pains to see that all bills, even those of a private nature, due in Charleston were fully paid by the officers and men of his command; but many leading merchants in the city were not so scrupulous. They gladly took advantage of the war to repudiate the claims of their northern creditors. . . . [A] number of the officers of the army who resigned to join the rebellion first deliberately drew their month's pay in advance and then left the pay-master, as a penalty for his kindness, to make good the deficiency from his . . . private funds in order to settle his accounts.

The midnight move angered Governor Pickens, and that gave Captain Doubleday enormous satisfaction.

Captain Abner Doubleday

The hot headed Governor, however, irritated at our change of station [to Sumter], took the responsibility of commending hostilities against the Union, without the co-operation of the Legislature and this at a time when the state was also destitute of war materials and funds.

William T. Sherman, in Louisiana, applauded Anderson's decision. Anderson had once been Sherman's captain.

William Tecumseh Sherman

Anderson has spiked the guns at Fort Moultrie, destroyed it and taken refuge in Sumter. This is right. Sumter is in mid-channel, approachable only by boats, whereas Moultrie is old, weak, and easily approached under cover. If Major Anderson can hold out until relieved and supported by steam frigates, South Carolina will find herself unable to control her commerce and will feel, for the first time in her existence, that she can't do as she pleases.

Some Southerners, though, saw the evacuation of Moultrie and the "taking" of Sumter as an act of war against the South.

Carolinian

Upon the whole it is fortunate that the first act of aggression is removed from the shoulder of our gallant little state.

Editor, *Charleston Courier*

Let the strife begin. We have no fear of the issue.

Major Anderson ceremoniously claimed the fort when they arrived.

Captain Abner Doubleday

Major Anderson, who was a very religious man, thought it best to give some solemnity to our occupation of Fort Sumter by formally raising the flag at noon, with prayer and military ceremonies. The band played "The Star Spangled Banner," the troops presented arms and our chaplain, the Rev. Matthias Harris, offered up a fervent supplication invoking the blessings of heaven upon our small command and the cause we represented.

When Anderson's men awoke the next morning, though, they found Sumter in far worse condition than they had imagined.

Captain Abner Doubleday

It was in very unfinished condition, and would require an immense amount of labor to render it safe against an assault.

The Union troops moved from Moultrie to Sumter at Christmas time, a season celebrated quietly and sadly after the move on December 26, as noted by a Camden, South Carolina, diarist.

Diarist

Another Christmas has come around in the circle of time but it is not a day of rejoicing. Some of the usual ceremonies are going on, but there is a gloom on the thoughts and countenances of all the better portion of our people.

The move of the Union Army from Moultrie to Sumter, right under the nose of the governor, gave the people of Charleston another reason to dislike Governor Pickens.

Charleston businessman

The dilemma is the result of his own negligence and bad management. The state . . . is disgraced every day.

Mary Chestnut

Major Anderson has moved into Fort Sumter while Governor Pickens slept serenely. One of the things which depressed me was the kind of men put in office at the crises. Invariably some sleeping dead head long forgotten or passed over, young and active spirits ignored. Places for worn out politicians seemed the rule.

Charlestonians were very annoyed by their state leader. Many referred to him as "the South's dictator" and others called him "Louis XIV."

Henry Ravenel, Charleston plantation owner and botanist

He is overbearing, haughty and rude & has given offense in numerous cases. He has caused many resignations & has made himself so unpopular since his election that if it were not for the critical state of affairs now existing, he would be called to account & perhaps impeached.

Foreigners could not stand him, either.

Robert Bunch, British Consul

He is a noisy, vulgar beast. [He has] absurd pomposity of manner. There is has not been time yet to get the secret history of his election but I suppose he has sold himself to the extremists.

Our Governor, I regret to say, is a hopeless fool. People talk very seriously of impeaching him before the legislatures. He is quite demented, everyone tells me, turns people out of his room by the shoulders, orders a thing at one minute and countermands it the next. It is not everyone who can manage a revolution even if he be in a teapot.

One of the things Pickens loved to do was read to Charlestonians letters to the editor of the Mercury *written by military academy cadets who favored secession.*

Carolinian cadet at West Point

I would like to hear something positive about what our state is going to do in the event of Lincoln's election. I think that she should leave the Union at all hazards, let come what may, and if she does, I am coming home instantly.

Carolinian living in Texas

I hope Lincoln will be elected and that we will come face to face with the damned Yankees. If he is elected, and my native state faces the music, I will be home by the first train.

On the Union side, Pickens infuriated Doubleday.

Captain Abner Doubleday

He is a military dictator.

For his part, Governor Pickens paid no attention to any of the criticism.

Governor Francis Pickens
I believe it is my destiny to be disliked by all who know me well.

◆

The next day the Confederates seized the abandoned Fort Moultrie, defeating a small group of men left there. Union troops saw the assault as an act of war.

Captain Abner Doubleday
While this [Moultrie attack] was going on, Major Anderson and myself stood side by side on the parapet watching the scene through our spy glasses. From his expression of indignation, I was in hopes he would take prompt measures to close the harbor against any further encroachments of the state troops.

Anderson did not. However, he and Doubleday, who had been at Sumter with him since their evacuation of Moultrie on December 26, were pleased that when the Confederates assaulted the unoccupied Moultrie they found a destroyed fortress.

Captain Abner Doubleday
The newcomers were exceedingly cautious upon making an entrance. They were looking out for mines in all directions and had brought ladders with them, on the supposition that there might be torpedoes in front of the main gates. It was a clear, beautiful evening and the moon was at the full. They were greatly enraged to find the flag staff cut down for they had hoped to run up their own flag on the very spot where ours had formerly waved. They found, too, the gun carriages burned, and the guns, which had gradually settled down as the carriages gave way resting with their breeches on the platforms, and the muzzles leaning against the walls. Out of the mouth of each hung a

small, white string. As many of the guns had been kept loaded for a considerable length of time, these strings had been tied by me to the cartridges in order that the latter might be pulled out and sunned occasionally, as precaution against dampness. The men imagined that these strings were arranged with a view to blow up the guns the moment anyone attempted to interfere with them and each soldier, as he passed, avoided the supposed danger.

Secession and Fort Sumter dominated all the conversations in the city of Charleston. Lawyer Edward Wells, who had been gone for a long time, noticed this as soon as he disembarked from the train. He wrote his brother:

Edward Wells

The air smells strongly of gunpowder. The excitement here is intense. The all-absorbing question here at present is secession. Men, women and children talk of nothing else.

Mary Pringle of Charleston, who owned thirty-nine slaves, wrote to her sons, assuring them that all was well.

Mary Pringle

Do not distress yourselves with apprehensions, my sons, God is over all. "Not a sparrow falls to the ground without his knowledge." We are anticipating but one battle and that will be over before this [letter] reaches you.

The governor's attitude about his role as "head" of the Confederacy and military, and his ability to ignite that "gunpowder," scared all of those people in Charleston. It also scared President Jefferson Davis. Pickens, on a whim, could start a war at any minute, using the cannons around Moultrie to bombard Sumter, sending ships out to attack it, and dispatching hundreds of state troops in a crazy assault. His bluster and bravado could wreck all the careful planning being done by the Southern president and his advisors in Montgomery. Davis had his Secretary of War send Pickens an urgent telegram.

L. P. Walker, Confederate Secretary of War, to Governor Pickens
The government assumes control of the military operations of Charleston and will make demand of the fort when fully advised.

The South Carolina governor was not the only important Southerner clamoring for war. Judah Benjamin, who would soon become the Confederacy's Secretary of the Treasury, was another one. So was William Porcher Miles, a South Carolina businessman, who urged an early attack on Sumter.

Judah Benjamin
At neither [Forts Pickens and Sumter] can it be long delayed.

Madison Perry, Governor of Florida, in a letter to Governor Pickens
Will you open at once upon Fort Sumter?

The orders from the War Department in Washington that the Union leader in Charleston, Major Anderson, so desperately sought finally arrived. But they were incomprehensible.

Captain Abner Doubleday
The orders [the courier] brought back [from the War Department] were to the effect that they had the utmost confidence in Major Anderson and that they left everything in his judgment.

This "leave it to Bob" policy continued for weeks. Anderson was about to run out of flour and tried to get some instructions from Washington on what to do, but they just told him to get by somehow.

Major Robert Anderson

I told Mr. Gustave Fox that if I placed the command on short notice I could make the provisions last until after the tenth of this month, but as I have received no instruction from the department that it was desirable that I should do so, it has not been done.

Union officer's wife

I feel too indignant. I can hardly stand the way the little garrison is treated by the heads of government. Troops and proper accommodations are routinely refused and yet the commander has orders to hold and defend the fort. I suppose the [White House] intends the Southern confederacy to be cemented with the blood of this brave little garrison. . . . [W]hen the last man is shot down, I presume they will think of sending troops.

If there was one thing Governor Pickens and Major Anderson shared, it was a feeling of being betrayed by the new administration.

Governor Francis Pickens

We [had] the executive [President Buchanan] with us and the Senate and in all probability the h[ouse] of R[epresentatives], too. Besides, we had repealed the Missouri line and the Supreme Court, in a decision of great power, has declared it, and all kindred measures on the part of the federal government unconstitutional, null and void. So, that before our enemies can reach us, they must first break down the Supreme Court—change the Senate and seize the Executive and by an open appeal to Revolution restore the Missouri Compromise, repeal the Fugitive Slave Act and change the whole government. As long as the government is on our side, I am for sustaining it and using its power for our benefit and placing the screws upon the throats of our opponents.

The Missouri Compromise Pickens referred to was passed by Congress in 1820. It drew a line from east to west along the 36th parallel, allowing slavery below the line but not above. In 1857, in Dred Scott v. Sandford, the Supreme Court ruled that the Missouri Compromise was unconstitutional because Congress had no power to prohibit slavery in the territories, because the Fifth Amendment guaranteed slave owners could not be deprived of their property without due process of law.

The feeling of betrayal ran deep. A Southern group called The Minute Men, named after the rebels of the American Revolution, had a constitution that said:

Minute Man Constitution

[A] "black Republican" President . . . must end in the destruction of or property and the ruin of our land. . . ."

EIGHT

Charleston, South Carolina

The Jewel in the Crown

When the Fort Sumter crisis began, Charleston, South Carolina, was considered one of the most beautiful cities in the United States. It was the twenty-second largest city in size, with about 40,000 people. It had one of America's prettiest and largest harbors. The sprawling harbor ran from the city's battery on the west four long miles to the eastern side on the Atlantic Ocean, where it ended in a pincer-shaped pair of peninsulas. Right in the middle of the harbor between those pincers was the unfinished brick Fort Sumter, built to thwart any foreign attack. It towered over the water in daylight and stood dark, gloomy, empty, and very menacing at night.

Charleston was a large transportation seaport for the shipping industry, with many vessels arriving from Britain and Europe. There were trains from New York, stagecoaches, carriages, and buggies of all shapes and sizes. The Ashley and Cooper Rivers emptied into Charleston Harbor and the larger plantations were on their banks. Rivercraft, large and small, sailed down them.

It was a religious city, and you could see the spires of its many churches from miles away. The city was riddled with slave auction sites and produce markets for shoppers. It had some of the finest theaters in the country, some quite elegant, and was host to the most talented traveling theater troupes in the United States. The city also had an opera house and its own symphony. It had fine schools and a new military college, the Citadel.

It was a rich city, too, and women paraded through its streets in expensive gowns and hats. Men wore the latest suits from the best shops in the

United States and Europe. Families owned lavish carriages, most driven by slaves. The battery was home to the mansions of the wealthy, usually men involved with the shipping industry or plantation lords with farms outside of town—some of whom owned a plantation house and a city house, too.

Charleston was famous for its parties that extended into the wee hours of the morning, where the best food and wine were served. Rich people who lived elsewhere in the South tried to vacation in Charleston for a week or so each year in order to meet the powerful and influential people of the South and spend time at their elegant parties.

The prospect of a war with the North bothered no one. Charleston had been a key site in the American Revolution, overrun by the Redcoats amid much weeping by its residents. The Americans won that war, though.

Throughout Charleston, the wealthy continued with their dinner parties and balls and men and women flirted with each other relentlessly under magnificent chandeliers to the strains of orchestral music, despite the trouble brewing at Fort Sumter.

Mary Chestnut

Fortunately for the men, the beautiful Mrs. Joe Heyward sits at the next table, so they take her beauty as one of the goods the Gods provide. And it helps to make life pleasant with English grouse and venison, not to speak of the Salmon from the lakes which began the feast. They had me to listen to an appreciative audience while they talk and have Mrs. Joe Heyward to look at.

A Mrs. Haynes felt great sorrow for the older married men of Charleston who sat by at all of the society balls in town, watching their wives dancing with much younger men. She wrote about this to Mary Chestnut.

Mrs. Haynes

What are your feelings to those of the poor old fellows leaning there with their beautiful young wives waltzing as if they could never tire and in the arms of every man in the room? Watch their haggard weary faces, the old boys. . . .

At church [changing topics] I had to move my pew. The lovely Laura was too much for my boys . . . they all made eyes at her and nudged each other and quarreled so, for she gave them glance for glance. Wink, blink and snicker as they would. She liked it. I say, my dear, the old husbands have not exactly a bed of roses; their wives twirling in the arms of young men, they hugging the wall.

The elites of Charleston enjoyed their lavish receptions and balls. After returning home from a ball, Mary Chestnut wrote in her diary:

Mary Chestnut
Certainly, this has been one of the most pleasantest days of my life.

There may have been glorious nights in the ballrooms of Charleston, but there was gloom throughout most of the South and in the North in those first two weeks after Lincoln took office and the Sumter crisis grew.

Mary Chestnut
I have just come from Mulberry, where the snow is a foot deep—winter at last after months of apparently May or June weather. Even the climate, like everything else, is upside down. . . .

Eliza Browne, Montgomery, Alabama, in a letter to a friend
Since you left, gaiety of every description has fled the city. The Ware ball was the last festivity of the season. Perhaps after Lent, they of the fashionable world will begin anew and try to eclipse that incomparable entertainment.

The situation was the same in the nation's capital.

Mrs. Jacob Thompson, wife of the Secretary of the Interior

The same gloom and depression is still over this city—no parties, no dinners, everybody looks sad.

Mary Chestnut

Mrs. Stephen Mallory received a letter today from a lady in Washington who said that there have recently been several attempts to be gay in Washington, but they proved to be dismal failures. The Black Republicans were invited [to a party] and came and stared at their entertainers and their new Republican companions, looked unhappy while they said they were enchanted, showed no ill temper at the hardly stifled grumbling and growling of our friends who thus found themselves condemned to meet their despised enemy.

There was tension everywhere as the Sumter crisis continued with no conclusion in sight. Fathers in the North and South worried that their sons would soon be in the Army and in harm's way. The secession of South Carolina brought about the immediate formation of new local militia companies. Two of the first Charleston-area men to enlist in their local company were John and Joseph Haskell, who left their hometown to join a company run by Colonel Maxey Gregg and wound up on the islands next to Fort Sumter. Their younger brother, William, who was underage, wanted to join too, but his irate father, fearful of a bloody war and the safety of his sons, stopped him.

William Haskell, South Carolina farmer, on his father

He did not care to hear anything further on the subject.

Many in South Carolina believed a fight was coming over Fort Sumter.

Susan Rutledge

Capt. Humphrey folded the United States army flag just before dinnertime. Ours [the Confederate flag] was run up in its place. You know the arsenal is in sight. What is the next move? I pray God to guide us. We stand in need of wise counsel, something more than courage. The talk is "Fort Sumter must be taken."

James D. Johnson, free black living in Charleston

Things look so dark and gloomy at home. What will be the issue, I fear to think. I am afraid it will come to leaving [home].

James Chestnut, at Charleston

A line of enemies is closing around us.

Mary Chestnut

We move on into the black cloud ahead of us.

Rumors flew everywhere in Charleston, believed by even high-ranking city and state officials. Governor Francis Pickens heard a wild one and wrote to Jefferson Davis about it as if it were true.

Governor Francis Pickens

A war steamer is lying on the Charleston bar laden with reinforcements for Fort Sumter. And what must we do?

Jefferson Davis gave him the same answer that he gave all rumormongers.

Jefferson Davis

Use your own discretion.

Oh no, cried other rumormongers, the ships were not carrying troops. They were carrying top-secret shipments of food for the Fort Sumter soldiers.

Mary Doubleday, wife of Captain Abner Doubleday

A crisis is very near—within a few days, we hear—and from so many sources we cannot doubt it—that the Charlestonians are erecting two batteries.

Abner Doubleday heard an even worse rumor.

Captain Abner Doubleday

We learned that cannon had been secretly sent to the northern extremity of the island. Two thousand of the best riflemen in the State were engaged to shoot us down the moment we attempted to man our guns.

◆

Rumors also swirled around the new Confederate general in Charleston, P. G. T. Beauregard, age forty-three. One was that when he traveled to Charleston from Montgomery he had a wagon full of champagne that he drank all day and all night, and that he had another wagon, a large one, filled with prostitutes, whom he visited frequently. Another rumor was that he was—absolutely was—unfaithful to his wife back in Louisiana. A fourth was that his hair was so dazzlingly black because he dyed it early in the morning so no soldiers would see him do it.

Rumors flew in Washington, too. One was that a secret Confederate Army of nearly 100,000 men was in northern Virginia preparing for an immediate invasion of Washington. Another was that the Confederates were planning a nighttime attack on the nation's capital in which they would set all the city on fire. Yet another was that an anonymous Congressman would raise an army of 20,000 men and attack and destroy not all Northerners, but just abolitionists. He said he knew where they were. He claimed the South had agreed to remain in the Union if he succeeded. One wild rumor was that a regiment of Confederate troops would seize the Electoral College and prevent it from electing Lincoln.

A former Congressman charged that in mid-January representatives of all the seceded states held a secret caucus where they decided to seize all political and military power in their states, and had actually sent telegrams to state militias ordering them to seize all forts, arsenals, and customs houses in their states and prepare to take control. In New York, saloons were rife with the rumor that secret Confederate forces planned to attack and destroy the Brooklyn Navy Yard.

A wild rumor, printed as the truth by the Richmond Dispatch, *was that Lincoln was about to send "the divorce act" to Congress. The act, certain to be passed, the newspaper proclaimed, would declare null and void any existing marriages between spouses from the North and South. They would have to get divorced and remarry people from their own half of the country.*

There were daily rumors that Lincoln would be murdered, and that Washington would soon be attacked by Southern forces. Henry Adams, the grandson of John Quincy Adams, wrote about them in a letter to his father.

Henry Adams

The people of Washingtonians [sic] are firmly convinced that there is to be an attack on Washington by the Southerners or use a slave insurrection, and in either case, or in any contingency, they are sure of being ruined and murdered.

The rumor of an attack on the nation's capital was believed by just about everybody. Secretary of State Seward wrote Lincoln in December about it.

William Seward
A plot is forming to seize the capitol on or before the 4th of March.

He added, reminding Lincoln yet again that he was the best-informed man in town:

William Seward
. . . Believe I know what I write.

Letter to the Editor, *National Intelligencer*
They have possessed themselves of all the avenues of information in the South—the telegraph the press and the general control of the postmasters.

After the Star of the West, *a steamship carrying supplies and reinforcements to Fort Sumter, was fired upon in January 1861, rumors abounded that the U.S. Army would attack Charleston.*

Ed Ludwig, at Charleston telegraph office
Rumors today that federal government sending troops to re-inforce Fort Sumter. Preparations made to resist.

Mary Chestnut
The air is red hot with rumors; the mystery is to find out where these utterly groundless tales originate.

There were crazy charges, too. Andrew Johnson, who would become Lincoln's second vice president, argued in Congress that Southern lawmakers were illegally using official US letterhead pages on which to write salacious statements—and, worst of all, not paying for the stamps.

Senator Andrew Johnson, Tennessee
Treasonable letters!

Many people believed these rumors. One lawyer in New York described a backdoor deal worked out to prevent a war.

George Templeton Strong
A friend has authentic, private, confidential information that Seward, Crittenden, Sen. Robert Hunter agreed last night on certain conciliatory measures and the whole slavery question is settled.

If people had no good rumors to spread, they would twist the words of famous people to suit their agenda. In the 1850s, General Winfield Scott used to joke that if he had an army of Virginia officers in command of Northern troops, he could lick any army in the world. In the spring of 1861, his words were twisted to claim he said that Virginians made the best commanders and Northerners the worst soldiers.

Many people are just tired of the rumors.

Evelyn Ward, a young girl from Tappahannock, Virginia
All the time there was war talk going on. I had grown used to it and did not cry over it anymore.

The Fort Sumter commander heard these rumors too, but tried to just remain vigilant.

Major Robert Anderson
I shall go steadily on, preparing for the worst, trusting hopefully in the God of Battles to guard and guide me in my course.

However, Anderson did believe from local newspaper accounts that the fort would be attacked.

Major Robert Anderson
I hear that the attention of the South Carolinians appears to be turned more towards Fort Sumter than it was and it is deemed probable that their first act will be to take possession of that work.

Mary Chestnut
Now we may be sure the bridge is broken.

NINE

Montgomery, Alabama
The Capital of the Confederacy

Montgomery, Alabama, which sat snugly on the banks of the Alabama River, became the state capital in 1846. The town originally was established by the Creek Indians. When they moved south, white settlers began to arrive and the community thrived. It was a quaint, pretty, quiet little town, despite being the state capital, and was chosen rather quickly as the capital of the new Confederate States of America at the suggestion of famed Alabama Congressman William Lowndes Yancey, a fervent supporter of states' rights and one of the country's best orators.

Main Street, the center of the community, was a wide dirt avenue that rose from the banks of the river toward the State Capital building. The street had a slave auction house and was lined with peddlers selling their wares. The city was populated with streets lined with trees, and many of the homes had substantial front and backyards. The bigger homes were on the river. It was a city of mild temperatures year-round, but it became oppressively hot in the summer and was always infested with bugs.

Secession was not overwhelmingly popular in Alabama. It passed by only nine votes at the state's Secession Convention. Jefferson Davis, the new president, was given a two-story white clapboard mansion on the outskirts of town as his house. The goat hill in town was where they built the stark-looking state house, a red brick building that overlooked the city. Davis was sworn in on its steps. The Exchange House Hotel in the downtown business district was turned into the Confederacy's administrative building, and there, in Davis's office, all decisions about Fort Sumter were made. Nearby was an old red brick warehouse that had been renovated into a second office building for the new national government.

Davis had electrified a crowd in Vicksburg, Mississippi, earlier when he said he would work hard to keep peace in the new Southern nation, but warned that there might be war.

Jefferson Davis

Our safety and honor [might require] us to dissolve our connection to the United States. I hope that our separation may be peaceful. But whether it be so or not, I am ready, as I always have been, to redeem my pledge to you and the South by shedding every drop of my blood in your cause. . . .

Davis was not only one of the South's staunchest defenders of slavery but its best spokesman on why the peculiar institution had always been recognized by both North and South. He stressed that the importation of slaves had been outlawed in 1808. So, he asked, what was the complaint?

Jefferson Davis

Property in slaves, already existing, was recognized and guaranteed just as it was by the Constitution of the United States; the rights of such property in the common territories was protected against any such hostile discrimination as had been attempted in the Union. But the "extension of slavery," in the only practical sense of that phrase, was more distinctly and effectually precluded by the Confederate than by the Federal Constitution. This will be manifest on a comparison of the provisions of the two relative to the slave trade. There are found at the beginning of the ninth section of the first article of each instrument. . . . The Confederate Constitution: . . . The importation of Negroes of the African race from any foreign country other than the slaveholding states of territories of the United States of America is hereby forbidden and Congress is required to pass such laws as shall effectively prevent the same.

Davis was an experienced and skilled speaker who had been in the public eye for nearly twenty years. One Virginia newspaper editor said of him:

Edward Pollard, Editor, *Richmond Examiner*
He seldom stormed, he seldom spoke loudly, or impetuously; but he often filled the heart of his hearers with unspeakable passion and captured their entire sympathies by that evidently forced moderation of tone and language.

Lucius Lamar, lawyer and later a Supreme Court Justice
I never saw him worsted in a debate. He was an off hand speaker and debater and always thoroughly up on every question that he discussed.

James Ryan, Editor, *Vicksburg Daily Sentinel*
[People] anticipate a proud and noble career should a sphere for the display of his oratorical talents, once be presented.

Editor, *Macon (Mississippi) Jeffersonian*
He is dignified with a bold and noble countenance, commanding attention, using chaste and beautiful language, giving no just ground for offense even to his opposition, who are at the same time, withering under his sarcasm at every sentence.

Even Republican party powerbroker Horace Greeley, who was the editor of the New York Tribune, *one of the nation's most influential anti-slavery newspapers, gave Davis his due as a speaker.*

Horace Greeley

Mr. Davis is unquestionably the foremost man of the South today. Every Northern Senator will admit that, from the Southern side of the floor, the most formidable to meet in debate is the thin, polished, intellectual looking Mississippian with the unimpassioned demeanor the habitual courtesy and the occasional unintentional arrogance, which reveals his consciousness of the great commanding power. . . . He belongs to a higher grade of public men with whom formerly the slave holding democracy was prolific.

Davis had been using his oratorical skills for years to defend slavery, and since 1851 had been considered the peculiar institution's most forceful champion. In 1851, he had rather concisely explained his embrace of slavery to a crowd in Aberdeen, Mississippi.

Monroe (Mississippi) Democrat

Colonel Davis said that he always thought and sincerely believed that the institution of slavery, as it now exists among us, is necessary to the equality of the white race. Distinctions between classes have always existed, everywhere, and in every country. . . . [D]estroy them today and they will spring up tomorrow. Menial services have to be performed by someone and everywhere the world over persons by whom menial services have been performed as a class, have been looked upon as occupying and are reduced to a state of inferiority.

The rich, by siding with the party in power . . . will always be safe. Not so with the poor. Their all is suspended upon their superiority to the blacks . . . the social equality of their wives, daughters and sons are all suspended and involved in this question.

Can anyone believe, does anyone hope, that the southern states in this confederacy will continue . . . to support the Union, to bear its burdens, in peace and in war, to a degree disproportioned to their numbers, if that very government is to be arrayed in hostility against an institution so interwoven with its interests its domestic peace and all its social relations?

Jefferson Davis
Obstacles might retard, but they cannot long prevent, the progress of a movement sanctioned by its justice and sustained by a virtuous people.

At times, Davis went much further.

Jefferson Davis
If slavery is to be a sin, it is not yours. It does not rest on your action for its origin, on your consent for its existence. It is a common law right to property in the service of man: its origin was Divine decree.

African slavery, as it exists in the United States, is a moral, a social and a political blessing.

Southerners said that Lincoln and his anti-slavery crusaders were wrong to believe that "all men are created equal." Many Southerners believed that they were not, and that in the new Confederacy you could have a strong nation built on the unequal principle upon which slavery rested.

T. S. Gourdin, Editor, *(Florida) Southern Confederacy*
We must abandon the old idea of our forefathers that "all men were born free and equal" and teach the doctrine of the diversity of the races, and all the supremacy of the Anglo-Saxon race over all others. We must take the ground never dreamed of by the men of '76, that African slavery is right in itself and therefore should be preserved.

Davis supporters did not see themselves as rebels, but as patriotic men and women who were building a new nation, separate from the old nation to which they had belonged. Mrs. Jefferson Davis wrote James Buchanan that he was probably the very last American President.

Varina Davis
I fear greatly, my dear old friend, that you are really the last of an illustrious line.

Southerners were joyful about their new country.

South Carolinian
We're making a nation and at record speed, too. They tell me the permanent Constitution will be ready in another week. We'll adopt it unanimously, just as we've taken all important steps unanimously. If we only had more states.

John Slidell, of Louisiana
At this point, there is unanimity of feeling at which you can form an idea without passing some time amongst and mixing, freely, with our people.

William Browne
Knowing as we do here the temper of the people, not the politicians—their hopes, aspiration, resolution, and resources—we look upon Union as impossible as the annexation of the Confederate States to Great Britain in their old colonial condition.

Many Southerners did not see Lincoln himself as the enemy of their new nation, but the North overall, despite the four-way presidential vote split. Since Lincoln was not the enemy, the South had no fear of a war, according to Henry Hilliard of Alabama.

Henry Hilliard
It is supposed, very generally, that we apprehend some mischief from Mr. Lincoln's administration, some direct and plain interference with

our rights, and we are appealed to by our northern friends to await some hostile demonstration on his part; we are reminded that his character is conservative. . . . Now all of this may be conceded and yet if the whole southern mind could be brought to yield implicit faith in these assurances, still the attitude of the southern states would remain unchanged. It is not any apprehension of aggressive action on the part of the incoming administration, which rouses the incoming administration to resistance, but it is the demonstration which Mr. Lincoln's election by such overwhelming majorities affords, of the supremacy of a sentiment hostile to slavery in the non-slaveholding states in the Union.

Herschel Johnson, of Georgia

I look with intense anxiety to the action of the border states. If they join us, we will constitute a respectable power among nations and shall be able to maintain an advancing career. If they adhere to the old Union, I shall regard it as a precursor of their emancipating at an early day. That will be a calamity on us. Without expansion, slavery must be limited in duration. But with a Southern Confederacy of fourteen states, we can maintain the Monroe Doctrine and acquire, when necessary, other lands suited to slave labor.

Northern newspapers chided that the South had failed to attract those border states.

Reporter, *New York Tribune*

Here are eight of the fifteen states, declaring that they wish and mean to stay in the Union, and not follow the defeated and bankrupt office-holders into the abyss of secession, treason and civil war.

Davis waved his hand to the crowds, had dinners, lunches, and breakfasts with well-wishers, but realized right away what a troubled place he was in. He wrote a secret letter to his wife, Varina, soon after he was inaugurated.

Jefferson Davis

The audience was large and brilliant. Upon my weary heart was showered smiles, plaudits and flowers; but beyond them saw troubles and thorns innumerable. We are without machinery, without means and threatened by a powerful opposition, but I do not despond and will not shrink from the task imposed upon me.

Still, he was buoyed by the public reception he received.

All along the route [from home to Montgomery], except when in Tennessee, the people at every station manifested good will and approbation, by bonfires at night . . . shouts and salutations in both.

Davis had his critics, though, and one of them was the Charleston Mercury's *editor, Robert Rhett Jr. He was the son of the wealthy and powerful Robert Rhett, a leader of the Democratic Party in South Carolina and a former US Senator. His son had assumed the editorship of the newspaper in the late 1850s. Rhett Jr. had often blasted Davis whenever he seemed to be making peace with Northern "enemies." He did that in 1858, when Davis had been hailed during a trip to New England where he told listeners that slavery had to stay but that Southerners could always get along with Northerners.*

Robert Rhett Jr.

[Davis was] a Union Mormon, a pitiable spectacle of human weakness. Of all the signal examples of Southern defection that the venality of the times has afforded, is there one that can at all compete with this? . . . [T]he Jefferson Davis we knew is no more.

◆

Whether Southerners disliked Davis or Northerners disliked Lincoln, they all agreed that by the winter of 1861 slavery had become the overriding issue in

America's political life and that the dispute over Fort Sumter was symbolic of the entire slavery argument. Slavery, and the nation, would rise or fall on Fort Sumter.

Most Southerners feared the whole governmental apparatus Lincoln would build and the influence it would have all over America. Georgia Governor Joseph E. Brown was one of them. Brown, the only man to ever serve four terms as governor of Georgia, said this about Lincoln.

Governor Joseph E. Brown

Mr. Lincoln is a mere mote in the political atmosphere of the country which, as it floats, only shows the direction in which the wind blows. He is the mere representative of a fanatical abolitionist sentiment—the mere instrument of a great triumphant political party the principles of which are deadly hostile to the institution of slavery, and openly at war with the fundamental doctrines of the Constitution of the United States. The rights of the South, and the institution of slavery, are not endangered by the triumph of Mr. Lincoln as a man but they are in imminent danger from the triumph of the powerful party he represents, and of the fanatical abolitionist sentiment which brought him into power as the candidate of the Northern section of the Union, over the united opposition of the Southern section against him. The party embracing that sentiment has constantly denied, and still denies, our equality in the Union and our right to hold our slaves as property; and avows its purpose to take from us our property as soon as it has the power. Its ability to elect Mr. Lincoln as its candidate shows that it now has the power to control the executive branch of the government. As the President, with the advice and consent of the Senate, he appoints the judges of the Supreme Court of the United States when vacancies occur. Its control of the executive power will, in a few years, give it the control of the judicial department, while the constant increase in abolition sentiment, in the Northern states, now largely in the majority in Congress, together with the admission of other free states, will very soon give it the power in the Legislative department. The whole government will then be in the hands of our enemies.

Brown was alluding to the fact that as president, Lincoln would pick just about every jobholder in the federal government and that all of them would surely be anti-slavery champions, as he was. Lincoln would, in effect, create an official army of anti-slavery crusaders.

Editor, *New York Herald*
With men holding these views [anti-slavery] as Judges and officers of the federal courts, as postmasters and collectors of customs, as district attorneys and marshals . . . there will commence an agitation of the slavery question such as the world has never witnessed. . . . [T]he abductors of slaves, the fomenters of servile incendiarism and the coming of John Browns will pursue their inquisitous labors in the full confidence that, if arrested and brought to trial, it will be by marshals, prosecuting attorneys, juries and judges that sympathize with them.

Lincoln had never questioned the rights of slaveholders in states and territories where slavery currently existed (this was a compromise to his opposition to slavery), but he held a hard line against slavery in new territories. And there were going to be a lot of new territories.

Lincoln did not want Southerners to think he would ever eradicate slavery in their states. He wrote a letter to that effect, a few weeks before the secession of Georgia, to his old friend Alexander Stephens, the short, thin, nearly emaciated US Senator from Georgia and soon-to-be vice president of the Confederacy.

Abraham Lincoln
I fully appreciate the peril the country is in and the weight of responsibility on me. Do the people of the South really entertain fears that a

Republican Administration would, directly or indirectly, interfere with the slaves or with them about the slaves? If they do, I wish to assure you, as once a friend, and still, I hope, not an enemy, that there is no cause for such fears. The South would be in no more danger in this respect than it was in the days of Washington. I suppose, however, this does not meet the case. You think slavery is right and ought to be extended while we think it is wrong and ought to be restricted. That is, I suppose, the rub. It certainly is the only substantial difference between us.

On December 10, even before South Carolina seceded, Lincoln told political colleagues and friends to remain with him on his "no new territories" slavery policy. In a letter to Lyman Trumbull he said:

Abraham Lincoln
No compromise on the question of extending slavery. If there be, all our labor is lost and, ere long, must be done again. . . . Stand firm. The tug has to come, and better now than any time hereafter.

Lincoln was frustrated with the preaching about how slavery had, and would, unify the nation. He warned that because the Supreme Court had upheld slavery in its Dred Scott decision, the South could continually press the North to expand slavery into the new territories.

Abraham Lincoln
A year will not pass till we shall have to take Cuba [a slave nation] as a condition upon which they [the slave states] will stay in the Union.

In the early days of the Fort Sumter crisis, Jefferson Davis's old friend William Seward not only disagreed with him on slavery, but argued that people, North and South, should stop paying attention to boundaries on a map and look at the life of the people in and around them for guidance on how both halves of the nation could move on and prosper together.

William Seward

I remain of the opinion that physical bonds, such as highways, railroads, rivers and canals, are vastly more powerful for holding civil communities together than any mere covenants, written on parchment or engraved upon iron. I remain, therefore, constant in my purpose to secure the construction of two Pacific railways, one of which shall connect the ports around the mouth of the Mississippi and the other on the towns of the Missouri and the lakes with the harbors on our western coast.

Seward had been telling people for months that the movement toward civil disruption was stronger than people thought and was no longer limited to speeches printed in newspapers. In January 1861 he wrote:

William Seward

The Union cannot be saved by claiming that secession is illegal or unconstitutional. Persons bent on that fearful step will not stand long enough on forms of law to be dislodged; and loyal men do not need such narrow ground to stand upon.

I dread, as in my innermost soul I abhor, civil war. I do not know what the Union would be worth if saved by the use of the sword. Yet, for all of this, I do not agree with those who, with a desire to avert that great calamity, advise a conventional or unopposed separation, with a view to what they call reconstruction; destruction goes before reconstruction.

Senator Charles Sumner, Massachusetts

The North . . . will surely die. It can no longer rule the Republic as a plantation . . . can no longer fasten upon the Constitution an interpretation that makes merchandise of men and gives a disgraceful immunity to the brokers of human flesh and butchers of human hearts. . . . [I]t must die, it may be, as a poisoned rat dies of rage in its hole.

Lincoln asked all Republicans what the point of the election was if now they were asked to abandon the platform upon which they campaigned.

Abraham Lincoln
We have just carried an election on principles fairly stated to the people. Now we are told in advance the government shall be broken up unless we surrender her to those we have beaten, before we take the offices. In this they are either attempting to play upon us, or they are in dead earnest. Either way, if we surrender, it is the end for us, and of the government. They would repeat the experiment upon us *ad libitum*.

As 1860 ended, many Southerners became more strident in their defense of slavery. Jefferson Davis had feared that winter that secession was coming over Fort Sumter, and lectured his fellow Senators for not understanding the gravity of the situation.

Jefferson Davis
Senators, we are rapidly drifting into a position in which this is to become a government of the army and the navy in which the authority of the United States is to be maintained not by law, not by constitutional agreement between the states, but by physical force: and you will stand still and see this policy consummated?

TEN

Fort Sumter

The March to Battle

The march of North and South to a clash at Fort Sumter began with the departure of Senator Jefferson Davis from the government of the United States in the winter of 1860.

Jefferson Davis

I am sure there is not one of you, despite whatever sharp differences there may have been between us, to whom I cannot now say, in the presence of my God, I wish you well and such, I am sure, is the feeling of the people whom I represent.

Leaving the US Senate was an emotional experience for him.

Jefferson Davis

I see now around me some with whom I served long. There have been points of collision but whatever of offense there has been to me, I leave here. I carry with me no hostile remembrance. . . . I go hence unencumbered by the memory of any injury received, and having discharged the duty of making the only reparation in my power for any injury received. . . . [I] bid you a final adieu.

The Senators in the chamber, and all the spectators, roared with enthusiasm; the applause was deafening. Davis, sensing what the future held, sat down heavily in his chair, put his head in his hands, and wept.

The man who soon would lead a new country looked very sick that day. Davis had just recovered from yet another debilitating herpes attack and was barely able to stand to deliver his farewell speech.

Murat Halstead, journalist

Why, that is the face of a corpse, the form of a skeleton. Look at the haggard, sunken, weary eye—the thin, white wrinkled lips clasped close upon the teeth in anguish. That is the mouth of a brave but impatient sufferer. See the ghastly white, hollowed, bitterly puckered cheek, the high, sharp cheekbone, the pale brow, full of fine wrinkles, the grisly hair, prematurely gray; and see the thin, bloodless, bony nervous hands? He deposits his documents upon his desk and sinks into his chair, as if incapable of rising.

Visiting British journalist William Russell, who interviewed Davis right after he was inaugurated, did not think much of him.

William Russell

[His face] was thin and marked on cheek and brow with many wrinkles . . . [his left eye is nearly blind] the other is dark, piercing and intelligent. He did not impress me as favorably as I had expected.

In fact, President Davis suffered from herpes simplex, which closed over one of his eyes and debilitated him when he was under stress, particularly throughout the Fort Sumter crisis.

When Abraham Lincoln was inaugurated as President in 1861, Fort Sumter—and what to do about it—was the number one priority of his administration. He continually consulted his cabinet and, in the end, decided to re-supply the Charleston fort that was running out of food. That decision brought on the attack from the Confederate soldiers surrounding the fort that began the Civil War. *From the Library of Congress.*

Probably no officer on either side at Fort Sumter was as elegantly dressed, impressive, and charming as General P. G. T. Beauregard of the Confederacy. The women of Charleston loved him when he arrived in the city. He was invited to numerous parties and some women even brought flowers to his office. It was on his orders that Confederate cannon fired on Fort Sumter. *From the National Archives.*

Captain Abner Doubleday, the second in command of the Union troops at Fort Sumter, was the latest in a long line of army veterans in his family. During the American Revolution, his great grandfather was a Minuteman, his paternal grandfather was a solider, and his maternal grandfather served as one of George Washington's messengers. Doubleday's father, Ulysses, had fought in the War of 1812. Doubleday graduated from West Point in 1842 and served with the army in numerous places before he was transferred to Charleston. Later, he fought at Gettysburg and by the time the war ended had been promoted to General. *From the Library of Congress.*

James Chestnut served as a US Senator from South Carolina prior to the war. He resigned when South Carolina seceded from the Union in 1860. When Fort Sumter was surrounded by Southern forces he was appointed as an aide to Confederate General Beauregard. He and his wife Mary had traveled throughout the South before the war and both were members of Southern aristocracy. *From the National Archives.*

Jefferson Davis, the President of the Confederacy, had been the hero of not one, but two American wars prior to Fort Sumter. He had served in the Black Hawk War and in the Mexican War, earning praise in both. Later, he served as the US Secretary of War and as a US Senator. Southerners elected him their President thinking that if a civil war did start, his military background made him the perfect man to lead the Confederacy. *From the National Archives.*

Laurence Keitt was notorious as the man who helped US Representative Preston Brooks beat up Senator Charles Sumner of Massachusetts with a cane in the Senate chamber in 1856. He held a gun on Senators preventing them from breaking up the fight, which left Sumner badly injured. Conversely, Keitt prevented a crowd from attacking Ward Lamon, a Lincoln emissary to Charleston, in that city just before the attack on Fort Sumter. *From the Library of Congress.*

Major Robert Anderson had owned slaves prior to the war and sold them. He was a veteran army officer and had served in many locations. He was in command at Fort Sumter during the bombardment. He fell ill later and left the US for medical treatment in France. He died there in 1871. Ironically, General Beauregard, head of Confederate forces in Charleston, was one of Anderson's students at West Point. *From the National Archives.*

Mary Chestnut was one of the leaders of South Carolina's high society prior to the war and knew hundreds of people. Her access to them made it possible for her to write her rich and highly detailed diary about Fort Sumter and the war. The diary notes about Fort Sumter were full of her love of the South and fear that her world would change forever by whatever was to happen there.

ABOVE: On the 100th anniversary of the attack that began the Civil War, a special postage stamp was issued to commemorate the event. *From iStock.* BELOW: Confederate army cannons were strategically placed across the harbor from the fort and bombarded it for most of the 36 hour attack. *From iStock.*

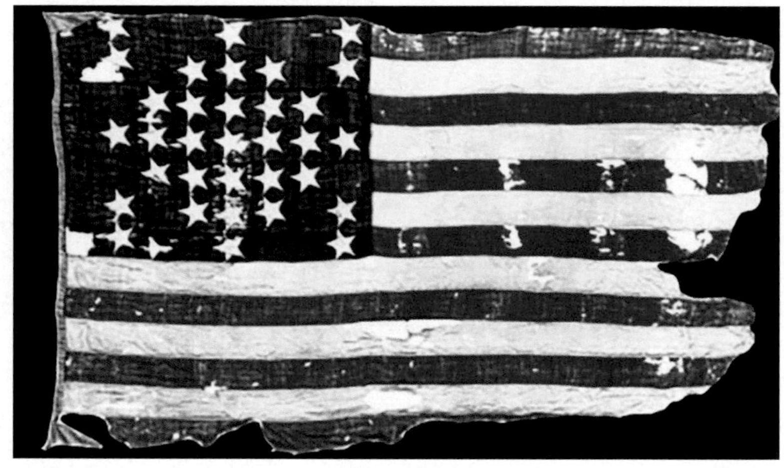

ABOVE: One of the flags flown at the fort in April, 1861. BELOW: Prior to the attack, Fort Sumter looks serene and sailboats drift past it in the harbor. *Both from iStock.*

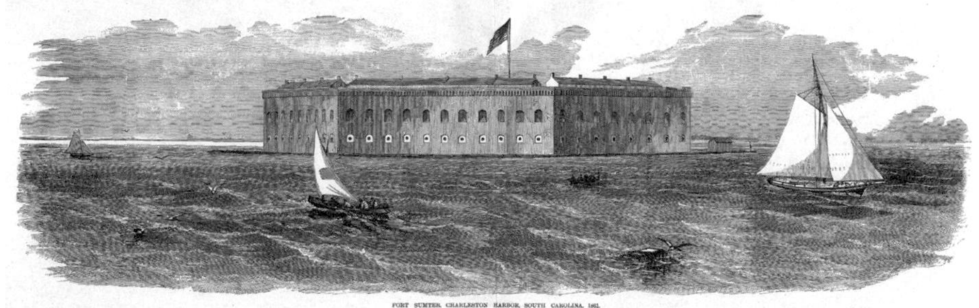

On September 8, 1863, after the Confederates had held the fort for two years, the Union Navy and army attacked it. There is a flotilla of Union ships advancing on the fort here. The Confederates repulsed the assault and held the fort. *From iStock.*

ABOVE: A stamp commemorating the 150th anniversary of the Fort Sumter battle was issued in 2011. *From iStock.* BELOW: This is one of the best illustrations of Fort Sumter, sitting on its tiny island, prior to the attack. *From iStock.*

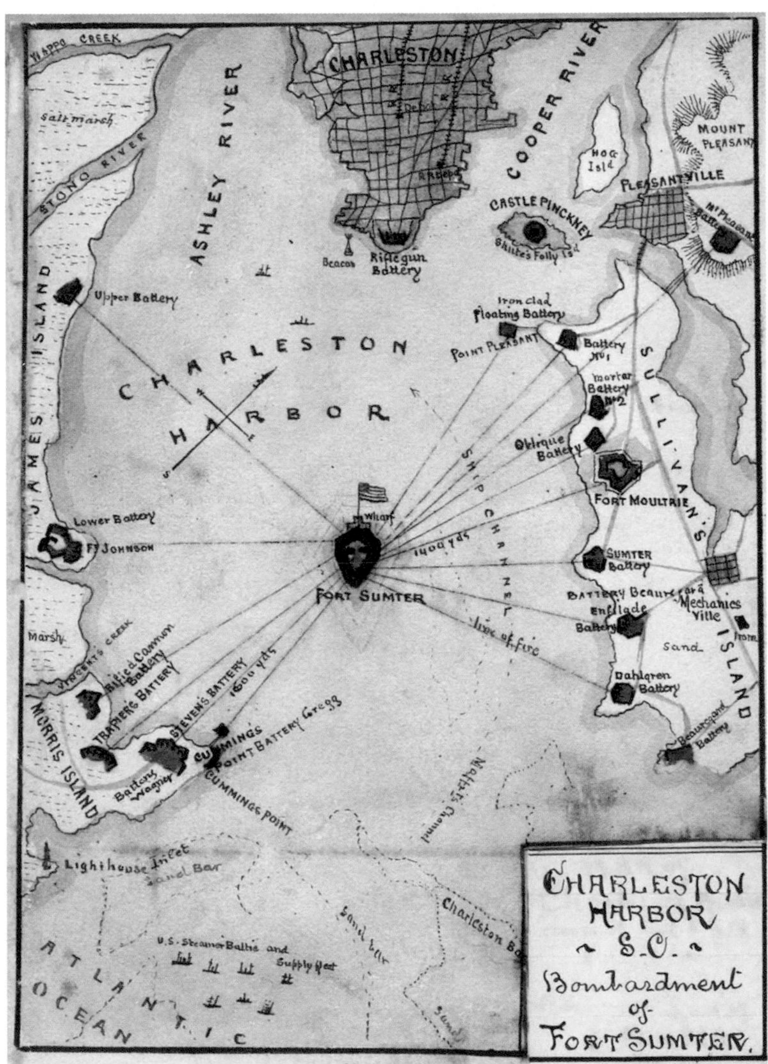

This map of the greater Charleston area shows the city darkened. It sits between two rivers, the Ashley and the Cooper. Four miles eastward is Fort Sumter, at the bottom of the map. *From iStock.*

ABOVE: The big guns at the fort were painstakingly put in place shortly after Union troops moved there from Fort Moultrie. This is one of them firing during the assault. *From iStock.* BELOW: Union troops scrambled to get their cannons firing. Here, men lift cannonballs from boxes to sustain the defensive firing of the guns. *From iStock.*

SCENE ON THE FLOATING BATTERY, CHARLESTON HARBOR, DURING THE BOMBARDMENT OF FORT SUMTER.

ABOVE: The fort under siege at night. Some of the shells are splashing in the harbor's water. *From iStock.* BELOW: This is battle weary Major Anderson depicted by an artist as a young and vibrant soldier and a good contrast to other illustrations and photos of the Union commander, one of which is shown in this work. *From iStock.*

ABOVE: Jefferson Davis as a younger man. *From iStock.* BELOW: The fort under attack, with the city of Charleston shown in the background. It is actually four miles from the facility. *From iStock.*

ABOVE: A recent photo of Sumter shows some battered walls and tourists strolling through it. *From iStock.* BELOW: Union soldiers were originally stationed at Fort Moultrie, but were moved to Sumter by Major Anderson. *From iStock.*

FORT MOULTRIE, CHARLESTON, WITH FORT SUMTER IN THE DISTANCE.

ABOVE: Union troops evacuating Moultrie in large rowboats and sailing to Sumter under the cover of darkness. The swift evacuation was not noticed by Charlestonians until daybreak. Major Anderson was angry that the war department never gave him credit for the brilliant transfer of troops. *From iStock.* BELOW: Fort Sumter under full Confederate siege. *From the Library of Congress.*

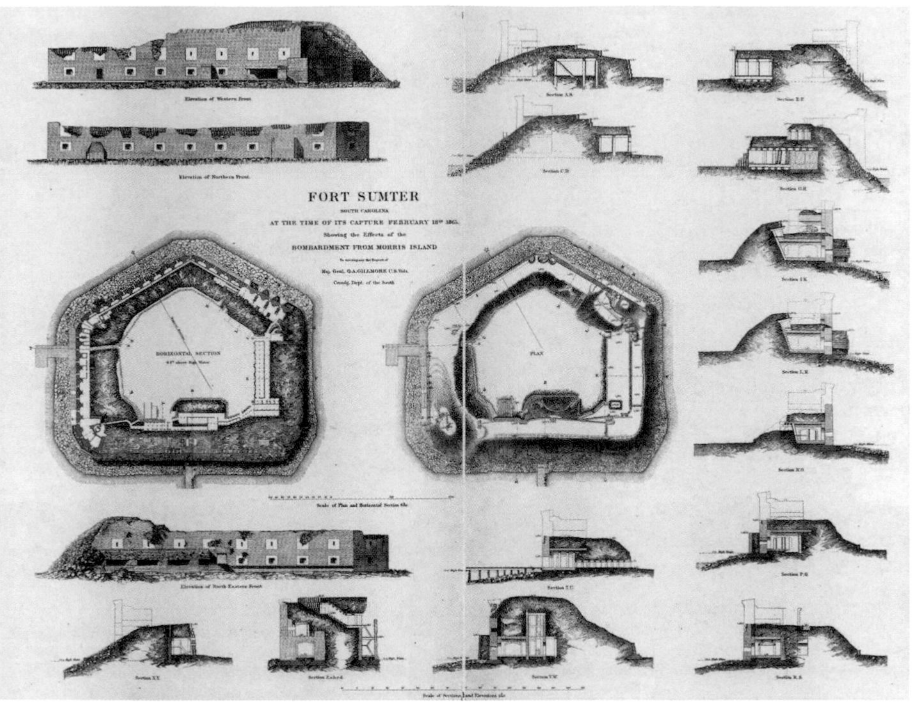

ABOVE: Diagrams and drawings of Fort Sumter before the battle. *From iStock.*
BELOW: Cannons being operated and fired during the bombardment itself. *From iStock.*

Fort Sumter in ruins. *From iStock.*

Jefferson Davis

I am suffering under a painful illness which has closely confined me for more than seven weeks and leaves me quite unable to read or write.

Many others who met him for the first time in Montgomery, Alabama, had vastly higher opinions of him. The new Confederate president was always glad to meet people; he told them all what they wanted to hear. He said to one group:

Jefferson Davis

Our people are a gallant, impetuous, determined people. What they resolve to do, that they most assuredly persevere in doing.

He told others that if the North wanted a fight, he was ready to give it to them. But he, himself, was not sure of the extent of his power.

Jefferson Davis

To me, personally, all violence is abhorrent. As President of the Confederate states, my authority is, in many respects, more circumscribed than would be my authority as Governor of Mississippi.

Davis had his problems. When Varina Davis first met her future husband, she wrote to her mother:

Varina Davis

He impresses me, a remarkable kind of man, but of uncertain temper and has a way of taking for granted that everybody agrees with him when he expresses an opinion, which offends me. He is the kind of person I should expect to rescue one from a mad dog at any risk, but to insist upon a stoical indifference to the fright afterward. I do not think I shall ever like him as I do his brother Joe. It was this sincerity of opinion which sometimes gave him the manner to which his opponents saw as domineering.

The new Confederate president also had a short, violent temper. He exploded at slight provocations. He was a perfectionist and wanted everybody to do what he thought was best, even if they did not agree with him. He never understood that someone with another opinion simply saw things a different way; people who did not agree with him were just wrong. He expected more and better work from everybody, regardless of circumstance or illness. Davis wanted everybody to be punctual and would stand outside the door to their office in the morning and tell them if they were a single minute late.

One of his biggest faults was that he would humiliate someone and then not understand why they felt humiliated. His wife helped him all she could, and put up with his imperfections. She always believed, though, that he did not have the personal skills to be a leader of any kind, much less the head of a new country.

In February 1861, Davis received a telegram from Robert Toombs, a tall, blustery Senator from Georgia, informing him of his election as President of the Confederacy. He read it to his wife.

Varina Davis
He spoke of it as a man might speak of a sentence of death.

She advised him not to take the job. Yet Varina Davis was a good first lady and performed well for someone thrust into the job. She had been an admired hostess back in Washington and would be again in the Confederacy. She was intelligent, gracious, friendly, and possessed a good sense of humor.

New Friend
She is as witty as she is wise.

◆

Davis always defended the South's new Constitution.

Jefferson Davis

It was a model of wise, temperate and liberal statesmanship. Intelligent criticism, from hostile as well as friendly sources, has been compelled to admit its excellence and has sustained the judgment of popular northern journals.

No, it did not. Northern journals were outraged by the secessionists and lambasted them in editorials—calling them scoundrels, at best.

Editor, *Detroit Daily Advertiser*

Every horse thief, murderer, gambler, robber and other rogue of high and low degree, fled to Texas when he found that the United States could no longer hold him. The pioneers of that state were all threats of one kind or another. . . . [T]hose of them that have escaped hanging or the state prison, and their descendants, are the men who have led the secession movement in that state.

Editor, *Boston Journal*

Secession is treason.

The Confederate president could see the war clouds forming in the Alabama sky. He blamed the Union.

Jefferson Davis

My mind has been for some time satisfied that a peaceful solution to our difficulties was not to be anticipated and therefore my thoughts have been directed to the manner of rendering force effective.

He understood that if war came, he would be asking men who did not own slaves to lay down their lives to defend slavery. He justified doing so by defending the institution.

Jefferson Davis
A government, to afford the needful protection and exercise proper care for the welfare for a people, must have homogeneity in its constituents. It is this necessity which has divided the human race into separate nations and finally has defeated the grandest efforts which conquerors have made to give unlimited extent to their domain.

Jefferson Davis
The slave must be made fit for his freedom by education and discipline and thus made unfit for slavery. And as soon as he becomes unfit for slavery, the master will no longer desire to hold him as a slave.

And he made an accurate prediction about the coming conflict.

Jefferson Davis
A Civil War will be long and bloody.

It was not just the South that was worried, but the West, too, and no one in the West was more concerned than Sam Houston, the governor of Texas. In November of 1860, he expressed his fears in a letter to a friend.

Governor Sam Houston, Texas
When I contemplate the horrors of Civil War, such as a dissolution of the Union will shortly force upon me, I cannot believe that the people will rashly take a step fraught with these consequences. They will consider well all the blessings of the government we have and it will only be when

the grievances we suffer are of a nature that, as free men, we can no longer bear them, that we will raise the standard of revolution. Then the civilized world, our own consciences and posterity will justify us. If that time should come, that will be the day and hour. If it has not—if our rights are yet secured, we cannot be justified. Has the time come? If it has, the people who have to bear the burden of revolution must affect the work.

When their new peaceful homes are the scene of desolation, they will feel no pang of regret. Moved by a common feeling of resistance, they will not ask for the forms of law to justify their action. Nor will they follow the noisy demagogue who will flee at the first show of danger. Men of the people will come forth to lead them who will be ready to risk the consequences of revolution.

If the Union is dissolved now, will we have additional security for slavery? Will we have our rights better secured? After enduring Civil War for years, will there be any promise of a better state of things than we now enjoy?

◆

As tensions heightened over Fort Sumter, both Abraham Lincoln and Jefferson Davis began to examine their options—and their consciences.

Jefferson Davis
God forbid if the day should ever come when to be true to my constituents is to be hostile to the Union.

Abraham Lincoln
I am not a war man. I want peace more than any man in this country.

Davis settled into his new home in Montgomery. He missed his wife, Varina, and his children. He wrote to them during the journey to his inauguration.

Jefferson Davis

I miss you and the children even more than usual, and when the military came en route including a company of boys, I wished the children could have seen it, to be remembered in after years. . . . Kiss my children and tell them to be good and love one another. Farewell, dear wife. May God hold you in his holy keeping.

Looking back on that time, Varina had little faith in the South to prevail in a conflict.

Varina Davis

The South did not have the material resources to win the war and white southerners did not have the qualities necessary to win it.

◆

President-elect Lincoln wrote in a letter to friend Lyman Trumbull in 1860 that if President Buchanan did give up the Charleston forts, including Sumter, as rumor had it, he, Lincoln, would take them right back, especially Sumter.

Abraham Lincoln

Dispatches have come here two days in succession that the fort in South Carolina will be surrendered by the order, or consent at least, of the President. I can scarcely believe this, but if it proves true I will, if our friends in Washington concur, announce publicly at once that they are to be retaken after the inauguration. This will give the Union a rallying cry.

He said in another speech:

Abraham Lincoln

All the power in my disposal will be used to reclaim the public property and places which have fallen, to hold, occupy and possess these, and all other property and place belonging to the government.

The government will not assail you unless you first assail it. With you and not with me is the solemn question of "shall it be peace or the sword."

And in a letter to General Winfield Scott, Lincoln said:

Abraham Lincoln

According to my present view, if the forts should be given up, before the Inauguration, the General must retake them afterwards.

Lincoln was so angry that Buchanan was giving thought to surrendering the forts in Charleston that he gasped when his secretary in Springfield read him a news story that Buchanan planned to do just that.

Abraham Lincoln

If that is true, they ought to hang him!

About the only thing Lincoln felt more strongly about was how pigheaded he thought Southerners were about slavery.

Abraham Lincoln

About one sixth of the whole population of the United States are slaves! The owners of these slaves consider them property. The effect upon the minds of the owners is that of property and nothing else—it induces them to insist upon all that will favorably effect its value as property to demand laws, institutions and a public policy that shall increase and secure its value and make it durable, lasting and powerful.

As things stood, Jefferson Davis did not see any option other than secession.

Jefferson Davis

It is not by crimination and recrimination that the sense of the people is likely to be changed. . . . [T]he occasion for such arguments has passed by. We have to deal with events which are now transpiring and about to be consummated. I trust there is to be no collision. . . . Had he [Buchanan] withdrawn his troops from Sumter, it would have been such a conspicuous act of conciliation that the other states would not, I believe, have called conventions to consider the question of secession.

Jefferson Davis

The argument is exhausted. All hope of relief in the Union . . . is extinguished. . . . We are satisfied that the honor, safety and independence of the Southern people are to be found in a Southern confederacy.

But others still believed there was a way out of war. Edmund Ruffin, a Virginia politician, saw a possibility for peace under President Davis.

Edmund Ruffin

Taken altogether, this is a most singular state of war. Fort Sumter surrounded by batteries prepared to batter or shell it. Nearly the like state of things exists at Fort Pickens [in Florida]. . . . The officers of the fort and the besieging Confederate army even exchange friendly visits. And dine at each other's quarters. Two different governments are now existing and the new one completely organized and established. Peaceful relations have continued between the two peoples despite the violent animosity of the communities and still more with individuals of the two sections. While every participation and aid of secession in the South is denounced in the North as treason . . . and even so declared judicially, Southern and northern men freely visit and travel anywhere in the other section, without being interfered with by any legal restraint or penalty. The mails are uninterrupted, as are the railway trains, express transportation and telegraph lines.

Many Southerners simply did not believe that Lincoln would risk a war over a single uncompleted fort and that, in any case, he did not have the legal right to make decisions about the fort.

A South Carolinian

Lincoln won't give Sumter up for two reasons. First, the eyes of the country are on Sumter as a test case, the eyes of every Republican Governor, every Republican Senator. Second, he has no power to give it up. Joseph Holt put that in a nutshell for Buchanan. The President can no more cede Sumter back to South Carolina constitutionally than he can cede the District of Columbia back to Maryland.

To the very end, Jefferson Davis hoped for a peaceful resolution of the Fort Sumter issue.

Jefferson Davis

Republics have often been cradled in war, but more often they have met with a grave in that cradle. Peace is the interest, the policy, the nature of a popular government. War may yet bring benefits to a few, but privation and loss are the lot of the many.

Just a week after New York City Mayor Fernando Wood was inaugurated, Davis wrote to him.

Jefferson Davis

There is nothing that can ever bring me willingly to consent to the destruction of this union. . . . So long, then, that it is possible that the prosperity and the liberties of the people can be preserved in the Union it shall be my purpose at all times to preserve it.

But he did not really believe that. He wrote just after he left the US Senate, long before Lincoln's inauguration, that there would be war.

Jefferson Davis

When Lincoln comes in, he will have but to continue in the path of his predecessor to inaugurate a Civil War.

Back in the middle of January, while he was still a US Senator, Davis wrote to South Carolina Governor Francis Pickens that he was determined to keep the peace, but was fearful of war.

As he traveled toward his own inauguration in February, he told cheering crowds the same thing. In his inaugural address, Davis also said there would be a conflict, brought about by the Union.

Jefferson Davis

Anxious to cultivate peace and harmony with all nations, if we may not hope to avoid war, at least expect that posterity will acquit us of having needlessly engaged in it. Doubly justified by the absence of wrong, on our part, and by wanton aggression on the part of others.

Davis had warned the Southern hotheads for months that a peaceful secession was probably impossible because he had known the Northern leaders for years while he was in Congress.

Jefferson Davis

With such opportunities of ascertaining the power and sentiments of the Northern people, it would have shown an inexcusable want of perception if I had shared the hopes of men less favored with opportunities for forming career judgments in believing with them that secession could be or would be peacefully accomplished.

Jefferson Davis

I see nothing short of conquest on one side or submission on the other. They will soon feel southern steel. . . .

Oh really? Northerners were not deterred.

Charles Eliot Norton, philosopher

We shall come, at length, to the rifle and the sword as the arbitrators of the great quarrel, I have no fear of the result.

Oh really? Jefferson Davis affirmed in his inaugural address:

Jefferson Davis

Obstacles may retard but they cannot long prevent the progress of a movement sanctified by its justice and sustained by a virtuous people.

Jefferson Davis

The time for compromise has now passed, and the South is determined to maintain her position, and make all who oppose her smell Southern powder and feel Southern steel if coercion is persisted. We ask nothing and want nothing. We have no complications.

Jefferson Davis

I will meet force with force.

Davis, his Cabinet, and Southern politicians had badly underestimated Lincoln's resolve. People who knew Lincoln swore he was tough. Henry Villard, a reporter for the New York Herald *in Springfield, who saw Lincoln often, wrote on the day after South Carolina seceded:*

Henry Villard, journalist

I cannot resist the conviction that the passage of the secession ordinance by the South Carolina Convention has, instead of intimidating the President-elect, only made him more firmer and more decided in his views on the reckless and unjustifiable attempt to break up the Union. He will not swerve from the conscientious and rigorous fulfillment of what he considers his Constitutional obligations.

The South Carolina Secession Convention of 1860 did pump fire into Southerners, though.

Robert Rhett Jr.

The tea has been thrown overboard. The Revolution of 1860 has been initiated.

Davis said that he saw his defense of the Confederacy as on par with President Lincoln's defense of the Union. Meanwhile, his vice president, Alexander Stephens, gave several speeches in March 1861 that predicted a long life for the Southerners' new nation.

Alexander Stephens

We are now the nucleus of a growing power which, if we are true to ourselves, our destiny and high mission, will become the controlling power on this continent.

ELEVEN

Fort Sumter

Blaming Major Anderson

The future of Fort Sumter remained just across the harbor in the person of South Carolina Governor Francis Pickens. In December, when Major Anderson and his men were still at Fort Moultrie and Sumter was unoccupied, Pickens, fearing trouble of some kind, boldly asked for permission from President Buchanan to seize the then-empty Sumter himself.

Governor Francis Pickens

I am authentically informed that the forts in Charleston harbor are being thoroughly prepared to turn, with effect, their guns upon the interior and the city. I would most respectfully and from a sincere devotion to the public peace, request that you allow me to send a small force, not exceeding twenty-five men, and an officer, to take possession of Fort Sumter immediately in order to give a feeling of safety to the community. There are no United States troops in that fort whatever or perhaps only four or five. If Fort Sumter could be given to me as Governor . . . then I think the public mind might be quieted under a feeling of safety.

The request was turned down, but that did not bother Pickens at all. As governor, he ordered his state militia to take action if it appeared Anderson was moving his men from Moultrie to Sumter.

Governor Francis Pickens
Forbid it, and if persevered in, to resist it by force and then immediately to take Fort Sumter at all hazards.

There were people in the South—important people—opposed to an assault on Sumter. One was former US President and Virginian John Tyler, a delegate to the Virginia Secession Convention. He wrote to Pickens:

John Tyler
Can my voice reach you? If so, do not attack Fort Sumter. You know my sincerity. The Virginia Delegates have earnestly united.

William Porcher Miles, a South Carolina delegate to the National Secession Convention in Alabama, held the same view.

William Porcher Miles
All of the hottest Southern men advise against the immediate attack upon Sumter.

Many Confederate military men were also opposed to an attack. Jefferson Davis sent General P. G. T. Beauregard to take charge of all Confederate troops in Charleston, and he concurred.

General P. G. T. Beauregard
Everyone here seems to be gradually becoming aware, through my cautious representations, that we are not yet prepared for this.

A few days later, however, on Pickens's orders, the Confederates seized the federal arsenal in Charleston.

By the end of 1860, all compromises discussed in Washington had failed. Senator Judah Benjamin, soon to be in the Confederate Cabinet, was furious with the US government and ready for a clean break.

Senator Judah Benjamin, Louisiana

You do not propose to enter into our states, you say, and what do we complain of? You do not pretend to enter into our states to kill or destroy our institutions by force. Oh, no . . . you propose simply to close us in an embrace that will suffocate us. . . . The day for adjustments has passed. . . . We desire, we beseech you, let this parting be in peace. . . . You can never subjugate us; you can never convert the free sons of the soil into vassals, paying tribute to your power. And you never, never, never can degrade them to the level of an inferior and servile race. Never! Never!

Benjamin was not alone in his hatred of the Union. Confederate state governments began seizing federal arsenals and munitions yards. Mississippi seceded on January 9, and the vote to do so was met with a huge cheer. Those who were there claimed there was no roar louder anywhere.

Delegate to the Mississippi Secession Convention

A great wave of excitement swept the audience and grave and dignified men, swayed by common impulse, joined in the deafening applause. In an instant the hall was a scene of wild tumult.

Captain Doubleday believed that Major Anderson was torn between the North and South. After all, Anderson's wife was from Georgia, and until a year or two earlier he had owned a plantation and slaves. But he had decided to get rid of them.

Captain Abner Doubleday

In my opinion, if he [Anderson] could have been satisfied that no other states would join South Carolina in her mad attempt, he would have done everything that lay in his power to punish her; for he looked upon her as a spoiled child that needed correction. Having married a lady from Georgia, he had almost identified himself with that state. He did own a plantation and Negroes there but had recently sold them. The purchaser afterward refused to pay for them on the ground that Anderson had destroyed their value by virtually warring against slavery. In this period, the feeling in many parts of the South was strong against South Carolina. This was particularly the case among the young men of Georgia who looked upon the leaders of secession in the Palmetto State as very presuming because these leaders thought and acted as though they were the only representatives of Southern sentiment.

On the Southern side, government spokesmen and newspaper editors said it was peace, not war, that they wanted. As both sides seemed to race toward a conflict, many Southerners still hoped for peace.

Mary Chestnut

We are always frantic for a good sign. Let us pray that a Caesar or Napoleon may be sent us. That would be our best sign of success. But they still say "never." Peace let it be, kind heaven!

Anonymous editor

We hope for the continuation of peace and unity between this Commonwealth and the government at Washington.

James McCarter, Charleston bookseller

I have always been a great lover of the Union, and have clung to it, with a sincere devotion. Even now, I do not give up any hope that some fortunate person may find out some way of escape from the evils of dissolution! But my fears are now greatly in advance of my hopes.

◆

The Fort Sumter debate did little to affect the life of Charleston. The slave auctions in the city, for example, went on as usual.

Mary Chestnut

I have seen a Negro woman sold on the block of auction. I was walking and felt faint, seasick. The creature looked so like my good, little Nancy, bright mulatto with a pleasant face. She was magnificently gotten up in silks and satins.

Slave auctions in Charleston angered her because she assumed the men who bought female slaves wanted them for sexual purposes.

Mary Chestnut

Men and women are punished when their masters and mistresses are brutes & not when they do wrong and then we live surrounded by prostitutes. An abandoned woman is sent out of any decent house elsewhere. Who thinks worse of a Negro or Mulatto woman for being a thing we can't name? God forgive us, but ours is a monstrous system and wrong and iniquitous. This only I see, like the patriarchs of old our men live all in one house with their wives and concubines and the mulattoes one sees in every family exactly resemble the white children. Every white lady tells you who is the father of all the mulatto children in every house, but those in her own she seems to think drop from the clouds or pretends so to think.

Elizabeth Van Lew, a Richmond, Virginia, abolitionist who ran a spy ring during the war, took things much further.

Elizabeth Van Lew

Slavery takes away a man's moral courage.

Mary Chestnut's husband, and her wealthy friends, including Jefferson Davis, did not agree.

Jefferson Davis

Slavery has its evils and abuses . . . [yet] we recognize him as our inferior, fitted expressly for servitude. . . . You cannot transform the Negro into anything one tenth as useful or as good as what slavery enables them to be.

Abraham Lincoln also saw the slippery moral slope slavery presented.

Abraham Lincoln

If I saw a venomous snaked crawling in the road, any man would say I might seize the nearest stick and kill it, but if I found that snake in bed with my children, that would be another question. I might hurt the children more than the snake. But if there was a bed newly made up to which the children were to be taken, and it be proposed to take a batch of young snakes and put them there with them, I take it no man would say there was any question how I ought to decide.

He disagreed with politicians like Stephen Douglas, who always seemed to embody both sides of the argument on slavery. In his famous 1860 speech at the Cooper Union in New York City, he addressed "Republicans."

Abraham Lincoln

Let us be diverted by none of those sophistical contrivances wherewith we are so industriously plied and belabored—contrivances such as groping for some middle ground between the right and the wrong, vain as the search for a man who should be neither a living man nor a dead man—such as a policy of "don't care" on a question about which all true men do care—such as Union appeals beseeching true Union men to yield to Disunionists, reversing the divine rule, and calling, not the sinners, but the righteous to repentance. . . .

Let us have faith that right makes might and in that faith, let us dare to do our duty as we understand it.

Lincoln also disagreed with Douglas's stand that popular sovereignty must prevail.

Abraham Lincoln
When the white man governs himself, that is self-government; but when he governs himself and also governs another man that is more than self-government; that is despotism. No man can logically say he does not care if a wrong is voted up or voted down. He cannot say people have a right to do wrong. He who would be no slave must consent to have no slave. Those who deny freedom to others deserve it not for themselves and under a just God cannot long retain it.

Confederate President Jefferson Davis, of course, sided with Douglas's views.

Jefferson Davis
Secession belongs to a different class of remedies. It is to be justified on the basis that the states are sovereign. There was a time when none denied it. I hope the time may come again, when a better comprehension of the theory of our government and the inalienable rights of the people of the states, will prevent any one from denying that each state is a sovereign, and thus they reclaim the grants which it has made to any agent whatsoever.

He also argued that one man's version of history is not necessarily another's.

Jefferson Davis

Tradition usually rests upon something which men did know; history is often the manufacture of the mere liar.

The beliefs of statesmen such as Lincoln and Davis, and countless Senators and Congressmen, North and South, started to matter little as the winter of 1860–1861 dragged on and Fort Sumter was hurtling toward an explosion. Neither president knew who would light the fuse or where the explosion would take place, but they were sure it was coming.

Men and women throughout the South were tired of talking and wanted action. They wanted their newly established Confederacy to separate from the Union and become its own thriving country. Many who lived below the Mason–Dixon line thirsted not only for a new Confederacy, but a new Southern empire. That empire would stretch north to Ohio and west to the shores of the Pacific. It would include Arizona, New Mexico, and the Great Plains states. Some went so far as to dream of annexing Caribbean islands, such as Cuba, whose residents were slaveowners and had always seemed eager to join a Southern union. Some saw the northern area of Mexico as part of that empire, and parts of Central America as well. It was time to get started, they howled. Thousands in the South pushed Davis and pushed him hard to get into a war to reach those grandiose goals.

All those dreams revolved around preserving slavery. Anyone trying to overturn slavery was an enemy of the South, and had to be dealt with harshly.

As the Fort Sumter crisis deepened over the slavery issue, many Charlestonians remembered the celebrated 1822 hanging of a slave, Denmark Vesey, in Charleston, for fermenting a slave revolt.

Woman who witnessed the hanging of Vesey

Ah! Slavery is a hard business and I am afraid that in this country we shall know it to be a bitter cost some day or other.

Hangings of all sorts was popular in the South. A minister happily applauded it as a good way to get rid of abolitionists.

Reverend John Bachman

God help me, I would rather have them [abolitionists] hanged first, and forgive them afterwards.

Elizabeth Van Lew

People were, if anything, more morbid than ever on the subject of slavery and I heard a member of the Virginia Legislature say that anyone speaking against it, or doubting its divinity, ought to be hung. Yes, hung as certainly and as truly as he would be for murder.

The Northerners had a yen for hanging Southerners, too.

John C. Winter, northern businessman

To catch them at it & hang the ringleaders as Pirates will be a terrible blow upon their prestige—let them make the fights & let Uncle Sam whip them.

One group of people who wanted to do some whipping—a lot of it—were residents of Charleston, who by February had developed a deep hatred for the Union troops living behind the walls of Fort Sumter out in their harbor.

Captain Abner Doubleday

Talbot stated that he had great difficulty making transit through Charleston; for while the leaders seemed to be more pacific than ever, the populace had become more violent. He brought me the pleasant information that the mobs were howling for my head, as that of the only "Black Republican" in the fort.

A few days later, Doubleday received a letter from a Charlestonian.

Captain Abner Doubleday

[It was] informing me that if I were ever caught in the city arrangement had been made to tar and feather me as an abolitionist.

By the winter of 1861, Anderson and Doubleday at Sumter, and everyone else, knew that Charleston was full of spies.

Thomas Gunn, friend of British Consul Bunch

There is a system of espionage as complete as that organized by the first Napoleon. The gentlemanly stranger who, learning you are from the North, claims it is his own birthplace and sounds you with some mild Union sentiments, intimating in his private conviction that "we have gone too far here." The barman who mixes your "cocktail," the colored waiter who attends assiduously upon our party at the hotel dinner and is much interested in the inevitable political conversations, the loungers in its hall or under its piazza—beware of each and all of them. Charleston is one vigilante committee.

Even though tensions remained high, Fort Sumter was the scene of genuine oddities, such as the visit of a Major Anderson—not the commander, but the director of the Tredegar Iron Works, a US munitions arsenal in Richmond, Virginia, that would soon become the largest arsenal of the Confederate Army. That Major Anderson was transporting a train filled with shot, shell, heavy guns, and mortars for the South Carolina militia to use against the Union troops at the fort. He knew that Major Robert Anderson was commanding Fort Sumter, and being that they had the same last name (they were not related), he wanted to pay his respects.

Captain Abner Doubleday

To my surprise, instead of being summarily expelled he was met with a most cordial reception, was invited to stay to dinner, and when he left he was dismissed with a "Goodbye! God Bless you!"

That time also brought out the generosity of people eager to help the troops stuck at Fort Sumter. Mr. Haight, a wealthy New Yorker, sent boxes of delicacies to the troops. Governor Pickens, who believed the false stories that the fort would be evacuated, allowed them to be delivered. And there was more.

Captain Abner Doubleday

The great tobacconist, John Anderson, of New York, also sent a large supply of the best quality of tobacco, having learned that the men felt the loss of their smoking more than anything else.

But right after that, the scene in Charleston returned to preparing for war.

Captain Abner Doubleday

On the 9th of February, the enemy's batteries were completely manned and ready for action.

On that same day, the Confederate government was duly organized by the election of Jefferson Davis as president. The next day, Lieutenant Hall returned from a visit to Washington, D.C.

Captain Abner Doubleday

As Hall passed through Charleston, one of the young men there told him there was quite a revulsion of feeling with regard to attacking Fort Sumter. Hall inquired the reason. The reply was that a schooner which had just come in had been in great danger from one of the infernal machines which had exploded and whitened the water.

Three days later, a Charleston friend stunned the garrison.

Captain Abner Doubleday

Captain Edward McCready, who had formerly been very intimate with the officers of the garrison, wrote a letter urging them to throw off their allegiance to the United States and enter into the Confederate service. No one took the trouble to answer it.

Even stranger, the soldiers read in various newspapers that the Fort Sumter crisis had become high-level theater up north.

Captain Abner Doubleday

Dramas founded on our occupation of Fort Sumter, and confinement there, were being acted in both Boston and New York. It was quite amusing to see our names in the playbills and to find that persons were acting our parts and spouting mock heroics on the stage.

Major Anderson had become a hero to the Republic as he and his men hung on day after day. He received hundreds of letters from well-wishers. Old men who had fought in the War of 1812 wrote him notes, as did giddy grade-school children. The legislatures of five states officially honored him. Babies were named after him and songs written about him. One town raised money to buy him an engraved sword. Towns accorded him thirty-three-gun salutes. There were laudatory notes from Republicans—and from Democrats, too.

This admiration was shared by many in Charleston. Their quarrel was with the government in Washington, not with the man caught in the middle.

Robert Rhett Jr.

The people of South Carolina have been measurably disarmed by their sympathy for Major Anderson.

TWELVE

Charleston, South Carolina

The Drumbeat for War Grows Louder

The sympathy for Major Anderson did not last long. As Confederate troops and South Carolina militiamen poured into Charleston and long trains of ammunition, weapons, and supplies arrived, the populace girded itself for war. All the Charleston area was getting ready, and so were nearby states and cities. Hundreds of men ordered militia uniforms, bands were organized, colors of battle flags selected, and soldiers drilled on city streets and in town squares. Cannon were fired in practice and bands of teenagers played "Dixie" from one end of Charleston to the other.

Major Robert Anderson

They take every preparation [drilling nightly, etc.] for the fight which they say must take place and insist on our not doing anything.

Mary Chestnut

We were busy and frantic with excitement, drilling, marching, arming and wearing high blue cockades. Red sashes, guns and swords were ordinary fireside accompaniments. I saw at a grand parade of the home guard a woman, the wife of a man who says he is a secessionist, driving about to see the drilling of this new company, although her father was buried the day before.

State militias were forming in every Southern state.

Elizabeth Van Lew

Many [Virginians] had already formed themselves into volunteer companies. These belonged to the State and found themselves in the army before they knew it. The whole South became one great military school. We were told that it would only require six per cent of our male population to whip the Yankees, a cowardly set who had only to believe us in earnest to yield to all of our demands.

Evelyn Ward

In those days, there was a regular militia force trained and drilled in [Tappahannock] Virginia, and we loved to see General Upshur, dressed in his blue uniform with brass buttons and wearing a great floating-top plume in his hat, lead out his soldiers and drill them on Main Street. Then Captain Walter Jones would come with his cavalry. My! How good he looked with his plume, his buttons, his epaulets and sash and his long sword.

There was regimental drill every morning and dress parade in the evening. All of the people in Tappahannock dressed up in their best to see the dress parade. We thought father looked splendid, dressed in his dark blue clothes [the Virginia uniform] with a rather high hat. He stood before the line very tall and straight. A mulatto with a flute and a little drummer boy who beat his drum quite well made very good marching music.

Robert Bunch

Everyone, old and young, is enrolled in some military company and drilling is going on at all hours. The public excitement is kept alive by the constant arrival of telegrams, many of the most absurd and mendacious character. Nothing is spoken of except bloodshed and reasonable counsels are entirely disregarded.

Another Southern custom at the time of the Fort Sumter crisis was the presentation of battle flags to newly drawn-up volunteer regiments. Usually a young lady from the community would present the flag to a local regiment as hundreds cheered or lined the streets for a grand parade. One such company was the Louisiana Rifles. The battle flag was presented by a local young woman.

Miss Idelea Collens

Receive then from your mothers and sisters those whose affections greet you with these colors, woven by our feeble but radiant hands. And when this bright flag shall float before you on the battlefield, let it not only inspire you with the brave and patriotic ambition of a soldier aspiring to his own and his country's honor and glory, but also may it be a sign that cherished ones appeal to you to save them from a fanatical and heartless foe.

Miss Collens was thanked by the regiment's color sergeant, who marched with his corporals to accept it.

Color Sergeant

Ladies, with high beating hearts and pulses throbbing with emotion, we receive from your hands this most beautiful flag, the proud emblem of our young republic. . . . To those who may be returning from the field of battle bearing this flag in triumph, though perhaps tattered and torn, this incident will always prove a cheering recollection, and to him whose fate it may be to die a soldier's death, this moment, brought before his fading view, will recall your kind and sympathetic words. . . . May the God of battle look down upon us as we make a soldier's vow that no stain shall ever be found upon thy sacred folds except the blood of those who attack thee or those who fall in their defense.

The local militias were an example of why the South thought it would win a war. But up North, just about everybody, military or civilian, believed the North would win—and handily. William Tecumseh Sherman did not. He had pointed out as early as 1856 that a victory over the Southerners would be hard-fought.

William Tecumseh Sherman

Unless people, North and South, learn more moderation, we'll see signs in the way of civil war. Of course, the North has the strength, and must prevail, though the people of the South could and would be desperate enough. . . . [S]urplus steam is threatening to blow up the Union.

A man in Montgomery, Alabama, tired of all the talk about a North–South conflict, let everybody at a party know how he felt after a few drinks.

Angry Man

This war talk is nothing. It will soon blow over. It is only a fuss gotten up by that Charleston clique.

Georgia Senator Robert Toombs, listening to him, cut him off.

Robert Toombs

A man who uses such language is a suspicious character.

Toombs then demanded that the man give him his passport and thrust it into his pocket. A chill ran through the crowd.

As the days passed in the Fort Sumter crisis, animosity toward the North, in the South and in Charleston, intensified. A Northern woman visiting relatives in Charleston sat down at a piano in the living room of her host, near a window that overlooked the harbor and, far off in the distance, Fort Sumter, just before breakfast and played the normally spirited patriotic tune "Yankee Doodle." Sad about events, though, she played it very slowly, striking just one key at a time with her fingers. Her host, upset, ran into the room and glowered at her.

The Host
Leave out the "Yankee" and play the "doodle." The "Yankee" did not fit the climate in South Carolina.

Myra Inman celebrated her seventeenth birthday the week that Lincoln took office and the Sumter crises exploded in Charleston.

Myra Inman
I wonder where I will be on my eighteenth?

William Russell, of the London Times, *wrote about the sentiments of the people of Charleston.*

William Russell
There is nothing in all the dark caves of human passion as cruel and deadly as the hatred South Carolinians profess for the Yankees.

His fellow Brit, Robert Bunch, agreed.

Robert Bunch
That the dislike to the Union now existing in the Southern country is more intense than it has been at any former period is, I think, unquestionable. . . . Now, scarcely a voice is raised in favor of the Union—everybody, including those who were the most energetic Union men . . . is in favor of immediate separation if the South fails to secure from the present congress some effective guarantee, not only against attacks, a la John Brown . . . but against any interference at all with slavery on the part of the free state.

He was not telling Southerners anything they did not already know.

Elizabeth Van Lew

Our people required blood, the blood of all who were of the John Brown party. They thirsted for it. They cried out for it. It was not enough that one old man, Brown, should die. No pleas of the people intellecting would be listened to.

And that hatred was becoming more intense, like lava in a volcano. An Englishman, James Stirling, on a tour of Charleston and other cities, expressed it best.

James Stirling

The whole South is like one of its cotton steamers, filled from the hold up to the topmost deck with the most inflammable matter, everything heated up to the burning point.

There was a political point that Southerners were missing in discussing the legality of slavery, insisted many Northerners, including Congressman John Sherman of Ohio. Sherman, a Republican, was finishing up his third term in Congress during the Fort Sumter crisis. He would later be elected to the Senate. The popular Sherman was almost elected Speaker of the House in 1859, losing after a political dispute took place. As a congressman and senator, during and after the war, he was one of America's most influential public figures, and author of the Sherman Anti-Trust Act.

John Sherman

The question is not whether this or that policy should prevail, but whether we should allow the government to be broken into fragments by disappointed partisans condemned by four-fifths of the people. . . . [T]he Union must be preserved.

Something people on both sides of the question neglected to consider was a military takeover of the United States during or after a Civil War. It scared

William T. Sherman, as did the Southern states hurtling toward secession. He wrote his congressman brother about his concerns.

William Tecumseh Sherman

I don't like the looks of the times. This political turmoil, the sending of commissions from state to state, the organization of military schools and establishments, and the universal belief in the South that disunion is not only possible but certain—are bad signs. If our country falls into anarchy, it will be Mexico, only worse. I was in hopes the crisis would have been deferred till the states of the northwest became so populous as to hold both extremes in check. Disunion would be Civil War and you politicians would lose all charm. Military men would then step in the tapis, and you would have to retire. Though you think such a thing absurd, yet it is not so, and there would be vast numbers who would think the change for the better.

◆

The ill-fated voyage to Charleston of the supply ship Star of the West *caused tremendous controversy. The ship was sent to Fort Sumter in the middle of January 1861, when Buchanan was still president. The ship was fired upon by Confederate forces. Southerners felt betrayed that President Buchanan had sent the vessel into the harbor. He was accused of duplicity and treason by many Southern leaders, and ordinary citizens as well.*

The wife of planter Patrick Edmondson of Halifax County, North Carolina, wrote to her sister Margaret about it.

Catherine Edmondson

[*Star of the West*] was Mr. Buchanan's treachery. Everywhere [news] was received with surprised dismay, the feeling almost universally being to leave South Carolina to herself, give her the fort if she required it.

Margaret's exclamation when she heard the news about the Star of the West *was, "Why Kate, you have been seeing history!"*

Catherine Edmondson

The ladies of South Carolina displayed an enthusiasm and earnestness in their preparations for war that was almost sublime in its unity and self-devotion. They spent their whole time scraping lint, making bandages and even learned to make cartridges. One lady in Aiken made 300 with her own hands.

An example of the heated feelings is an exchange of letters between President Buchanan and Jacob Thompson, the Secretary of the Interior, right after the ship was fired upon and had to turn around without reaching Fort Sumter.

Jacob Thompson, Secretary of the Interior

It is with extreme regret that I have just learned that additional troops have been ordered to Charleston. . . . I distinctly understood you that no orders of that kind would be made without being previously considered and decided in Cabinet, but certainly no conclusion was reached and the war department was not justified in ordering re-inforcements without something [more] than was said. I learn, however, this morning, for the first time, that the steamer *Star of the West* sailed from New York on last Saturday night with two hundred and fifty men under Lieut. Bartlett bound for Fort Sumter. Under these circumstances, I feel myself bound to resign my commission.

James Buchanan

You are certainly mistaken in saying that no conclusion was reached. In this your recollection is entirely different from your four oldest colleagues in the Cabinet. Indeed, my language was so unmistakable that the secretaries of war and the navy proceeded to act upon it without any further intercourse with myself than what you heard, or might have heard, me say. You had been so emphatic in opposing these reinforcements that I thought you would resign in consequence of my decision. I deeply regret that you have been mistaken in point of fact, though I firmly believe, honestly mistaken.

When Texas Senator Louis Wigfall heard of the Star of the West*'s turnaround, he was jubilant, and took a poke at Northerners.*

Louis Wigfall

Your flag has been insulted; redress it if you dare.

The troops at Fort Sumter heard that a supply ship was on its way, but they did not know when it was scheduled to arrive. Just after dawn on January 9, it slipped into Charleston Harbor.

Captain Abner Doubleday

I was on the parapet with my spy glass for I fancied from a signal I had observed the previous evening, on a pilot-boat, that something must be wrong. As I looked seaward, I saw a large steamer (*Star of the West*) pass the bar and enter the Morris Island channel. It had the ordinary United States flag up, and as it evidently did not belong to the Navy, I came to the conclusion it must be the *Star of the West.*

Major Anderson himself was still in bed. When the vessel came opposite the new battery, which had just been built by the [Citadel] cadets, I saw a shot fired to bring her to. Soon after this, an immense United States garrison flag was run up at the fore. Without waiting to ascertain the result of the firing, I dashed down the backstairs to Anderson's room to notify him of the occurrence. He told me to have the long [drum] roll beaten and to post the men on the guns on the parapet. I ran out, called the drummer, and had the alarm sounded. It took but a few minutes for men and officers to form at the guns in readiness for action. The battery was still firing, but the transport had passed by and was rapidly getting out of range. At the same time, it was approaching within gun shot of Fort Moultrie. The latter immediately opened fire from one of two guns. Anderson would not allow us to return the fire and the captain of the vessel, wholly discouraged by our failure to respond, turned about and made his way back to New York.

It was plainly our duty to do all that we could. For anything we knew to the contrary, she might have been in a sinking condition. Had she gone down before our eyes, without an effort on our part to aid her, Anderson would have incurred a fearful responsibility by his inaction.

Just two weeks after the Star of the West *was shelled, Major Anderson made arrangements to have all the women and children at Fort Sumter taken by ship to New York City, where churches and local residents would care for them, since they left Charleston with no money. The women and children sailed to Charleston and then boarded the steamer* Marion, *which departed for New York on February 3, 1861. Abner Doubleday's wife was among those on the ship.*

Captain Abner Doubleday

As they passed the fort, outward bound, the men gave them repeated cheers as a farewell and displayed feeling; for they thought it very probable they might not meet them again for a long period, if ever.

Doubleday told a marvelous story about a boy on that ship.

Captain Abner Doubleday

Among those children was a little waif called Dick Rowley, afterwards known as "Sumter Dick." He had been abandoned by his mother and thus thrown out upon the world. After a time, he was sent—after his arrival in New York—to the house of Dr. Stewart, who was a family connection of mine. After supper, he reminded the ladies that he had not heard tattoo yet and wished to know at what hour they beat the reveille. He evidently thought that every well-regulated family kept a drummer and fifer on hand to sound the calls. He was very unhappy until he had procured a small stick and a miniature flag. Every morning at sunrise he hoisted the flag and carefully lowered it and put it away at sunset.

All of Charleston was thrilled that the cadets from the Citadel had opened fire on the Star of the West.

Robert Rhett Jr.

Yesterday morning was the opening ball of the Revolution. We are proud that our harbor has been so honored.

Troops at Fort Sumter agreed on the first point. One was Captain John Foster, a career Army man who would later become a Union general.

Captain John G. Foster

The firing upon the *Star of the West* by the batteries on Morris Island opened the war.

While Southerners saw the cadets as heroes, many in the North branded them as traitors. Just two weeks later, Congressman Samuel Blair of Pennsylvania blasted Charlestonians.

Representative Samuel Blair, Pennsylvania

Will the generations that are to succeed us believe that at such a time we sat out a whole winter with these guns still pointed at us, trying how far we might go to comply with the demands of traitors, and what new securities we might devise for the protection and spread of human bondage?

THIRTEEN

Washington, D.C.
Rumors of War

In Washington, rumors flew everywhere. Some said the Navy was ready to attack Pensacola. No, another rumor insisted, the Navy had already set sail for Charleston. A full-scale attack on Santo Domingo, in Haiti, was yet another story circulating. The rumor that the U.S. Navy was going to sail to both Pickens and Sumter and fire on the nearby cities was getting stronger every day.

Atop the red brick walls of Fort Sumter, Major Anderson was swamped by all the rumors, too. He shook his head a lot, because by this point there was really not much he could do. The new president and his Cabinet in Washington were formulating a strategy to either resupply the fort or give it up—Anderson did not know which—and Confederate commanders were preparing to attack it. He was the pawn in the middle.

Major Robert Anderson

My course has been to pray daily to God to give me a clear understanding of my duty and to give me strength of purpose & resolution fully to perform it. I confess that I would not be willing to risk my reputation in an attempt to throw reinforcements into this harbor within the time for our relief rendered necessary by the limited supply of our provisions . . . with a force of less than 20,000 good and well-disciplined men.

A confrontation appeared to be looming. The story of that confrontation would be written soon, and written by the South, not the North and their infernally slow and confused president, who was lambasted by the editors of pro-Southern Charleston newspapers. One of the most colorful and loudest Southern rabble-rousers was the editor of the Charleston Courier, *who unsheathed his sword in just about every edition. In the middle of all his shouting and fuming, though, he warned his readers that Fort Sumter had an incredible amount of firepower.*

Editor, *Charleston Courier*

Twenty-five well drilled men could hold [Sumter] against all of Charleston. Its batteries could level Fort Moultrie within a few hours and shell the city effectively if turned against us.

A reporter for the Courier, *like his editor, not knowing what the real condition of Fort Sumter was, gushed over its power.*

Reporter, *Charleston Courier*

The grim fortress featured defiance on every side—the busy noise of preparation resounded through its unforgiving walls. . . . Major Robert Anderson has achieved the unenviable distinction of opening a Civil War between American citizens by an act of gross breach of faith.

People had no idea the weak shape that crumbling old Sumter was in. Major Anderson, inside it, constantly bemoaned the fate of his garrison, but the enemy saw Sumter in a very different light. Residents of Charleston feared the prospect of a bombardment of the city by federal the guns at Sumter.

Alfred Ravenel

The occupation of Fort Sumter by the federal troops from its commanding & almost impregnable position has been regarded by our people with great apprehension. . . . We are in a state of anxious suspense as to the next act in the drama. . . . It would seem that we have been treacherously dealt with . . . the die has been cast and we may now look for Civil War.

A Southern general, arriving later in the North–South standoff in Charleston, like other Charlestonians, genuinely feared the big guns on the top of the walls of Fort Sumter.

Anonymous General, Confederate Army

The enemy can demolish our other posts when he pleases from one of the most impregnable fortresses in the world, and so our posts live at his will, and remain in our possession at his sufferance.

What the newspaper people, citizens of Charleston, and Union soldiers did not know was that the Confederates had been hard at work to prepare for a surprise attack. They cloaked gun batteries with trees and built tent camps as large as they could to make the Union troops believe they had more men than they did. In a stunning move, they built a house around a gun battery, then startled the Union soldiers when they revealed it.

Captain Abner Doubleday

On April 10, a house directly opposite to us in Moultrieville was suddenly removed, disclosing a formidable masked battery, which effectually enfiladed two rows of our upper tier of guns . . . and took a third tier in reverse. It was a sad surprise to us, for we had our heaviest metal there. I set to work immediately to construct sand bag traverses but it was difficult to make much progress as we had no bags and were obliged to tear up sheets for the purpose and had the pieces sewed together. . . . Anderson ordered us to abandon all guns on the parapet . . . it deprived us of the most powerful and effective part of our armament.

That same day, April 10, Major Anderson received news from Washington that the much-talked-about Navy supply fleet was on its way to Charleston.

Captain Abner Doubleday

The fighting was about to commence. The news acted like magic upon them. They had previously been drooping and dejected; but they now sprung to their work with the greatest alacrity, laughing, singing, whistling, and full of glee. They were overjoyed to learn that their long imprisonment in the fort would soon be at an end.

L. P. Walker, the Confederate Secretary of War, in far-off Montgomery, Alabama, knew supplies at Sumter were running low. But he believed if the reinforcements arrived, the fort could become very dangerous indeed.

L. P. Walker, in a letter to General P. G. T. Beauregard

Re-inforcements must be prevented at all hazards, and by the use of every conceivable agency. Fort Sumter is silent now only because of the weakness of the garrison. Should re-inforcements get in, her guns would open fire upon you.

He later said the stress of being Secretary of War and overseeing the Fort Sumter situation ruined his health.

Mercury *editor Robert Rhett Jr. had watched the work at Fort Sumter and come to a different conclusion.*

Robert Rhett Jr.

[Whoever held Sumter] could defy any fleet of vessels . . . [but] an entrance, say, at the present state of construction [could] be easily made.

Rhett added that at the same time a frontal assault was launched, hundreds of men could climb ladders and get into the fort over its walls.

All this talk about whether or not South Carolinians could take the fort made Major Anderson quite nervous.

Major Robert Anderson

I hear that the attention of the South Carolinians appears to be turned more towards Fort Sumter than it was, and it is deemed probable that their first act will be to take possession of the work.

These reports, and fears, from the Charleston press and the Confederates bolstered the confidence of the Union troops in Fort Sumter.

Captain John Foster, in a letter to his father

Morale is very high. You need not be in any unnecessary anxiety on my account for, to tell the truth, despite all of their [Confederate] bluster, I am almost sure they will never fire a shot at us. Indeed, I think they are only too glad to be let alone.

That morale was buoyed by patriotism.

Wylie Crawford

How trifling party differences appear in view of the great danger to our country now. We here have forgotten them all as we stand around our flag, unfurled every morning over our guns, dearer than ever to us now that we know and feel that it is in danger.

Crawford, the surgeon, felt that troops in Sumter could fire on Charleston with its guns whenever they wanted.

Wylie Crawford

The truth is we are the government at present. It rests upon the points of our swords. Shall we use our position to deluge the country in blood?

One enlisted man at Sumter wrote a letter to the New York Herald *on April 5, 1861, assuring them the troops were fine and ready for a fight.*

Enlisted Man

We have enough to eat and drink. Our fuel is scarce, but that is nothing. . . . Major Anderson is a true soldier, and so are the other officers. The men would die for him. I only wish we had a chance to give the rascals hell.

Sergeant James Chester

There was never a happier or contented set of men in any garrison than the Sumter soldiers.

Major Robert Anderson

The command is in excellent health and in fine spirits.

Anderson believed, right to the end, that politicians would resolve the secession issue and there would be no attack on Sumter—and certainly no Civil War.

Major Robert Anderson

Our errant sisters thus leaving us as friends, may at some future time be back by conciliation and justice.

The return of soldiers from Washington, always with no news at all, now produced excitement. One, Theodore Talbot, found himself a hero for simply getting back.

Theodore Talbot

My return as been a cause of great rejoicing to the command on account of pleasant tidings that I brought with me. . . . Major Anderson cried like a child when I gave him all the affectionate greetings sent him by his companions in arms.

Talbot also brought a letter to Anderson from the Secretary of War.

Joseph Holt, Secretary of War

[I wish to] express the great satisfaction of the government for the forbearances, discretion and firmness with which you have acted amid the perplexing and difficult circumstances in which you have been placed. In every way admirable, alike for its humanity and patriotism, as for its soldiership. You will continue to act strictly on the defensive to avoid, by all means compatible with the safety of your command, a collision with the hostile forces by which you are surrounded.

After that letter, though, there was nothing but silence from Washington, and the lack of orders depressed Anderson.

Holt also said the move to Sumter from Moultrie was "brilliant." The Confederates would later charge that it was the first overt "act of war" and that the Union, not the South, was the aggressor. Jefferson Davis hinted at Moultrie as the cause of the war in his February inaugural address, and blamed the North.

Jefferson Davis

[We are] anxious to cultivate peace and harmony with all nations. If we may not hope to avoid war, we may at least expect that posterity will acquit us of having needlessly engaged in it. Doubly justified by the absence of wrong on our part, and by wanton aggression on the part of others.

Many Southerners, in Charleston and elsewhere, no longer believed the federal government was on their side, but instead wished to totally control them.

Robert Rhett Jr.

Charleston and Savannah will be mere suburbs of New York and Boston.

Many Charlestonians agreed.

William Porcher Miles
The South can never know peace and security again in the Union.

Miles was one of the most frustrated men in the South, and was soon to be a Confederate general.

William Porcher Miles
I am sick and disgusted with all of the bluster and threats and manifestos and resolutions. Let us act if we mean to act without talking.

Robert Rhett Jr.
There exists a great mistake . . . in supposing that the people of the United States are, or ever have been, one people. On the contrary, never did the sun shine on two people as thoroughly distinct as he did people of the North . . . and South. . . . Like all great nations of antiquity, we are slaveholders and understand free governments. The North does not. They are a people wrapped up in selfishness. They have no idea of free government. Their idea of free government is this, that when three men get together, the two are to rule the one; when five men get together, the three are to rule the other two. . . .

The sense that there were two nations was illustrated earlier at the 1860 Democratic Convention in Charleston, where the Southern delegates walked out rather than support the nominee, Stephen Douglas of Illinois. When he could not get the required votes, the convention was moved to Baltimore, where he got the nomination.

Robert Newman Gourdin, Charleston merchant
If the South sustains Douglas in any circumstance, she abandons all she has struggled for and contended for years past . . . abandons herself to the contempt and to the spoilation of the relentless enemies. If we

falter now and compromise our principles for party we seal our fate [and] a bloody revolution will be our only hope of redemption. The result of the Charleston Convention will tell the future of the South for weal or woe.

Gourdin was one of Charleston's most prominent, and popular, residents. He stood out at parties with his full white beard and expensive suits. He was also a bachelor. He lived in the city with his bachelor brother, Henry, and his widowed sister, Anna, and her three sons in a mansion on the Charleston battery that had one of the city's largest wine cellars. He had been unhappy about North–South politics for months. In late summer he told a friend:

Robert Gourdin
I am in despair.

Robert Rhett Jr. had been pushing the state government and new Confederate Army to seize Sumter. R. S. Holt, the brother of Lincoln's holdover Secretary of War, and a Kentucky man, had as well.

R. S. Holt
Submission by the South is now death. We must resist or perish miserable.

The South's first effort to do that came on April 10.

Captain Abner Doubleday
About 3 P.M., a boat came over with Colonel James Chestnut and Captain Stephen Lee, both aides of Beauregard. They had a demand for the surrender of the fort. Anderson politely declined to accede to this request, but stated in conversation he would soon be starved out.

This gratuitous information should never have been given to the enemy, in view of the fact that a naval expedition was on its way to us. It was at once supposed that Anderson intended to surrender without fighting.

Major Robert Anderson
God grant that neither I nor any other officer in our army may be again placed in a position of such mortification and humiliation.

Over the next two days, the Confederates prepared for an attack.

Captain Abner Doubleday
The enemy's batteries on Sullivan's island were so placed as to fire directly into the officer's quarters at Fort Sumter; and as our rooms would necessarily be untenable, we vacated them and chose points that were more secure. I moved my bed into a magazine that was directly opposite Cummings Point and which was nearly empty.

South Carolina's former governor, William Gist, preparing for a war he was certain would come, sent Thomas Drayton to Washington to purchase 10,000 new rifles. He had to settle for an older model.

Thomas Drayton
Better do this than be without guns at a crisis like the present.

Governor Pickens continually complained about the rejection of his offer to seize and occupy the fort to keep the peace.

Governor Francis Pickens
If something of the kind be not done, I cannot answer for the consequences.

Although few people liked him, none could criticize Pickens's Southern patriotism.

Mary Chestnut
Governor Pickens is a fire-eater down to the ground.

Pickens was routinely criticized in both local Charleston newspapers, however, and accused of getting in the way of President Davis and the Confederate Army and impeding progress on all fronts.

Editor, *Charleston Courier*
Pickens does nothing for the benefit of the state, but much to produce confusion. Conflicting and incomprehensible orders were emanating from the military department and indiscreet and injurious proclamations from the Executive. Everything was in confusion and everybody complaining.

Union troops were insulted by Pickens's demand that the Union leave Sumter and go back to Moultrie or he would order the South Carolina militia to storm the fort—something Union troops considered not only illegal, but abhorrent. Many Union officers wanted Anderson to fiercely refuse, and in strong language. Anderson did refuse, but quietly.

Captain Abner Doubleday
As commander of the defense of Charleston, Pickens thought he had an inherent right to occupy any fort in the harbor. He stated that he, too, was a Southern man; that he believed the whole difficulty was brought on by the faithlessness of the North . . . but as regards of returning to Fort Moultrie, he [Anderson] could not and he would not, do it.

I have always felt that this was a most insolent demand. If the Governor considered himself aggrieved by our change of station, his redress lay in an appeal to Washington. This attempt to assume command of us, and order us out of a United States fort, was an assumption of authority that merited a more spirited reply.

Doubleday's anger at Pickens did not deter the governor at all in his efforts to claim everything in Charleston that belonged to the federal government. He had his militia seize Moultrie and Castle Pinckney, the other forts that had been in federal hands, on December 27, and the Customs House and all other US forts and buildings the next day. Union troops were further incensed when the captain of a US revenue cutter turned over his ship to Confederate authorities, in full view of the troops stationed inside Sumter.

Captain Abner Doubleday

Previous seizures [of US ships] made without a declaration of war had been justified on the ground that the forts and public buildings were fixtures within the limits of the State. To retain this vessel was simply an act of piracy.

Later, after the war was over and Union troops paraded in triumph and Southern troops staggered back to their homes, President Buchanan, whose critics charged he had done nothing right in his four years in office, made one of the most cogent statements about the Civil War. He reminded people that when he was elected in 1856, he predicted all of this.

President James Buchanan

We have so often cried wolf that now, when the wolf is at the door, it is difficult to make the people believe it.

Even out of office in April 1861, Buchanan still hoped the country could be saved. When he reached his Lancaster, Pennsylvania, home just after Lincoln's inauguration, he told a welcoming crowd:

James Buchanan
God grant that the Constitution and the Union shall be perpetual.

A farmer outside of Charleston was not so sure.

Local farmer
I fear that we will have a long, Civil, bloody war—and perhaps an insurrection among the slaves. The Lord save us from such a horrid war.

FOURTEEN

(Still) Blaming Major Anderson

Major Anderson was taken to task relentlessly by his political and military bosses in the nation's capital. They even blamed the sand dunes on him. Anderson wanted to level the sand dunes to offer Fort Sumter more protection from cannonading, if it commenced, but the government said that if he did that, he would just stir up trouble.

Anonymous Military Commander
[You will] betray distrust and prematurely bring on a collision. . . . [The problems] demand the coolest and wisest judgment.

Major Anderson constantly complained that no one in Washington ever gave him any credit for evacuating Fort Moultrie late at night on December 26, 1860, and, unseen, taking all of his men and their wives out to Fort Sumter—something all in the Union garrison saw as heroic. His note to the War Department reported on abandoning Fort Moultrie.

Major Robert Anderson
I have the honor to report that I have just completed, by the blessing of God, the removal to this fort [Sumter] of all my garrison. The step which I have taken was in my opinion necessary to prevent the effusion of blood. I removed them on my own responsibility, my sole object being to prevent bloodshed. I cannot and will not go back.

Major Anderson, like just about everyone, had prayed that there would not be any conflict over Fort Sumter. As the new year began, though, he started to worry about relief ships as he watched Confederate troops and local militia, who appeared to be building a battery on nearby Morris Island.

Major Robert Anderson
At present, it would be dangerous and difficult for a vessel from without to enter the harbor in consequence of the batteries which are already erected and being erected. . . . We are now, or soon will be, cut off from all communication, unless by means of a powerful fleet, which shall have the ability to carry the batteries at the mouth of this harbor. I shall not ask for any increase in my command because I do not know what the ulterior [undisclosed] motives of the government are.

Anderson's worries were deep. Disgusted with everyone and everything at one point, he lamented:

Major Robert Anderson
[I feel like] a sheep tied, watching the butcher sharpening a knife to cut his throat.

Residents and visitors to Charleston had been afraid for months that there were so many soldiers in town that the slightest incident would start a battle.

Robert Bunch
Fort Sumter is perfectly surrounded by men—there are certainly six or 7,000 on the various islands. My fear is that even if the U.S. supplies and re-inforcements do not arrive, an attack will be made by the Southern troops. As the Irishman says: Everyone is *spoiling* for a fight.

Men on the nearby islands were so close that soldiers in Fort Sumter could hear shouts from military meetings and gatherings of secession groups. Abner Doubleday observed a large gathering on Sullivan's Island.

Captain Abner Doubleday
A secessionist meeting was held in our immediate vicinity—accompanied by many threats and demonstrations.

Confederate officers often drove past Fort Sumter in carriages on inspection tours, and their wives worried about them traveling in the line of fire. Mary Chestnut's husband went on one of those tours.

Mary Chestnut
I hope that Anderson will not pay them the compliment of a salute with shotted guns as they pass Fort Sumter, as pass they must.

The desire of Charlestonians to seize Fort Sumter fit with the enthusiasm they all showed back on December 20, the night the state seceded from the Union and put its people on the path that led to the standoff in the harbor. Diarist Murat Halstead wrote on the evening of the state's secession:

Murat Halstead
There was a Fourth of July feeling in Charleston last night—a jubilee. There was no mistaking the public sentiment in the city. It was overwhelmingly and enthusiastically in favor of the seceders. In all of her history, Charleston had never enjoyed herself so hugely.

Robert Bunch
My city is wild with excitement—bells ringing, guns firing and scarcely one man in a thousand regrets the dissolution.

Some who witnessed the parades or read about them in overseas newspapers were not so certain of that.

Lord John Russell, England, late 1860

Things look indeed very serious in America. I don't see how the North is to bridle its tongue about slavery, but if the South does not wish secession she may be content with a pledge that the President will not propose abolition. I fear there is no hope, or hardly any hope, of a compromise. For ourselves, unless we are asked to mediate, we can do nothing more than deprecate collision. The South may have much to be thankful for that they have yet two months before they finally decide. I hope they will use them wisely.

Henry William Ravenel, Charleston planter

Our people do not reflect enough upon these things for themselves, but are led on by politicians, and made to think that safety, honor, self-respect and our very existence depend upon these issues.

Some in the city—just a handful—disagreed with the secessionists.

James Pettigrew

My unhappy fellow citizens talk of seceding from the Union. It is impossible, but they will not hear reason. I foresee nothing but disaster and ruin for them.

Many in Charleston, and throughout the South, saw secession as the first step on a new road.

Jefferson Davis

The past is dead; let it bury its dead, its hopes and its aspirations. Before you lies a future—a future full of golden promise.

Davis felt that the course of history had changed forever.

Jefferson Davis

A restitution of the Union has been rendered forever impossible.

December of 1860, the month South Carolina seceded from the Union, now seemed so long ago. It was the turning point for many Northerners who did business with the South or worked there. Hundreds started to leave and went home to their Northern cities and villages. In Louisiana, William T. Sherman left his job as superintendent of the Louisiana Seminary at the urging of his brother. Ironically, Sherman had lamented to his brother that he had been forced to leave four jobs in four years because of "calamity," never admitting that he was just not suited for those jobs. He would soon get back into the one profession for which he was incredibly well-suited: the U.S. Army.

John Sherman, to his brother William

You ought not to remain much longer at your present post. You will in all human probability be involved in complications from which you cannot escape with honor. Separated from your family and all your kin, and an object of suspicion, you will find your position unendurable. A fatal infatuation seems to have seized the Southern mind during which any act of madness may be committed. . . . If the sectional dissensions only rested upon real or alleged grievances, they could readily be settled, but I fear they are deeper and stronger. You can now close your connection with the seminary with honor and credit to yourself, for all who know you speak well of your conduct. While remaining you not only involve yourself, but bring trouble upon those gentlemen who recommended you.

It is sad state of affairs, but it is nevertheless true that if the convention of the Southern States make anything more than a paper secession hostile collisions will occur and probably a separation between the free and slave states.

And then John Sherman changed the history of the United States.

John Sherman, to his brother William

When you return to Ohio, I will write you freely about your return to the army, not so difficult a task as you imagine.

William T. Sherman resigned his position in Louisiana on January 18, 1861.

The tension over the fort and the arrival of thousands of Confederate and state troops to the town brought many problems for Charlestonians, not the least of which was greatly increased drinking. Alcoholism became so severe in the Army that Confederate General James Pemberton forbade any drinking in the city or in the Army camp. The order annoyed civilians as well as soldiers and crippled the taverns in the city.

General James Pemberton

All distillation of spiritous liquors is positively prohibited and the distilleries will forthwith be closed. The sale of spiritous liquors of any kind is also prohibited.

There was no government clampdown on drugs, though, and that relieved a number of people in Charleston. Mary Chestnut was one of them.

Mary Chestnut

We had a madwoman ranting about being separated from her daughter [on the train]. It excited me so that I quickly took opium. It enables me to retain every particle of mind or sense of brain I ever have & so quiets my nerve that I can calmly reason and make rational views of things.

Some women in Charleston even bragged that when they went to militia camps to visit their husbands serving in the military, they had sex with them, all for "the cause," of course.

Despite their enthusiasm for the Southern cause, many Southerners complained about their leaders.

Mary Chestnut

Everywhere that I have been people have been complaining about war and their lukewarm leaders.

The secession of the state had thrilled some and alarmed others.

Mrs. Charles Lowndes, on secession

God help us.

James Pettigrew

We are here in such a disturbed condition that the things that are going to happen in a week are uncertain as if they belonged to the distant future.

One large problem for the Confederacy was Governor Pickens. He continually upset President Davis by telling him that his men in Charleston would attack Sumter with or without orders from the Confederate president.

Governor Francis Pickens

I will go on with the same activity as ever in preparing our defense for any event that may arise. We would desire to be informed if when thoroughly prepared to take the fort shall we do so or shall we await your orders and shall we demand the surrender or will that demand be made by you?

In the North, thousands pleaded with the new President, Lincoln, to come up with a plan of some kind for Fort Sumter. Many had been Lincoln supporters in the election, such as Carl Schurz of Wisconsin. Schurz had been an activist in the German revolution in 1848. He moved to the United States in 1852 and later became a Republican and gave numerous speeches in support of Lincoln.

Carl Schurz

There is a general disconnect pervading all classes of society. Everybody asks, what is the policy of the administration? And everybody replies: any distinct line of policy, be it war or a recognition of the Southern Confederacy, would be better than the uncertain state of things. Our defeat at the recent elections has taught us a lesson which can hardly be misunderstood. The Republicans are disheartened, groping in the dark not knowing whether to support or oppose the administration. . . . Foreign governments seem to take advantage of our difficulties, the Spanish invasion of San Domingo is an indication of what we may expect. . . . There is but one way out of this distressing situation. It is to make short work of the secession movement and then to make front against the world abroad. . . . As soon as one vigorous blow is struck, as soon as, for instance, Fort Sumter is reinforced, public opinion in the free states will at once rally to your support.

During the campaign, Schurz met Lincoln and went home to tell his wife how much he admired him.

Carl Schurz

[Lincoln] is a whole man, firm as a stone wall and clear as crystal. . . . He himself will not hear of concessions and compromises, and says so openly.

Many others, who did not share Schurz's admiration for Lincoln, argued that "the time has come" for action in Charleston.

Ralph Waldo Emerson, philosopher

The hour has struck, so long predicted by philosophy, when the civil machinery that has been the religion of the world decomposed to dust and smoke before the new adult individualism and the private man feels like he is the State.

Other philosophers believed the entire nation was collapsing.

Henry W. Bellows, Theologian

I am not without serious apprehension that the loosening of the staple at Washington . . . might precipitate the whole chain of order into confusion and righteous chaos. [I fear] the possible insecurity of life and property if secession and revolution should occur, driving our populace into panic for bread and violence toward capital and order. . . .

But if the North did plunge into a war, Bellows and many other intellectuals thought the whole nation would emerge strengthened.

Henry W. Bellows

When threatening and anxious times come upon us, then all great realities begin to shine out. Citizenship and nationality . . . obedience to law and order . . . oaths of office and solemn compacts with man and God that have been, perhaps, lightly and half consciously taken on renewed meaning.

Philosopher James Russell Lowell agreed.

James Russell Lowell

Slavery is no longer the issue of debate and we must beware of being led off upon that side issue. The matter at hand is the re-establishment of order, the re-affirmation of national unity and the settling, once and for all, whether there can be such a thing as a government without the right to use its power in self-defense. . . . [T]his government, like all others, rests upon the everlasting foundation of just authority.

Poet Walt Whitman also agreed.

Walt Whitman
The Negro was not the chief thing. The chief thing was to stick together.

Echoing a theme of Lincoln's, poet John Greenleaf Whittier declared that if there was a Civil War, it would be God's revenge for slavery.

John Greenleaf Whittier
It will be the chastisement which Divine Providence is inflicting on the nation.

◆

If Northerners were feeling that something had to be done, the feeling in the South was even stronger. Fort Sumter had to be leveled as a show of force, many argued, and as a way to keep already jittery Southerners united in the cause. Southern pride had replaced slavery as the dominant cause.

Editor, *Mobile (Alabama) Mercury*
The country [the South] is sinking into a fatal apathy and the spirit and even the patriotism of the people is oozing out under the do-nothing policy. If something is not done, pretty soon, decisive, either evacuation or expulsion, the whole country will become so disgusted with the sham of Southern Independence that the first chance the people get at a popular election they will turn the whole movement topsy-turvy, so bad that it will never on earth be righted again.

Alabamian

There is another way of avoiding the calamity of reconstruction and that is war. Now, pardon me for suggesting that South Carolina has the power of putting us beyond the reach of reconstruction by taking Fort Sumter at any cost.

Some Northerners understood this new view.

Editor, *Indianapolis Journal*

The seceded states are determined to have a war because they believe a war will drive to support the border slave states, and unite them all in a great Southern Confederacy. A policy of peace is to them a policy of destruction. It encourages the growth of a reactionary feeling. It takes out of the way all the pride and resentment which could keep the people from feeling the weight of taxation, and the distress of their isolated condition. . . . A war buries all of these considerations in the fury and glory of battle. War will come because the Montgomery government deems it the best way of bringing in the border states and of keeping down trouble at home.

No less an authority on statesmanship than former president Franklin Pierce assured Jefferson Davis and his Cabinet that a war would not be fought only on the fields of the South but also in the cities of the North.

Former president Franklin Pierce

If through the madness of Northern Abolitionists, that dire calamity must come the fighting will not be along Mason's and Dixon's line merely [but in Northern streets].

Those who defy law and . . . Constitutional obligations will, if we ever reach the arbitrament of arms, find occupation enough at home.

Some suggested that just a little sword-rattling in Charleston would scare off the Yankees; a few cannonballs now might prevent many more later.

Governor M. S. Perry, Florida, on Fort Pickens in his state
Let us arm for the contests and perhaps by a show of our force and our readiness for the combat we shall escape the realities of war. We have taken the field. Our flag is unfurled at Pensacola. . . .

In Charleston, General Beauregard hinted that if Sumter was not taken right away, it would become invincible and unattainable when reinforced by federal troops and with more cannon.

General P. G. T. Beauregard
If Sumter was properly garrisoned and armed, it would be a perfect Gibraltar to anything but constant shelling, night and day from the four points of the compass. As it is, the weakness of the garrison constitutes our greatest advantage.

Lincoln's envoy to Charleston, Stephen Hurlbut, agreed. Hurlbut, a native Charlestonian, was one of two men Lincoln sent to Charleston to interview people, take notes, and form an opinion on whether or not Fort Sumter should be supported. Ward Lamon was the other. Each visited the city for several days and then returned to Washington to speak with the president.

Stephen Hurlbut
The power in that state [South Carolina] and in the Southern Confederacy is now in the hands of the conservatives—men who desire no war, seek no armed collision but hope and expect peaceful separation & I believe that after separation the two sections will be more friendly. . . .

It is equally true that there exists a large minority indefatigably active and reckless who desire to precipitate collision, inaugurate war & unite the Southern Confederacy by that means. These men dread the effects of time & trial upon their institutions.

Lincoln entertained dozens of suggestions, transparent and secret. One that Lincoln thought would get everyone in the North into trouble was to send several supply ships into the harbor to Fort Sumter at night and, at the same time, send several troop transports to the area to unload thousands of soldiers to attack the Confederates as they watched the supply ships. That plan was soundly rejected.

Editors in the North screamed that the president had to break his silence on Sumter and come up with a plan of action.

Editor, *Boston Daily Evening Traveler*
Weakness, imbecility, cowardice and flunkeyism!

A New York lawyer went further—if that was at all possible.

Lawyer
[The American bald eagle is] now a debilitated chicken, disguised in Eagle feathers.

Peter Dye, friend of Secretary of State William Seward
The do-nothing policy of our government is disastrous.

FIFTEEN

Fort Sumter
Brother Against Brother

Young men all over America debated the Fort Sumter crisis, wondering if it would lead to war and if they would be pulled into it. This was a real dilemma for brothers, some living in Northern states and some in Southern states, who could wind up fighting one another.

Joseph Halsey, forty-one, and his brother Edmund, twenty-one, who grew up in Rockaway, New Jersey, were good examples of how badly the nation was divided as the Fort Sumter crisis grew. Joe had left New Jersey while he was a student at Princeton to marry a girl he met on a trip to Virginia. Her father owned several dozen slaves and was one of the wealthiest men in the state. Joe, who had a law office on his plantation, gradually came to champion the slavery cause. He was surrounded by slave owners, partied with slave owners, and had slave-owning relatives. His younger brother Edmund was a fierce anti-slavery advocate and a student at Princeton when the crises over Sumter started. The two brothers, when they met, or in letters to each other, argued constantly over slavery and states' rights. Their father Samuel, former speaker of the New Jersey State Assembly, played referee between them and fervently hoped that the Sumter crisis would be resolved without a war and that neither would become a soldier.

Joseph Halsey

All the South asks is let us and our servants alone that we may live in quiet and have some security for our lives, our families, and not convert our beautiful country into a desert peopled by the cursed children of

Ham [slaves] until the whole race, thus uncontrolled, would be swept from the earth.

Joseph Halsey

We do not meddle with you and abuse your class and your private matters and have no wish to dominate over the North, but the South has ever been, and still is, and must succeed so long as there is enough good sense left in the nation. The property and comfort of this union will be crushed and the ties of a suicidal civil war as the consequence.

Edmund Halsey

Can any impartial person take these facts and say that slavery is a blessing, a divine institution and state over and over again its advantages? Back it by scripture and think it strange the north does not fall down and worship it?

Samuel Halsey

None in my family will fire a shot at the South.

Edmund Halsey

Disunion would be followed by the most awful insurrections you ever heard of and no power on earth could stop them, either. War will not make it any better for then all will be abolitionists and the South cannot reduce the north to the state of a subjugated province.

There was no joy in the homes of the Halseys. The looming crisis similarly worried hundreds of brothers and their parents, North and South.

There was no joy in Charleston, either. There, even before the first shot of the war was fired, Mrs. Robert Gourdin discovered that her Confederate husband was facing her brothers from the North at Fort Sumter, all with guns loaded and ready to shoot. On March 5, 1861, the day after Lincoln's inauguration, a group of people raised a Confederate flag in Charleston. A glum Mary Chestnut watched them do it.

Mary Chestnut

We stood on the balcony to see our Confederate flag go up. Roars of cannon, etc. etc. Mrs. Sanders complained of the deadness of the mob. "It was utterly spiritless," she said. "No cheering, or so little, and no enthusiasm."

Mary Chestnut wrote in her diary that a friend showed her a letter from a girl who said she kept a rope handy to hang Lincoln if she ever encountered him.

Mrs. Gourdin's husband, popular with both sides in the city, did all he could to keep the peace between the North and South. He served on a committee that permitted the Union troops in the fort to keep buying food and supplies at Charleston stores. He came up with the idea of sending the supplies to Fort Johnson, a Confederate facility, so as not to raise suspicions. From there, with no one knowing it, they were put on ships and taken to Sumter.

After Fort Moultrie was overrun by the Confederates in late December, Charlestonians took down the US flag and raised a red flag they obtained at the state capital. Katie Skillen, sixteen, daughter of a U.S. Army sergeant, was present at the flag raising and wept as it went up.

Katie Skillen

I am mad to see our flag go down and that dirty thing in its place.

One captain of a steamer from New York angrily tore down his vessel's American flag when he sailed into the harbor at Charleston. On hearing this story, Edmund Ruffin commented:

Edmund Ruffin
Popular feeling is very strong.

Disrespect for the federal government had been growing for months. Back in November, even before secession, South Carolina Governor Gist had placed a twenty-man militia unit in front of the US arsenal in Charleston to help protect it against a possible attack.

Edmund Ruffin
The people will run ahead of the government.

That's precisely what Major Anderson feared.

Major Robert Anderson
The storm may break upon us at any moment.

He begged for help.

Major Robert Anderson
I would thank the department [of war] to give me special instructions as my position here is rather a politico-military than a military one.

Anderson's men felt that way too, and said the Southern soldiers who surrounded the fort had hair-trigger tempers. One told an officer:

Soldier at Fort Sumter
Anything that indicates a determination on the part of the general Government to act with an unusual degree of vigor in putting these works in a better state of defense will be regarded as an act of aggression.

Back in December 1860, even the wives of soldiers stationed in Charleston started to believe an attack on the fort was just a few days away. For them, despite the long-held public belief that there would be no war, the conflict seemed imminent.

Mary Doubleday

A crisis is very near, within a few days, we hear—and from so many sources we cannot doubt it—that the Charlestonians are erecting two batteries.

Her husband was even more certain of an assault.

Captain Abner Doubleday

We learned that cannon had been secretly sent to the northern extremity of the island . . . two thousand of the best riflemen in the state were engaged to shoot us down.

Yet Anderson kept hoping for peace.

Major Robert Anderson

I think an appeal to arms and to brute force is unbecoming the age in which we live. Would to God that the time had come that there should be no war, and that religion and peace should reign throughout the world.

General P. G. T. Beauregard's assessment of the problem of Fort Sumter was simple, direct, and flew in the face of Charlestonians' beliefs. He told his superiors, bluntly, that Lincoln would never surrender the fort. He would try to reinforce it with troops and supplies and those ships had to be stopped.

And at some point, he believed, Sumter had to be attacked. To do that, Beauregard went to work changing a lot of the gun positions the federals had held that were now in Southern hands. He had some cannon turned so they faced Sumter, and added more cannon batteries on the island and peninsulas around Sumter. He placed six thousand troops and numerous batteries of cannon in semicircles around the fortress ready to fire.

....

General P. G. T. Beauregard
In meantime, I will go on organizing everything around me.

Beauregard had also, in just a few weeks, commanded the respect of all Charlestonians because of his gracious manners, sophisticated appearance, pleasant personality, charm, and grim determination to hold the Southern line against Lincoln and the hated Northerners. Beauregard knew where he stood and was happy about his success in Charleston.

....

General P. G. T. Beauregard
I am . . . very well pleased with this place & its people, who are so much like ours in La. that I see but little difference in them.

He always hinted that he was the Napoleon of the South. Once, in describing the qualities of a leader, he said:

....

General P. G. T. Beauregard
Does it become his duty to put himself at their head and, colours in hand, if need be, like Napoleon at Arcola, show his soldiers the way to victory or to a glorious death!

Charleston might never have had the distinguished, debonair Beauregard at all. Just a year earlier he was getting off a boat in Louisiana when he plunged headfirst into a river. Several bystanders dove into the water to save him. Floundering in the river, he thought he was going to drown.

General P. G. T. Beauregard
I saw the face of God. He was not looking very pleased with me.

Around that time, he left his longtime job as an engineer for the city of New Orleans and reenlisted in the Army, ending up as a captain at West Point, where, an avowed secessionist already, he was put in charge of training troops for the Union against, possibly, the secessionists. When the Army realized who they had as head of training, they gave him another job. He plunged into the new job as he had plunged into the last one, and as he had plunged into all his jobs over the years. He was a Union patriot who might not be one soon, he told people around him, but was bound by honor to do a good job for the Union until something happened.

General P. G. T. Beauregard
I shall be most scrupulous in the performances of all my obligations to the govt. so long as I keep my opinions of the present unfortunate condition of our country to myself. I must respectfully protest against any act of the War Dept. that might cast any improper reflection upon my reputation or position in the Corps of Engineers.

There had been no more flag-waving, red-white-blue patriot than Creole-born Louisianan Beauregard. He exhibited that during the Franklin Pierce administration when someone criticized the president and the nation.

General P. G. T. Beauregard
The American star, far from having reached its calumniating point, has not commenced its brilliant ascent & that if we are only true to

ourselves centuries will yet elapse before it shall have obtained its meridian splendour!

The soldiers that Beauregard met in his new Confederate regiments were excited to be in Charleston and part of what might be the first battle of the Civil War. It was a real adventure for them—something to tell their grandchildren about years later. One of them was J. E. Hall from Alabama, who was joined on his railroad car for a part of the journey by schoolmates, all incredibly proud of him. So were all the Charlestonians he met during the Fort Sumter crisis. Part of that may be attributed to his never-ending praise of them and their soldiers.

Private J. E. Hall

They were all so glad to see me. I thought they would kill me. I could not shake their hands fast enough. . . . When the cars started, Henry Harris and some others said they couldn't leave me and went on to Opelika with me and there got off. All but H. Harris. He said he still must go on farther and went to West Point [Georgia] with me

Beauregard had this to say about Hall and others like him.

General P. G. T. Beauregard

A gallant and free people, fighting for their independence and firesides, are invincible, even against disciplined mercenaries at a few dollars per month. What, then, must be the results when its enemies are little more than an armed rabble gathered hastily on a false pretense and for an unholy purpose with an octogenarian [Union General Winfield Scott] as its head? None but the demented can doubt the result.

Union soldiers had mixed feelings about Beauregard's arrival.

Captain Abner Doubleday

As he had just left our army, where he had been highly trusted and honored, it is said he displayed a good deal of feeling at finding himself opposed to the flag under which he had served so long. He expressed much sympathy for his old friend, Anderson, who, he stated, was merely fulfilling his duty as a soldier in fighting for his own government and asserted that he would not attack us, even if we withdrew all our sentinels, but would force us to surrender by cutting off all our supplies.

Beauregard was determined to get all the monies he believed were owed him by the Union, no matter what the circumstances. As an example, his train ticket from West Point to New Orleans to join the Confederate Army cost $165. The US government would not pay it and Beauregard insisted, in letter after letter, that the government owed him the money. Even as he pointed his cannons at Sumter in March 1861, he kept writing letters demanding the $165 reimbursement.

He also had important friends write letters to Jefferson Davis urging Beauregard's appointment as a general, and he worked hard to show Davis they were right. He got the job—brigadier general—and arrived in New Orleans in March 3, 1861, the day before Lincoln's inauguration. He soon dazzled everyone.

T. Harry Williams, historian

He was five feet seven in height and weighed about 150 pounds. He had dark hair and eyes and a sallow, olive complexion. His features were marked by a broad brow, high cheekbones, a chopped moustache and a protruding chin. His eyes fascinated most people; large, melancholy with drooping lids, they were likened by one man to the eyes of a bloodhound with his fighting instincts asleep but ready to leap into instant action. In manner, he was courteous, grave, sometimes reserved and severe, sometimes abrupt with people who displeased him. His expression was fixed, impassive; associates saw him go for months without smiling. He was most likely to erupt into excitement, to show the fire beneath, by suddenly launching into an impassioned defense of the Southern cause. His voice was clear and pleasant, with a barely perceptible French accent. He impressed people as being modest, industrious, indomitable. Many who saw him thought that he looked like a French marshal or like Napoleon in a gray uniform—which was what he wanted them to think.

The ladies of Charleston adored him. They brought him letters, flags, scarves, and flowers. His desk was adorned with vases of flowers from women every day of his tenure in the city. Charlestonians regarded Beauregard as the hero of the hour.

Reporter, *Virginia Daily Sentinel*

The appointment [of Beauregard] has given great satisfaction in this state and nowhere more so than in camp. I have not yet heard a murmur against it. The soldiers all know that they have a man now at their head who will go to work in the proper manner and if an attack is to be made that it will be conducted in scientific style and in no useless sacrifice of life.

Many connected the appointment of Beauregard to the new Confederate government's early success.

Mary Chestnut

The southern confederacy must be supported now by calm determination and cool brains. We have risked all and we must play our best, for the stake was life or death.

Newspaper reporters who flocked to Charleston sized up the situation rather quickly—particularly when a Northern reporter was told to go home by a group of Charlestonians.

Reporter, *New York Tribune*
Be easy, gentlemen. I'm not going to stay much longer. Things are one way or another going to come to a close before long.

After his trip to the South, a clerk in the U.S. Treasury observed:

Richard Ela
The upshot is that every person I talked to, whether originally from the North or the South, expressed the firmest determination to support the Confederate states.

The people of Charleston were more strident with Beauregard leading the army there. The population of Charleston has become more violent [toward the Union army].

General Beauregard and Confederate leaders told General Pemberton and other generals to work with Governor Pickens.

General John C. Pemberton
I shall not consider it an interference with my authority if the Governor and council make preparations for the defense of this city. . . . [T]he disposition evinced by so many distinguished citizens of this state to defend Charleston to the last extreme meets with my entire sympathy and concurrence.

A wild late-March rumor that Lincoln had ordered the federal garrison at Sumter evacuated and announced that he would cede Sumter to the rebels was printed in most newspapers, North and South. Major Anderson was actually relieved.

Major Robert Anderson

God has, I feel, been pleased to use me as an instrument in effecting a purpose which will, I trust, end in making us all a better and wiser people.

The plan—if it had been true—would have relieved him of having to show anybody, particularly the Confederates, what a shambles the unfinished fort was. At more than thirty years old, the facility was already antiquated. Its walls, as an example, could not withstand the weight of the new, large Columbiad cannons. Most of the rooms in the fort were empty or unfinished. The heating system was very poor.

Later, after Sumter was taken by the Confederates, Southern General John Pemberton toured the fort and shook his head.

General John C. Pemberton

The forts should be destroyed. They will be of no use to us after the termination of this war in their present condition for I take it impregnable iron clad batteries must take the place of stone and mortar.

Anderson would discover later that his call for 20,000 troops for a rescue attack to save Sumter probably would not have succeeded. In fact, two years later, when the Confederates held Sumter, officers surveyed those islands and were disappointed. Any force would have had problems with the terrain and perhaps never even reached the fort.

Colonel Charles Simonton, Confederate Army, 1862

I caused a reconnaissance to be made last night for the purpose of examining the means of landing on Black Island. I found that all around the sides which could be reached the slope is gradual and the bottom very soft and boggy for about 300 yards. This must be traversed before the hard marsh is reached. A man walking on this sinks to above his knee and at times to his hips. . . . I do not think it is practical to land a large number of men on Black Island.

We must meet the enemy in thick woods, for which I can get no guide. It will be almost impossible at night to keep the command in hand after landing them in a scattered and somewhat disorganized condition through the marsh and [then] the thicket.

On the same day in March 1861 that the rumor of an evacuation spread through the Union garrison at Sumter and through the North, it also reached Charleston, where a smiling Colonel James Chestnut, so eager to get back to his wife Mary, confirmed it to the Reverend A. Toomer Porter.

James Chestnut
There will be no war. It will all be arranged.

Around the time of General Beauregard's arrival in Charleston, President Lincoln reread alarming letters from Ulysses Doubleday, who sent Lincoln the letters he had received from his brother, Captain Abner Doubleday, Anderson's second-in-command at Sumter. Doubleday, a personable man who had spent weeks talking to Charlestonians, many of whom became friends with him and his wife before the Army moved to Sumter, painted an entirely different picture of the situation than the diplomats and generals.

Doubleday and his wife had lived at Fort Moultrie since 1858, when he was transferred there. He was four years older than his wife, Mary, whom he had married in 1850 (he was thirty-six in 1861).

He told his brother that the South Carolinians were furious with the North and with Lincoln and were ready to attack at any moment. The letters shook Lincoln. Doubleday's portrayal of Charlestonians matched that of Postmaster General Montgomery Blair, who told the president that the Sumter issue went beyond military intentions and was a contest of Northern versus Southern manhood.

Montgomery Blair

[Southerners] saw Union men as factory workers and shopkeepers and saw Southern men as "warriors" looking for a fight.

Captain Abner Doubleday, to his wife

Secession with everyone I meet seems to be a foregone conclusion. They all say as a matter of course that they must have the forts [in the harbor]. The army would withdraw the troops . . . and give the forts to the South if secession takes place.

Doubleday also told his brother, in another letter, that hundreds of officers were ready to leave the U.S. Army and join the Southern forces.

Captain Abner Doubleday

The danger we anticipate will proceed from the decision of the secessionists to commence the campaign by driving us out to give themselves prestige . . . for their decision [to act at once]; they will not wait for the action of their own legislature.

Lincoln decided to see if Doubleday's wife, who had lived with him at Fort Sumter and earlier at Fort Moultrie, had any more of her husband's letters or could convey his opinions of the Sumter situation to the president. She and the other Union soldiers' wives had been sent home by Major Anderson for their safety.

Mary Doubleday was startled when President Lincoln knocked on her door in Washington, D.C. They talked for a long time and she showed him numerous letters from her husband in Charleston. Doubleday told his wife that while large supply ships could be spotted day or night, smaller ships could not.

When President Lincoln left Mary Doubleday's home, he was depressed.

SIXTEEN

Washington, D.C. Prime Minister Seward

Even as Lincoln was visiting Mary Doubleday and various Cabinet members and generals argued over whether or not Fort Sumter should be evacuated, Secretary of State William Seward was secretly holding talks with representatives from the Confederacy to avert war. He did this without Lincoln's knowledge and, critics would charge, in contempt of the president's authority. He was no longer operating as Secretary of State, but as America's "Prime Minister," intent on ruling the nation despite its elected president, just as British prime ministers had, for generations, ruled despite its kings and queens.

Seward had always been a powerful politician, whether as New York's governor or a US senator, but also as a friendly, kind, and generous man. People may have disliked his political stands, but they liked him personally. That was best exhibited in a letter written to him by Charles Francis Adams Jr., the grandson of John Adams, who spent time with him campaigning for Lincoln in the autumn of 1860.

Charles Francis Adams Jr.

I beg you not to suppose that the continual attention and kindness you showed to me, and the thoughtfulness, which so often led to me being brought forward when there was a chance for me to show that I had anything in me & and at moments, too, when all your thoughts might well have been taken up by your own position—do not suppose that this was unnoticed by me, or that for it I did not feel deeply grateful. I had no claim on you, but you could not have taken greater interest in me had I been your son.

Frederick Roberts

[You are] the Hector or Atlas not only of his Cabinet, but the giant intellect of the whole north.

Many relied on the veteran Seward, not political novice Lincoln, to preserve the Union.

Benjamin Taylor

Unionists look to yourself, and only to you, as a member of the Cabinet, to save the country.

One member of President James Buchanan's Cabinet told Seward:

Buchanan Cabinet Member

You will be the premier.

Although as president, Lincoln was the head of his party, Seward was so admired that many Republicans saw him as the real leader of the Republican Party. Seward wholeheartedly agreed he was that man.

William Seward

The actual direction of public affairs belongs to the leader of the ruling party.

Seward's influence did not escape the notice of Southerners, either.

Mary Chestnut
Seward is in ascendancy.

Robert Rhett Jr.
The friends of Seward say that he is preparing a plan of policy for the administration . . . for the preservation of peace, but fears are entertained that Chase and Greeley will defeat the whole scheme.

Seward agreed with all of them. He told a group of men just after Lincoln's inauguration:

William Seward
I have built up the Republican Party. I have brought it to triumph, but its advent to power is accompanied by great difficulties and perils. I must save the party and save the government in its hands. To do this, war must be averted, the negro question must be dropped, the irrepressible conflict ignored, and a Union party to embrace the border slave states inaugurated. . . . [T]hen the people in the cotton states, unwilling led into secession, will rebel [against their leaders].

Many reporters saw Seward as the new president, not Lincoln. It was Seward whom everyone visited at the White House, Seward whom everyone consulted. Some even thought the "presidency" was wearing Seward out.

Reporter, *New York Herald*
Seward looks worn down by the weight of his responsibilities.

The new Cabinet members did not like Seward and used the term "premier" as one of scorn when referring to him in those weeks just before Fort Sumter came to a head.

Gideon Welles

Mr. Seward, as the coming premier, was on the change of administration to carry forward the policy of non-reinforcement of Sumter. Until blood was spilled, there was hope of reconciliation. In fulfillment of this arrangement, Mr. Seward opposed any and every scheme to reinforce Sumter and General Scott, who was old, and much under the influence, if not a party to the understanding, seconded, or too a leading part in that opposition.

Welles was an eyewitness to Seward's overwhelming importance in the administration as "premier." Senator Stephen Douglas bumped into Welles in Washington and learned that one of the government's policies had been suddenly changed. He told Welles he needed to go right to the top to argue against it. Welles agreed to take him right to the top. He did not take him to the White House to see Lincoln, though, but to the State Department to see Seward.

Gideon Welles

The look of incredulity and astonishment which came over him I can never forget. Then you have faith in Seward? Have you made yourself acquainted with what he has been going on here all winter? Seward has had an understanding with these Southerners.

Ironically, the Fort Sumter mess boosted Seward's spirits. Even his Cabinet enemy, Welles, was impressed.

Gideon Welles

Mr. Seward possessed a hopeful and buoyant spirit which did not fail him in that dark period and at no time were his party feelings more decided than during that spring of 1861. Old Whigs he clung to and strove to retain all Democrats he distrusted, unless they became identified with the Republican Party.

Seward was also secretive, and during the last few weeks of the Buchanan administration he was especially so. What Lincoln, in far-off Springfield, did not know—could not know—was that Buchanan had put Seward on his secret team of aides to deal with the ever-growing Fort Sumter and secession crisis. Seward nodded his head knowingly and told friends he was up to the task of running the nation.

William Seward
If this whole matter [secession and Fort Sumter] is not settled within ninety days after I am seated in the saddle, and hold the reins firmly in my hand, I will give you my head for a foot-ball.

All of the members of the Cabinet resented the way Seward tried to bully the new president and them as the self-anointed "premier." It really irked them that the president let Seward decide when and where Cabinet meetings would be held and then send them memos with the information. The unhappiness grew and grew.

Finally, secretly, the Cabinet appointed Treasury Secretary Salmon Chase to talk to the president about calling their meetings. After a long-winded appeal by Chase, Lincoln stared at him and said, "Okay, Tuesdays and Fridays at noon?" Chase nodded and the skirmish was over.

Seward was often accused of having no real political stance and that his position on issues depended on which way the political wind was blowing. He was asked once by his friend Varina Davis if he ever spoke from convictions. He answered without a moment's hesitation.

William Seward
Never.

He was often criticized for becoming involved in other people's work.

Adam Gurowski, Seward's aide

[He tried] to meddle in everything.

He was accused of seeing movements where there were none.

Colonel John B. Baldwin, Virginia Unionist

He was earnestly engaged in the effort to secure peace and safety as a means of averting the military era which he thought he saw dawning upon the country.

Seward had been startled by Lincoln's nomination to an office he believed, along with millions of others, that he himself deserved. At the beginning of Lincoln's presidency, he often criticized the president and had little regard for him. He reluctantly wrote to his friend Thurlow Weed:

William Seward

The P. is all right . . . the President is the best of us but he needs constant and assiduous cooperation.

He told new friend, Charles Francis Adams Jr., that Lincoln was just not up to the presidential task.

William Seward

Lincoln had no conception of his situation—much absorption in the details of office dispensations, but little application to great ideas.

Adams, who admired Seward, agreed about Lincoln.

Charles Francis Adams Jr.
The man is not equal to the hour.

After a few weeks as Secretary of State, Seward had had it with Lincoln.

William Seward
He is a well-intentioned incompetent, a prairie lawyer fumbling his way towards disaster.

Seward played the role of president, dispensing official positions of the government as his own. At one party, when a judge raised the subject of Fort Sumter and its dangers, Seward laughed.

William Seward
Oh Judge, your mind is diseased on the subject. We shall never have a civil war.

Seward, a theatergoer like Lincoln, admired the theatrical work of actor Edwin Booth and his younger brother, John Wilkes Booth—as did the president. Once Edwin was a dinner guest at the Seward home. Seward's daughter wrote about the dinner in her diary.

Fanny Seward
Father said that if he would allow him he would tell him where he thought his acting might be improved. He accepted father's criticism—often saying he had felt those defects himself.

Seward's dinner parties were legendary. He and his wife invited the movers and shakers of the Senate and House, as well as merchants, bankers, authors, actors, playwrights, and numerous journalists. They all engaged in lively conversation, mostly led by Seward, and were regaled with his colorful stories. They enabled him to build a reputation as not only a skilled politician, but as a very likable and charming man.

At all the dinner parties before the attack on Fort Sumter, Seward always held out hope for some kind of reconciliation. He offered this toast at one.

William Seward

Away with all parties, all platforms, all persons committed to whatever else will stand in the way of the American Union.

Many of Seward's fellow Republicans were against conciliation if it involved the continuation of slavery, and warned that the Secretary of State did not understand the anger of the people on that issue.

Congressman John Sherman, Ohio

Should politicians and merchants [conciliate], the people will rebel. I assure you whatever may be the consequence, they will not yield their moral conviction by strengthening the influence of slavery in this country. Recent events have only deepened this feeling. The struggle to establish slavery in Kansas, the murders and mobbings in the South of Northern citizens, the present turbulence and violence of Southern society, the manifest fear of freedom of speech and of the press, the danger of insurrection and now the attempt to subvert the government.

Lincoln had always admired Seward from far-off Springfield, and admired him as his Secretary of State and new best friend. It was Seward who introduced the president-elect to Washington's power brokers when Lincoln arrived from Illinois. It was Seward who continually lobbied Virginia's politicians to the Republican cause, assuring them that Lincoln would not eradicate slavery where it was, just block it in the new territories. It was Seward who gave Lincoln invaluable advice on how to navigate the jungles of Washington politics. It was Seward who made Lincoln feel comfortable in this strange new land of national politics and even assisted him in writing his inaugural address.

There were those in Washington, though, who despite Seward's fame and power just hated him. Secretary of the Navy Gideon Welles was one. He continually smirked at Seward at dinner parties, and in his diary he often added Seward's lofty unofficial prime minister title or addressed him as His Premiership. Welles especially enjoyed ridiculing Seward for his prediction that the secession crisis would be over in ninety days.

Gideon Welles

While the great body of the people, and most of their leadership in the Northern states, listening to the ninety day prophecy of Mr. Seward, were incredulous as to any extensive, serious disturbance. There were not a few whose forebodings were grave and sad. All the calamities which soon befell the country these men anticipated. Yet of responsibility, would not permit themselves to despond or despair of the Republic. . . . [Seward] had probably overestimated his own power and ability to allay the rising storm. And had not the personal influence he supposed. He had prophesized during the winter peace and harmony, within a very brief period after the change of administration to be effected. These unfortunate prophecies, which became a matter of mirth with many of his friends, and of ridicule among his opponents, were not entirely vain imaginings or without some foundation. In his confident belief that he could, once in place of power effect conciliation and peace, it had been an object with him to tide the difficulties past the fourth of March.

Perhaps no anecdote describes how Americans saw Seward and his relationship to Lincoln than a story told by Seward admirer Charles Francis Adams Jr., who was with then-Senator Seward when his campaign-for-Lincoln train arrived in Springfield and the Republican presidential nominee boarded it to talk to Seward, whom he had not seen in thirteen years.

Charles Francis Adams Jr.

There was a rush into and about the windows of the car in which Mr. Seward was seated. [Then, at Lincoln's entrance] there he was, tall, shambling, plain and good natured. He seemed shy to a degree, and very awkward in manner, as if he felt out of place, and had a realizing sense that properly the positions should be reversed.

This idea that Seward should be the nominee and later the president was held by many Americans for months and was the foundation for the Prime Minister Seward movement, which hurt Lincoln's early presidency and undercut his leaderships during the Fort Sumter crisis. Henry Adams wrote as the Fort Sumter crisis grew that January:

Henry Adams

By common consent, all eyes were turned to him and he was overwhelmed by entreaties from men in all sections of the country to do something to save the Union.

◆

Just after Lincoln took office, Jefferson Davis sent three Peace Commissioners to Washington: Martin J. Crawford, John Forsyth, and A. B. Roman. Their mission was to meet with President Lincoln and reach a settlement that would result in the Southern acquisition of Fort Sumter following the evacuation of Union troops there and their successful, bloodless, departure from the Confederate states. Lincoln thought that even meeting with them would give the Confederacy legitimacy, and refused to do so. The three then went to Secretary of State Seward's office. At first he also refused to see them. The trio then sought out friends in power—US Supreme Court Justices John Campbell of Alabama, who had just resigned, and Samuel Nelson of New York, still on the court. They agreed to meet with Seward to press for a meeting with Lincoln, or have Seward settle the dispute—believing all the time that

Seward was speaking for Lincoln, which Seward told them and they told the three Peace Commissioners. It was not true.

Seward was certain that Lincoln would evacuate Fort Sumter, just as President Buchanan had wanted to do. If Lincoln was not certain about the evacuation, he, Seward, would talk him into it. If Lincoln needed the agreement of the Cabinet, he, Seward, would talk the Cabinet into it. He had been able to talk just about everyone into everything, so why should this be any different? Besides, it was a way that he could run the country as prime minister while Lincoln kept his chair in the White House warm for 1864, when Seward would be elected president—as everyone expected.

It set in motion a series of meetings and letters that ended in disaster—just so Seward could show off his own power.

He met with the two judges in mid-March and told them that he spoke for Lincoln and that he would get the president to evacuate the fort. Two days later, he met with them again and said that the fort would absolutely be evacuated. They relayed that message to Jefferson Davis, who was elated.

William Seward
The President may desire to supply Sumter, but he will not do so.

Seward bragged that the deal had been consummated and said the Southerners could assure Jefferson Davis of the evacuation.

William Seward
Before this letter reaches Davis, the fort [Sumter] will have been evacuated.

Seward was specific in his note and conversation with the Supreme Court judges. The fort would be abandoned in exactly five days. There was no doubt about it.

He was so certain that he could get Lincoln to leave Sumter that he told the judges:

William Seward

A Civil War might be prevented by the success of my mediation.

The judges and Peace Commissioners knew, as did everybody, that the Cabinet had been meeting on Fort Sumter each day and that Seward oversaw the Cabinet meetings. It had to be true.

This view of Seward's power is what drove the three Southern Peace Commissioners to trust him with their secret talks and agreements. They believed Seward to the very end, even as the cannons finally roared at Fort Sumter.

Jefferson Davis's Peace Commissioners

At our meeting on March 15, [we] were assured by a person occupying a high official position in the government [Seward] and who was speaking by authority [Lincoln] that Fort Sumter would be evacuated in a very few days. . . . [T]hese assurances were subsequently repeated.

The following day somebody, probably Seward, leaked the news of Lincoln's evacuation of Fort Sumter to the press and every paper in the country printed the story as true. There was happiness, North and South. George Summers, who was working to keep Virginia in the Union, was ecstatic.

George Summers

[It] acted like a charm. It gave us great strength. A reaction is now going on in the state.

Seward pushed as hard as he could to fulfill his pledge to the Southern Peace Commissioners. He went into the next Cabinet meeting and lobbied mightily.

William Seward

The facts of the case are known to be that the attempt must be made with the employment of military and marine force which would provoke combat and probably initiate a Civil War. I would not provoke war in any way now.

The newspaper articles about the evacuation were read by a startled Abraham Lincoln. Even though Lincoln knew nothing about Seward's agreement to abandon Fort Sumter, he did know that by March 15 the Cabinet was in favor of it, as Lincoln himself had been since he arrived in Washington. The president read his Cabinet secretaries' opinions on the Sumter evacuation question that day. The Cabinet voted five-to-two to evacuate the fort, pleasing Seward.

Union Officer at Fort Sumter

The news . . . seems to have caused an entire cessation of work on the batteries around us. Unless otherwise directed, I shall discharge my force when the orders for the evacuation arrive.

Many soldiers at Fort Sumter had believed since the start of the crisis that evacuation the only solution. Wylie Crawford was one of them.

Wylie Crawford

[Sumter] must be given up and the sooner the administration appreciates this the better. All this talk of "occupying, holding and possessing" the fort is nonsense. There is neither army enough to do it or is it likely there soon will be.

Crawford told his brother the best thing to do with Fort Sumter would be to blow it up. Even so, Crawford did have fond memories of the place.

Wylie Crawford

I cannot tell you how grieved I am at the thought of leaving this fort, where every stone and surrounding is so impressed upon my heart.

Crawford wrote about his feelings while watching the flag being raised at Sumter.

Wylie Crawford

[It is] yet undishonored. Weeks of excitement and toil have made it dear to us; and this old glorious fortress as yet untouched by the invader.

Edmund Ruffin, who had traveled to Charleston just to watch the attack, shrugged his shoulders and on March 18, 1861, told friends he was going to go home; there would be no fight.

Edmund Ruffin

I will wait no longer to witness it. I have not the least expectation of the occurrence of any fighting here. The public mind is becoming tranquilized under it and will become fully reconciled to it when the causes which have led to that necessity have been made public and are rightly understood.

Yet despite the news, people were apprehensive everywhere. Most still feared a conflict.

Salmon Chase

If the attempt to enforce it will influence a Civil War, I cannot advise it.

Emory Upton, a West Point cadet, warned his sister:

Emory Upton

You will, before the reception of this letter, have heard the war news. Troops are moving in every direction . . . an attack on Fort Sumter is highly probable. The *New York Times* and *New York Herald* today state that the provisions are on their way there and that Anderson has orders to open his batteries if a vessel is fired upon. . . . [W]e will be in the right, and let us maintain it as becomes free men.

And of course, the news about the evacuation was false. So the problem of how to get supplies to the fort was still pressing.

Letter to the *Richmond Enquirer*
No one now doubts that the ball will open as soon as the United States fleet attempts to enter the harbor of Charleston. All may look out for bloody work.

Montgomery Blair
[Re-supply] will in any event vindicate the determination of the people and their President to maintain the authority of the government and this is all that is wanting, in my opinion, to restore it.

Caleb Smith, Secretary of the Interior
If such a conflict should become inevitable, it is better that it should commence by the resistance of the authorities or the people of South Carolina to the legal action of the government in enforcing the laws of the United States.

Edwin Bates, US Attorney General and former Missouri Congressman
I am most unwilling to strike, I will not say the first blow, for South Carolina has already struck that, but I am unwilling under all circumstances at this moment to do any act which may have the semblance, before the world, of beginning a Civil War . . . the terrible consequences of which would, I think, find no parallel in modern times. . . . [T]o

avoid these evils, I would make great sacrifices—and Fort Sumter is one; but if war be forced upon us, causeless & pertinacious rebellion, I am for resisting it with all the might of the nation.

A few days later, on March 28, Lincoln was jolted by a memo from General Scott.

General Winfield Scott

It is doubtful . . . whether the voluntary evacuation of Fort Sumter alone would have a decisive effect upon the states now wavering between adherence to the Union and secession. It is known, indeed, that it would be charged to necessity and the holding of Fort Pickens [in Florida] would be adduced in support of that view. Our Southern friends, however, are clear that the evacuation of both forts would instantly soothe [feelings]. . . .

Simon Cameron, Secretary of War

Even if provisioned, Sumter cannot be maintained against the hostile troops and fortifications surrounding it. Take Scott's advice [and give it up].

Let them both go?

Lincoln, who had at first considered handing the fort over to the Southerners, now waffled. The president hosted his very first state dinner that night and it was an enormous success. Late in the evening, he herded his Cabinet secretaries into a room and told them of Scott's latest unsettling memo. He raised other considerations as well.

The president told his secretaries to think about the two forts one more time and come back to the White House the next day for another discussion.

What were the other considerations? First, the Northern press, initially happy to let the South secede and go its own way, certain the wayward states would quickly come crawling back, had changed its mind. Most editors now wrote that Sumter had to be held. Lincoln sensed, too, that the fort in Charleston Harbor had become the symbol of the Union and that if it was turned over the entire Southern Confederacy would be legitimized. Thinking back on his inaugural address, he now believed that he needed to hold both sections of the nation together for America to move forward. He was now the nation's trusted guardian. Lincoln also did not like to be bullied, and he felt that everyone, North and South, was trying to bully him.

He remembered his pledge to good friend and law partner Billy Herndon just before he left Springfield for Washington.

Abraham Lincoln

I am decided; my course is fixed; my path is blazed. The Union and the Constitution shall be preserved and the laws enforced at every and all hazards. I expect the people to sustain me. They have never yet forsaken any true man.

Montgomery Blair

[Lincoln is] playing politician.

Others in the Cabinet did not yet understand that unlike most people, Lincoln thought on several levels at the same time, always trying to meld them together. Lincoln did not see Sumter solely as a single fort in a harbor that had to be either evacuated or resupplied. He understood that the people had come to see it also as a symbol of freedom and liberty, something that South Carolina, or the entire South, could not take away from the American people just because they wanted to.

Sam Barlow

I am not joking . . . if ever have I known the entire people more unanimous on any question. We are ruined if Anderson is disgraced or if Sumter is given up.

What the president needed to do, somehow, was resupply the fort and retain it—without the North firing a shot and without the fort being fired upon by the South. He also needed to show the country that he was not a weak president, someone elected with just thirty-nine percent of the popular vote. He needed to show men and women from Long Island to the shores of California that he was a strong president, a resolute man completely in charge of the White House and the country.

And so he held back on Sumter.

By this time, too, efforts to achieve peaceful compromises in the House and Senate to avert secession and/or war had failed. John Crittenden, the House member who chaired one of the compromise committees, threw up his hands at the intransigence of Congressmen from both sides.

John Crittenden

If old Bunker Hill now had a voice, it would be, of course, as it should be, a voice like thunder, and what would she proclaim from her old and triumphant heights? No compromise with your brethren? No sir, that would not be her voice, but I fancy to myself if that venerated and honored old scene of American bravery, hallowed by the blood of the patriots who stood there, hand in hand, brethren of North and South, could but speak, it would be but one voice, a great and patriotic voice. Peace with thy brethren, be reconciled with thy brethren.

Lincoln had also had an angry visit from Francis Blair, father of Postmaster General Montgomery Blair and a powerful politician in his own right. He burst into Lincoln's office, right past his aides, and roared that abandoning the fort would be treason.

Gideon Welles

He touched a chord that responded to his invocation.

The crisis had worn Lincoln out. Everybody around him noticed it and was concerned. A Southerner who had watched him since before the inauguration told Jefferson Davis that Lincoln looked pale and had lost weight.

Southern observer
The thin lips had a straight line and closer compression.

Reporter, *New York Times*
Mr. Lincoln has a wiry physique that has enabled him to bear up under a pressure such as no other President has encountered.

One reporter was so shaken by his appearance on March 15 that he thought Lincoln would soon die in office.

Reporter, *New York Herald*
Mr. Lincoln will break down upon the pressure made upon him as General Zachary Taylor did before him.

A correspondent who talked to him during one of his all-day job interviews was stunned by his appearance and demeanor.

Anonymous reporter
I saw the President this morning and his whole air was that of not only a worried man, but an ill man. He would require a fortnight's rest, it seemed to me, to enable him to let off a joke or a jolly backwoods reminiscence.

Lincoln told family members he was exhausted. He signed a letter to a man, "Your tired friend."

The day after the state dinner, when he was scheduled to meet again with the Cabinet, was not a good one for Lincoln. He was exhausted and in bad humor.

Abraham Lincoln
I am in the dumps.

The president again put the Fort Sumter question to his Cabinet.

Abraham Lincoln
To send an armed force off Charleston with supplies of provisions and re-inforcements for the garrison at Fort Sumter. And, to communicate, at the proper time, the intentions of the government to provision the fort peaceably if unmolested.

Lincoln had asked, too, about holding Fort Pickens in Florida. They all agreed to do that. Sumter was different. The Cabinet voted five to two to resupply Sumter with food only.

Attorney General Bates saw Sumter as a large domino that, if it fell to Southern forces, would set off a chain of states that would secede.

Edwin Bates
South Carolina is the head and front of this rebellion & when that state is safely delivered from the authority of the U.S. it will strike a blow against our authority which it will take us years of bloody strife to recover.

Several secretaries predicted a violent reaction against any attempt to resupply the fort.

Gideon Welles

By sending, or attempting to send, provisions into Sumter, will not war be precipitated? It may be impossible to escape it under any course of policy that may be pursued, but I am not prepared to advise a course that would provoke hostilities.

If this is done, will it not be claimed that aggressive war has been commenced by us upon the state and its citizens in their own harbor?

Welles also astutely pointed out that this strategy could backfire on the South.

But armed resistance to a peaceable attempt to send provisions to one of our own forts will justify the government in using all of the power at its command to re-inforce the garrison and furnish the necessary supplies.

Meanwhile, most Southerners paid little attention to Lincoln, his politics, or his health. They were certain he would give in on the fort. Or were they?

Robert Rhett Jr.

[Exhibiting] a gentle exercise of legitimate power towards so many rebellious counties to bring them to their senses . . . Lincoln is a cool man, a determined man, a man [not] of words, but of action, who says what he means and means what he says, an earnest man withal, and no politician.

SEVENTEEN

Charleston, South Carolina
Sex, Sex, and More Sex in the Old South

Despite all the tension over secession and Fort Sumter, both Southerners and Northerners found some time to enjoy scandals—and the ensuing gossip—at the highest levels. In the middle of the Secession Convention in Montgomery, Alabama, Mary Chestnut was staying with her husband at a hotel. Security at the hotel was tight because everybody feared Union spies were prowling about the hallways trying to steal war plans or listening in on the conversations of people like Chestnut. For that reason, most of the rooms next to Confederate officials had been kept empty to prevent spies in adjoining rooms from putting their ears to the walls and picking up information. But sometimes there was a mix-up.

One afternoon when she returned from a luncheon at which the new Confederate States' future was discussed, Mary Chestnut was accompanied by a friend. Her friend explained the empty room arrangements and noted that families had rooms with interior connecting doors between two rooms. To make her point, Chestnut's friend went to the door between her room and the next and flung it open. The next room was not empty, though. It contained an attractive teenage girl and a married middle-aged man, who was a friend of Mary's, on a wide bed. They were still clothed, but had their hands all over each other and were kissing passionately.

When she saw Mary, the young girl jumped up from the bed.

Young girl
Oh, he is my cousin. . . . Er, he is married.

Mary was startled.

Young girl
He is taking me home from school.

Chestnut took a step into the room and looked at her older friend, still on the bed.

Mary Chestnut
He knew better and was terribly embarrassed. He might well be ashamed of himself.

Mary and her husband left Montgomery shortly afterward and traveled to Charleston. There, as she did on all visits to the city, Mary became a leader of the social scene and center of the whirl of parties. Mary Chestnut told friends that the women, married and single, of Charleston spent half the party chasing men and the other half bragging about it.

Mary considered herself one of the best-looking women in the South—and probably was. Her good looks attracted the admiration of men, and women too. She took great pride when other beautiful women admired her.

Mary Chestnut
I remember now her amazement at the attention Robert Campbell, then unmarried, devoted to me. Men did fall in love with me wherever I went.

She was very self-conscious about her looks. Upon their arrival in Charleston, she and her husband had their photographs taken, and she was not pleased at the result.

Mary Chestnut
Mr. Chestnut very good. Mine like a washer woman.

In the Charleston party world, across the bay from Fort Sumter, there was always talk of pregnancies and who had to get married.

Mary Chestnut
[They] counted the months on their fingers.

The women of Charleston, Montgomery, and other cities in the South were catty and judgmental of rich or important women, of whom they were jealous.

Mary Chestnut
Gossip was unrelenting and it seemed not to leave any woman unscathed. One woman criticized Mrs. Jefferson Davis' circle of women friends as "not young and they wore gaudy colors and dressed badly."

A friend of Mrs. Davis, who knew the accuser, shot back that "she is darkly, deeply and beautifully freckled and she wears a wig which is kept in place by a tiara of mock jewelry and she has the fattest of arms and wears black lead bracelets."

◆

In Charleston and throughout the South, the tension created by the Sumter crisis, the coming of possible war, and fear of the Union brought out the worst in many people. There seemed to be violence everywhere.

The Chestnuts' friend, William Taber, had been killed in a duel. When the Chestnuts were in Montgomery, another man had been shot dead in the street in an argument involving the prospective war. Fistfights had broken out in Charleston's bars over disputes about the fate of Fort Sumter. Isaac Hayne, of Camden, South Carolina, had been shot in the chest by Ben Allston in a duel across a dinner table, the blood flying all over the food.

Tension—and violence—had been mounting in the South since John Brown's seizure of Harper's Ferry in 1859. British consul to Charleston Robert Bunch had been reporting them regularly to his superiors and friends in London.

Robert Bunch

I do not exaggerate in designating the present state of affairs in the Southern country as a reign of terror. Persons are torn away from their residences and pursuits, sometimes tarred and feathered, "ridden upon rails," or cruelly whipped; letters are opened at the post office; discussion upon slavery is entirely prohibited and under penalty of expulsion with or without violence, from the country. The northern merchants and "travelers" are leaving in great numbers. . . . [O]n the part of individuals the sense of danger is evinced by the purchase of firearms, especially of revolver pistols, of which very large numbers have been sold during the last month.

One arms dealer, Captain Colt, of the famous Colt Manufacturing Company, had an altercation with a Charlestonian and the Southerner shouted at him with great hatred that he was "a damned Yankee." Colt was afraid the man would murder him and asked a local ship's captain, Charley Lamar, what he should do. To Lamar, the answer was quite simple, especially for that time.

Charley Lamar

If he gives you any trouble, call him out and shoot him.

Mary Chestnut's friend

It is the war fever. It is the temper of the times cropping out.

All this acrimony, sadness, and tension was put aside at the end of March, though, because it was race week, a time when a series of horse races in Charleston was accompanied by lavish parties from one end of the city to the other. One of the most elegant was at the mansion of Mrs. A. M. Vanderhorst, one of the wealthiest women in the South. She wrote of it in her diary.

Mrs. A. M. Vanderhorst

The music was fine, the gentlemen and ladies in high spirits and the supper under the shining silver with the sparkling champagne most enlivening.

Someone told her it was the party of the year, and she blushed.

Mrs. A. M. Vanderhorst

Out in the countryside, the wealthy were beginning to engage in fox hunts, to play cards and blind man's bluff, to dance. One rich planter's wife wrote her brother earlier that "If there is no war & I don't have another lung trouble, we plan to have a very gay spring."

But in the shadow of those elegant parties, Major Anderson saw the pieces of a coming conflict falling into place, one by one.

Major Robert Anderson

At present, it would be dangerous and difficult for a vessel from without to enter the harbor, in consequence of the batteries which are already erected and being erected. . . . [W]e are now, or soon will be, cut off from all communications, unless by means of a powerful fleet, which shall have the ability to carry the batteries at the mouth of this harbor. I shall not ask for any increase in my command because I do not know what the ulterior motives of the government are.

There were two Charlestons, Mary Chestnut said in her diary. One was the elegant mansions with large verandas, with ladies hosting tea parties in the afternoon and dinners and lavish balls at night. Men dressed as if they were going to be married, their suits from the most expensive clothing stores in the city. Wine and champagne flowed and men and women danced until midnight.

The other Charleston was a fortress, with eighty-five men inside Fort Sumter and six thousand Southerners massed on both sides of it, manning nearly one hundred cannons, prepared for an attack. Many of the women Mary met, old friends, told her that their husbands had either joined Governor Pickens's South Carolina Militia or the Confederate Army and were in uniform, waiting for orders.

They were some of the best troops the South would muster in the war. Later, General W. Porcher Miles would ask for more South Carolinian troops under his command because they were so skilled and showed great pride in their state.

General W. Porcher Miles

Now that the [tug of war] has come to us in the Palmetto State, cannot something be indulged to state pride and sentiment? This is a moral element that high statesmanship will not only refuse to ignore, but will eagerly avail itself of. I cannot overestimate the effect [of sending] South Carolina troops.

This early pride in the Palmetto State soldiers would fade within a year. In May of 1862, the South Carolina troops guarding Fort Sumter became so disenchanted with their commanders and Governor Pickens that they seemed ready to mutiny.

Colonel James Chestnut

[There is a] threat of mutiny and refusal to fire against the enemy if he should he appear.

General Robert E. Lee fired off a warning note to the soldiers.

General Robert E. Lee

It becomes necessary for you to make up in vigilance any want of physical force you may have to contend against. It is also of the gravest importance that the discipline of the garrison of the different works should be brought to the highest state of perfection [because] Charleston is to be defended to the last extremity. If the harbors are taken, the city is to be fought for street by street and house by house.

One problem with the plan Confederate generals in Charleston had to bombard Fort Sumter in 1861 was that it included the use of area slaves to assist the Army. Jefferson Davis had given orders to recruit all the black men in Charleston, slave or free, for that job. At first, unarmed slave laborers were considered but rejected. But General Beauregard pointed out that Southern soldiers could not be spared for ditch-digging. Why not use slaves?

General P. G. T. Beauregard

In this exigent hour, send your negroes with spades and shovels to this city without an instant of delay or hesitation, to the extent of 3,000 effective laborers. Each Negro should be provided with at least three days of subsistence.

Thomas Jordan, Confederate officer

Call on the planters, in good faith, to give you a list of their able-bodied male Negroes and a statement of the amount of labor several furnished on the works in South Carolina. [If that does not work] impress the slaves who hitherto have not furnished labor.

Most slaves, of course, did not want to participate in the Southern cause. But they had little choice. Hundreds of slave laborers arrived in the Charleston area in wagons for work in the middle of January 1861. They were quickly spotted by the Union troops at Fort Sumter.

Captain Abner Doubleday

About six hundred Negroes were now at work night and day, in perfecting the defense of Fort Moultrie. The enemy continued their hostile preparations with the utmost energy and zeal, in spite of the tacit truce which was supposed to exist.

After a few days, seeing their chance, the slaves began to flee under the cover of darkness. Many of their owners, angry that the blacks were working for the Confederate government and not for them, began to arrive in Charleston and, despite orders, took them back to their plantations. It was a sign of how integral slave labor was to the workings of the plantation and the survival of the Southern economy.

EIGHTEEN

Charleston, South Carolina
Lincoln's Envoys Plunge into a Hostile City

President Lincoln did not want to make a decision about going to war unless he had first-hand, on-the-ground, eyewitness reports from reliable people—people with no political agenda and who believed in the president. The first was Gustavus Fox, the second was Stephen Hurlbut, and the third was Ward Lamon.

Fox was chosen because he was the brother-in-law of Postmaster General Montgomery Blair, who pushed him relentlessly, and because he had submitted a sketchy plan to Lincoln for an invasion of Charleston Harbor by small Union supply ships. Fox went to the city, met with Major Anderson for two hours, and came home. He did not survey all the forts and harbors, as Lincoln had asked, but he did turn in a sixteen-page report full of speculation and ideas that Lincoln found most useful.

Hurlbut had inside knowledge to offer; he had married into a prominent family that had been in Charleston for years. His report was direct and detailed.

Stephen Hurlbut

I absolutely believe that the seven [seceded] states are irrevocably gone, except perhaps Texas and Louisiana, as to which I have no information.

Item: I have no doubt that a ship known to contain only provisions for Sumter would be stopped and refused admittance. Even the moderate men who desire not to open fire [and] believe in the safer policy of time and starvation, even those men, would approve of firing on a provisional expedition were one sent.

Item: I learned from one of the pilots, an acquaintance in former years, that the vessels sunk to obstruct the ship channel had not had that effect, but had been swept out by the force of the current, making but a slight alteration on the bar.

Item: If Sumter is abandoned, undoubtedly this will be followed by a demand for Fort Pickens and the keys of the Gulf, that is, Pickens and the other two forts in the Gulf.

Item: It is my deliberate judgment, from long acquaintance with the people and the country of South Carolina and . . . in a modified form with the other seceding states, that the attempt to fulfill the duties of the Executive Office in enforcing the laws and authority of the U.S. within their limits will be war, in fact, war in which the seceding states will be united and the others disunited.

Hurlbut added in his report that everyone in Charleston saw themselves as citizens of the Confederacy, not the Union.

Stephen Hurlbut

Separate nationality is a fixed fact . . . a unanimity of sentiment which is to my mind astonishing. . . . [N]o attachment to the Union . . . there is positively nothing to appeal to.

Finally, Lincoln chose his close friend and security guard, the gigantic Ward Lamon, one of the tallest and strongest men in Washington. He trusted Lamon implicitly. He told him to meet with Major Anderson, but also to see Charleston city officials, get an appointment with Governor Pickens, and mingle with the people to get a very broad-based feeling about people's opinions regarding the fort and its prospect of resupply.

Even as he was making plans to dispatch Lamon to Fort Sumter, numerous other forts—Camp Hudson, Fort McIntosh, Ringgold Barracks, Camp Verde, Fort Clarke, Fort Inge, Fort Lancaster, Fort Brown, Fort

Duncan, Fort Chadbourne, and Fort Bliss in Texas—had been taken by state authorities or given up by the federal government. In Mississippi, the state seized a fort and hospital without federal resistance. In Florida, state officials took a naval yard, an arsenal, and three forts. Officials in Alabama took a fort, an arsenal, and several federally owned ships without resistance. Georgia seized two forts and an arsenal. Louisiana grabbed two forts and an arsenal. Cabinet members grumbled that if Lincoln did not care about giving up all these forts, arsenals, and ships, why was he so insistent on holding on to one single unfinished fort in the harbor of Charleston? But many in the Army, and many former soldiers, were furious at the seizure of Army bases by Southern states and the willingness of Presidents Buchanan, and then Lincoln, to give them up.

William Tecumseh Sherman

I regard the seizure by Governor Moore [in Louisiana] of the United States arsenal as the worst act yet committed in the present revolution. I do think every allowance should be made to Southern politicians for their nervous anxiety about their political power and safety of slaves. I think that the Constitution should be liberally construed in their behalf, but I do regard this civil war as precipitated with undue rapidity.

Governor Moore did not deny his complicity in the crisis of 1860–1861 and acknowledged that the seizure of forts and arsenals, and the recent activity at Fort Sumter, was dangerous.

Governor Thomas Moore, Louisiana

It is war for the South to surround Anderson with batteries and it is shilly-shally for the South to cry "hands off!" "no coercion!" It was war and insult to expel the garrison at Baton Rouge and Uncle Sam had better cry "cave!" or assert his power.

Lincoln's plan to send the three envoys was strongly opposed by Seward, who was still secretly trying to fulfill his promise to the South to get the Union Army out of Sumter. He said at a Cabinet meeting:

William Seward

We can't spare Lamon and should feel very badly if anything dangerous should happen to him.

Abraham Lincoln

I have known Lamon to be in many a close place and he has never been in one that he did not get out of. I'll risk him.

Ward Lamon was a tall, burly man with a thick beard and a high forehead. Lincoln said he was the strongest man he had ever met—and Lincoln was considered a very strong man himself. Lamon had been a prosecuting attorney in Illinois in the 1850s and moved to the capital, Springfield, in 1858. He soon met Lincoln, who was a lawyer and state legislator there. The two became friends immediately, even though they were so unlike one another. Lamon was brusque, loud, profane, detested abolitionists, and had great sympathy for the Southern states and slaveholders. Lincoln was just the opposite. He enjoyed Lamon's stories and admired his blunt, fierce demeanor. The two became closer and closer.

At the Chicago convention, Lamon told Lincoln's convention handlers that he would do anything to get his friend the nomination. On the day of the crucial fourth ballot, Lamon personally supervised the printing and distribution of the thousands of counterfeit tickets handed out early in the morning to Lincoln supporters, whose vociferous support of their candidate on that ballot, it was said, helped get Lincoln the nomination.

Lamon assumed that President Lincoln would give him the ambassadorship to some foreign country, but Lincoln did not, asking him instead to move to Washington to serve as his aide and counsel. He sent Lamon as his representative to assessment meetings and trips such as the Fort Sumter expedition.

The president may well have owed Lamon his life. It was his friend who insisted, against Lincoln's wishes, that he accompany the president-elect to Washington, armed, for the inauguration. On that journey at least one murder plot was hatched against Lincoln—one so serious that detective Alan Pinkerton, with Lamon, spirited the president-elect into Washington in disguise late at night. Since Lamon had saved his life, Lincoln certainly believed he could do something as simple as travel in and out of Charleston without getting himself killed.

On instructions from Lincoln, Lamon went to see James Pettigrew, a lifelong Charlestonian and a Union supporter, at his home. Pettigrew, seventy, was one of the most important men of Charleston. He was a distinguished figure in both North and South.

Visitor to Pettigrew's home

[He is] a venerable figure with a noble face, his snowy hair falling on his shoulders, with something ancient with the fashion of his dress. He seemed like one of the Revolutionary fathers returned to earth.

Lamon was startled at what Pettigrew told him.

James Pettigrew

The whole people of Charleston were infuriated and crazed. . . . [N]o act of violence would surprise me. It is too late. Secession or war is inevitable.

Lamon, keeping as low a profile as possible and staying in his room at a hotel in Charleston at night, made secret arrangements to see Governor Pickens (who was staying at the same hotel with his wife) in the dining room for breakfast the next morning. What happened that morning was exactly what Pettigrew predicted. Charlestonians jammed the hotel hallways, shops, and porch to get a glimpse of Lamon. He wrote in his memoirs that more than a thousand people jammed the street outside, too, despite the early hour. His top-secret mission was very public now and he had to push his way through that crowd of residents, very unhappy to see the man they all called "Lincoln hireling."

Ward Lamon
The news had spread far and wide that a Great Goliath from the North . . . had come suddenly into their proud city, uninvited and unheralded. [Onlookers] were that class of dowdy patriots who, in times of public commotion, always find the paradise of the coward, the bruiser and the blackguard.

The governor immediately told Lamon that his mission was a waste of time.

Governor Francis Pickens
I see no way out of existing difficulties but to fight it out.

Lamon tried to cut him off, but the governor continued.

Governor Francis Pickens
Nothing can prevent war except the acquiescence of the President of the United States in secession and his unalterable resolve not to attempt any re-inforcement of the Southern forts. To think of longer remaining in the Union is preposterous. We have five thousand armed soldiers around this city, all the states are arming with great rapidity and this means war with all its consequences.

Lamon tried, and failed, to reason with Pickens.

Governor Francis Pickens

Let your President attempt to re-inforce Sumter and all the tocsin of war will be sounded from every hilltop and valley in the South.

Lamon felt his visit was worthless. Not only had Pickens been pushing for hostilities, but Robert Rhett Jr., the editor of the Charleston Mercury, *had been calling for an assault on the fort for six months. The next day, after another night of hiding in his room, Lamon sailed to Fort Sumter on a steamer provided by Governor Pickens and met with Major Anderson, whom he described as "despondent" and "as ready for war as Pickens."*

When Lamon returned to his hotel later that afternoon, the crowd of onlookers was even larger and rowdier than the previous day, despite the presence of a militia guard sent by the governor to protect Lamon. Many started cursing him.

Ward Lamon

All eyes were fixed upon the daring stranger, who seemed to be regarded not as the bearer of the olive branch of peace, but as the demon come to denounce the curse of war, pestilence and famine. . . . [It was] painful and embarrassing.

Lamon shoved his way through the crowd into the hotel's elegant reading room, where he saw a pile of rope curled up in corner of the room that Lamon assumed was to be used to hang him. An angry man was in the reading room waiting for Lamon. The envoy was thunderstruck at how ridiculous the old man looked in his most splendid clothes. He wore a fork-tailed coat with bright brass buttons and a bell-crowned hat that Lamon said appeared to have come from the days of Sir Walter Raleigh. He wore a red bandana cravat and a shirt collar of amazing amplitude.

Ward Lamon

He looked as if he had service at Thomas Jefferson's first reception.

The elderly man kicked the pile of rope to the center of the room.

Elderly man
Do you think this [rope] strong enough to hang a damned Lincoln abolition hireling?

Lamon ignored him and turned to address the angry crowd that had forced its way into the reading room.

Ward Lamon
I am a Virginian, by birth, and a gentleman. I was sent here by the President of the United States to see your Governor.

Elderly man
Damn your President!

Lamon put his hands on his hips in defiance and glowered at the old man, whom he towered over.

Ward Lamon
You are surrounded by your friends, a mob, and are brutal and cowardly enough to insult an unoffending stranger in the great city that is noted for its hospitality and chivalry, and let me tell you that your conduct is cowardly in the extreme.

Lamon had just insulted every one of the Charlestonians in the room, and they were angry. The crowd pressed toward him and Lamon took a step back, fearful that he would be beaten or killed.

Then, suddenly, emerging quickly out of the middle of the crowd of angry men and women strode South Carolina Congressman Laurence Keitt, an old friend of Lamon's and one of the most respected and popular men in Charleston. He was loved in that Southern city because in 1858 he had badly beaten, strangled, and nearly killed Northern Congressman Galusha Gale in a dispute, and later had aided Southern Congressman Preston Brooks in severely beating Senator Charles Sumner of Massachusetts with a cane right on the floor of the Senate. (Keitt held back Sumner's friends with a loaded pistol as Preston repeatedly hit the senator.) Keitt laid his hand on Lamon's shoulder and smiled at him.

Laurence Keitt
Why Lamon, old fellow, where did you come from? I am glad to see you.

The old man in the Sir Walter Raleigh cap stepped forward.

Elderly man
You speak to that Lincoln hireling?

Keitt cut him off.

Lawrence Keitt
Stop! You insult Lamon and you insult me. He is a gentleman and my friend.

The intervention of the highly respected Keitt quieted the crowd. He put his arm around Lamon and led him through the crowd, which backed off, to the hotel bar, where they had a drink. The rope stayed in the middle of the floor. Nobody was hanged with it that day.

The fury of Charlestonians should not have surprised Lamon. Just three months earlier, Robert Rhett Jr. wrote to the boss of a Northern reporter who wanted to come to Charleston with a stark warning.

Robert Rhett Jr.
Your reporter would run great risk of his life. Representing that paper he would certainly be tarred and feathered and made to leave that state.

So many rumors flew and so much misinformation was dispensed that just about everyone in Charleston and Fort Sumter thought they knew something but really knew nothing about the purpose of Lamon's mission.

Captain Abner Doubleday
Colonel Ward C. Lamon came over to visit us. It was given out that he was sent as an agent of the general government to see Governor Pickens in relation to post office matters but in reality he came to confer with Anderson and to ascertain the amount of provisions on hand.

The next day, Lamon interviewed the US postmaster in Charleston, who was as grim as everyone else he spoke to about Sumter. British Consul Robert Bunch was certain of a war, too.

Robert Bunch
We are in the most frightful commotion imaginable. It is fully believed that the U.S. government intends to re-inforce Fort Sumter and every man is under arms. If the news from Washington be true that re-inforcements are on their way, there will be a desperate fight here before we are, perhaps, many days, perhaps hours, older.

There was fear of war everywhere. In Northern newspapers, advertisers were tapping into the anxiety.

F. Williams & Co. advertisement
In consequence of the
PANIC! PANIC! PANIC!

We are determined to offer our very large stock of fall imports for the balance of the season at such price as will command an immediate sale.

W. J. F. Dailey & Co. advertisement

Owing to the troublesome times into which our country has fallen, we have made a

FURTHER REDUCTION

In our prices in order to convert our goods into cash before the

UNION GOES TO PIECES!

Northern newspapers made no secret of their feelings about the Southerners.

Michigan Newspaper

We have fed the Southern whiners with sugar plums long enough.

Editor, *New York Post*

If the rebels fire at an unarmed supply ship, and make a perfectly proper act the pretext for shedding the blood of loyal citizens, on their heads be the responsibility.

Minnesota Newspaper

Before this rampant fever of the Union will abate, THERE MUST BE BLOOD LETTING.

Bloodshed was also on the minds of people all across the South. They wanted a good fight. A young Alabama man reasoned it this way.

Alabama man
Unless you sprinkle blood in the face of the Southern people, they will be back in the Union in ten days.

Lamon boarded the 8 train to Washington that night and, to his surprise, met Stephen Hurlbut, Lincoln's other envoy, whom Lamon did not know was in Charleston. Hurlbut was so scared to be seen with Lincoln's man that he begged Lamon not to sit with him and his wife.

Stephen Hurlbut
Don't you recognize us until this train gets out of South Carolina. There is danger ahead.

There certainly was.

NINETEEN

Fort Sumter
The Cannons Roar

On March 20, 1861, as President Lincoln was under enormous pressure to act on Fort Sumter, the three Peace Commissioners sent by Jefferson Davis wired the president of the Confederacy.

Peace Commissioners
The war wing presses on the President; he vibrates to that side. . . . [T]herefore, of notice to us may be that of the coward who gives it when he strikes.

The Commissioners also wired General Beauregard in Charleston.

Peace Commissioners
Has Sumter been evacuated?

Charles Francis Adams Jr.
With which side would Lincoln be allied? That, North and South, was the question. These men had been brooding over the questions at issue and dwelling on them till their minds had lost their tone, and become morbid.

Toward the end of March, an angry Governor Pickens wrote the Peace Commissioners in Washington to ask why, if Seward had guaranteed an evacuation, were the Stars and Stripes still flying above Fort Sumter?

Adams wrote in his diary that William Seward looked like he had aged ten years over the last month. Seward was constantly confronted with the Fort Sumter issue at all the parties he attended. At one, a reporter asked him when Sumter would be evacuated. Seward snapped at him.

William Seward

That is a plain lie. No such orders have been given. We will give up nothing we have—abandon nothing that has been entrusted to us. If people would only read these statements by light of the President's Inaugural, they would not be deceived.

Everybody in Charleston believed such orders had been given and that the entire garrison at Fort Sumter would soon be sailing back to Washington, D.C. Residents there had been declaring each day Evacuation Day with great jubilation, much as they referred to Christmas and New Year's Day. No less an authority than General Winfield Scott had assured Emma Holmes's uncle, Edward, that the troops would be sent home from Sumter soon.

Emma Holmes

. . . and today telegraph was received appointing tomorrow [evacuation day] but scarcely anyone credits it.

All the newspapers carried the evacuation story except the New York Herald. *It first wanted to check numerous sources all over town. A day later, convinced it was true, it ran its own evacuation story, confirming all the others.*

Washington correspondent, *New York Herald*

I am able to state positively that the abandonment of Fort Sumter has been determined upon by the President and his Cabinet.

On April 6, at the height of the tension over Fort Sumter, Major Anderson wrote his former student, General Beauregard, an extraordinary letter.

Major Robert Anderson

I most earnestly hope that nothing will occur to alter, in the least, the high regard and esteem I have for so many years entertained for you. I am, Dear General, yours . . .

General Beauregard responded:

General P. G. T. Beauregard

Let me assure you, Major, that nothing shall be wanting on my part to preserve the friendly relations and impressions which have existed between us for so many years.

In Washington that month, Seward vented his frustration with the secession movement, which he saw as not only short-sighted but impertinent.

William Seward

I myself, my brothers, my sisters have been all secessionists. We seceded from home when we were young, but we all went back to it sooner or later. These states will all come back in the same way.

Seward was also appalled at the numerous conspiracy theories that flew around the nation's capital and in Charleston. One was that one of Lincoln's envoys, Gustavus Fox, had outsmarted a Confederate officer, Harrison, and spent time all by himself snooping around Fort Sumter. The real story was much more tame.

General P. G. T. Beauregard

Were you with Captain Fox all the time of his visit?

Harrison, Confederate officer

All but a short period, when he was with Major Anderson.

General P. G. T. Beauregard

I fear that we shall have occasion to regret that short period.

At this same time in the nation's capital, the president received a stunning memo from Seward that accused him of having no policy on Fort Sumter, foreign affairs, or just about anything else.

William Seward

1st. We are at the end of a month's administration and yet without a policy, either domestic or foreign.

2d. This, however, is not culpable and it has been unavoidable. The presence of the Senate, with the need to meet applications for patronage, have prevented attention to other and more grave matters.

3d. Change the question before the public from one upon slavery or about slavery—for a question upon Union or Disunion.

The occupation or evacuation of Fort Sumter, although not in fact a slavery or party question, is so regarded. Witness the temper manifested by the Republicans in the free states and even Union men in the South.

I would simultaneously defend and reinforce all the forts in the Gulf, and have the Navy recalled from foreign stations to be prepared for a blockade. Put the island of Key West under martial law.

His suggestions on foreign affairs were even more extreme.

William Seward

I would demand explanations from Spain and France, categorically, at once.

I would seek explanation from Great Britain and Russia, and send agents into Canada, Mexico and Central America to rouse a vigorous continental spirit of independence on this continent against European intervention.

And if satisfactory explanations are not received from Spain and France, would convene Congress and declare war against them.

But whatever policy we adopt, there must be an energetic prosecution of it. For this purpose it must be somebody's business to pursue and direct it incessantly. Either the President must do it himself and be all the while active in it or devolve it on some member of his Cabinet.

Lincoln responded with a rebuke that immediately ended Seward's role as prime minister.

Abraham Lincoln

[You wrote] either the President must do it himself and be all the while active in it or devolve it on some member of his Cabinet. . . . If this must be done, I must do it.

Seward immediately backed off.

The pressure on Lincoln eased somewhat when a longtime friend, Senator Lyman Trumbull, introduced a supportive resolution on the Senate floor.

Senator Lyman Trumbull, Illinois

The true way to preserve the Union is to enforce the laws of the Union . . . and that is the duty of the President . . . to use all the means in his power to hold and protect the public property of the United States.

Despite Trumbull's resolution, Lincoln was restless and told friends that he tossed and turned in his bed that night, March 28, and got no sleep for the first time in his life.

Meanwhile, William Seward again met with the Southern Peace Commissioners to assure them that Sumter would be evacuated. In a note to Judge Campbell he said:

William Seward
Faith as to Sumter fully kept.

Judge Campbell
The tone of the inaugural message will be followed and its recommendation will be allowed to slide, as are the expressions common to that class of thieves known as politicians.

That same day, March 29, the editor of the Charleston Courier *blasted Seward and the administration.*

Charleston Courier
[Policy] is double-dealing jugglery.

Everyone at the March 29 Cabinet meeting in Washington was glum. Different proposals were discussed and the reports and recommendations of Fox, Hurlbut, and Lamon gone over once more. This time three Cabinet members—Gideon Welles, Salmon Chase, and Simon Cameron—were for resupplying the fort, no matter what the cost. Others leaned toward a resupply, and Seward remained heatedly against it.

Salmon Chase
If war is to be the result, I perceive no reason why it may not best begin in consequence of military resistance to the efforts of the administration to sustain troops of the Union stationed under the authority of the government in a fort of the Union in the ordinary course of service.

I am clearly in favor of maintaining Fort Pickens and just as clearly in favor of provisioning Fort Sumter. If the attempt be resisted by military force, Fort Sumter should, in my judgment, be re-enforced.

In the Cabinet, and in his office, Treasury Secretary Chase was a brilliant tactician and a deep thinker, but he was socially awkward. He fumbled and stumbled in hosting dinner parties at his home, something Seward found so easy to do. Seward went to the library, and he read numerous newspapers, magazines, and books. Chase did not. His idea of an enjoyable evening was playing cards with friends. He did not drink or smoke. He was not a good conversationalist and had no sense of humor.

Friend of Salmon Chase
He seldom told a story without spoiling it.

Salmon Chase's personal life had been tragic. He had married three times, and buried three wives and four children. Chase, though, had a lovely daughter, Kate, said to be the most beautiful woman in Washington, who served as a successful and gracious hostess for him for years. He told people that his daughter would serve as his first lady if he was elected president. He had groomed her to be a proper young lady, and a first lady, too. When she was thirteen, he told her:

Salmon Chase
I desire that you may be qualified to ornament any society in our own country or elsewhere into which I may have occasion to take you. It is for this reason that I care more for your improvement in your studies, the cultivation in your manners and the establishment of your moral & religious principles, than for anything else.

With Kate's smiling help, he had been very successful as governor of Ohio and one of the founders of the new Republican Party.

Albert Hart, Chase biographer

There may have been abler statesmen than Chase, and there certainly were more agreeable companions, but none of them contributed as much to the stock of American political ideas as he.

William Gienapp, historian

In the long run, no individual made a more significant contribution in the formation of the Republican Party as did Chase.

Chase and others organized the Republican Party in 1855 at a time when every American finally started to see slavery as a major issue in the country. William T. Sherman was one of them. He had left the Army in 1853 and worked at a bank. In 1856, he told his brother, Congressman John Sherman, of his anxieties about slavery.

William Tecumseh Sherman

Slavery [is] rising more and more every year into a question of real danger, not withstanding the compromises. Having lived in the South [I understand] that if slavery were a new question no one now would contend for introducing it. But it is an old and historical fact that you must take it as you find it. Rice, sugar and certain kinds of cotton cannot be produced except by forced Negro labor. Slavery being a fact is chargeable on the past. It cannot, by our system, be abolished except by force and consequent break up of our present government. . . . It was a mistake to make Missouri a slave state, but it was done long ago and now there is no remedy except in the state itself. Slavery can never exist here [in the North] so the North now has the power and can exercise it in prudence and moderation.

When Lincoln's Cabinet next met in Washington several days later, Gideon Welles, too, was now convinced of the resupply plan.

Gideon Welles

I concur in the proposition to send an armed force to Charleston with supplies and provisions for the garrison of Fort Sumter, and of communicating, at the proper time, the intentions of the government to provision the fort peaceably if unmolested. The time has arrived when it is the duty of the government to assert and maintain its authority.

Throughout the Union, the newspapers were still split on what to do, and many politicians and newspapers suggested that it would be politically incorrect for Lincoln to resupply Fort Sumter without the approval of Congress, whose members were all home.

On March 29, the Cabinet vote to resupply Fort Sumter was six to three. Lincoln now had the majority of the Cabinet on the side of resupply—his own belief as well as, he thought, most of the Northern press and people.

President Lincoln's mind was made up. He was ready to send supplies to the fort and risk a war.

Abraham Lincoln

[Surrendering the fort would be] utterly ruinous . . . that, at home, it would discourage the friends of the Union, embolden its adversaries, and go far to insure to the latter, a recognition abroad.

President Lincoln immediately sent an order to Navy Secretary Welles and War Secretary Cameron.

Abraham Lincoln

I desire that an expedition, to move by sea, be got ready to sail as early as the 6th of April, the whole according to memorandum attached and that you cooperate with the Secretary of War [and Navy] for that object.

There was an enclosure—not in the president's handwriting.

Navy Dept.

Steamers *Pocahontas,* at Norfolk, *Pawnee* at Washington and Rev. Cutter *Harriet Lane* at N. York to be ready [under sailing orders] for sea with one month's stores [provisions, etc.]. Three hundred seaman to be kept ready for leaving the receiving ship at N. York.

War Dept.

Two Hundred men at N. York ready to leave garrison [to be ready to leave Governor's Island in New York]. Supplies for twelve months for one hundred men to be put into portable shape, to be ready for instant shipping. A large steamer and three tugs conditionally engaged.

Even as that fleet was preparing to sail, William Seward continued to put off the Southern Peace Commissioners. As late as April 7, he kept lying to them and insisted the fort would be evacuated. When they learned the truth, they were astonished by his nerve and duplicity.

Down at Fort Sumter, supplies were running out and the men worried that all food would be gone before they heard anything definitive from their government.

Captain Abner Doubleday

If the government delays many days longer, it will be very difficult to relieve us in time, for the men's provisions are going fast.

And what about Fort Pickens in Pensacola, Florida? Seward made a great effort to switch all conversations and memos to that fort, to cover his gaffes with the Peace Commissioners over Fort Sumter. As a diversion, Seward wrote on March 29 that the Cabinet and the president should hear from Captain Montgomery Meigs, supervising the building of the

Capitol dome, because a year earlier Meigs had worked at Fort Pickens and knew all about its defenses.

William Seward

I would call Captain Meigs forthwith. Aided by his counsel, I would at once, and at any cost, prepare for a war at Pensacola, and Texas, to be undertaken, however, only as a consequence of maintaining the possession and authority of the United States.

Fort Pickens was a very real problem for the president. Everything connected to it seemed to go wrong. He had sent the vessel Brooklyn *to Pickens with supplies, but through a mix-up in orders it sailed to Key West instead. The supplies never reached Fort Pickens. Unfortunately, the* Brooklyn's *trip to Key West was discovered and reported by the* New York Tribune, *and the story was then picked up by hundreds of newspapers.*

Lincoln felt better after meeting with Meigs, though, because Meigs assured him that Pickens could not be taken by Confederate forces. Its defenses were too strong. Lincoln sent Meigs to see General Scott.

Captain Montgomery Meigs

He with some effort directed us to read our papers to General Scott, tell him instructions of the President and that he wished this thing done and not to let it fail.

After his meeting with Lincoln, Meigs met with Seward, who told a bizarre story. Meigs wrote in his diary that night:

Captain Montgomery Meigs

The administration had been in a strait, Seward said. General Scott objected in relieving Fort Sumter or Pickens, thought it best to give them up and thus put a stop to all cry of coercion. For his own

[Seward's] part, his policy had been all along to give up Sumter as too near Washington and leaving a temptation to [Jefferson] Davis to relieve it by an attack on Washington. That he wished to hold Pickens and making the fight there, and in Texas—where he hoped the Unionist Governor, Sam Houston—would co-operate and thus make the burden of the war, which all men of sense saw must come, fall upon those who by rebellion provoked it.

Back on April 1, the mix-up in messages to the Brooklyn *was finally explained. The president got a letter from Captain Israel Vogdes, commander of the troops aboard the* Brooklyn, *that had been sent eleven days earlier.*

Captain Israel Vogdes

Our means of communication with the government are very uncertain. We do not feel certain that our communications have reached the department nor do we know whether the department's messenger to us may not have been intercepted.

There was more bad news about Fort Pickens. Vogdes, on the scene at the fort, disagreed with Seward's assessment that Pickens was impregnable.

Captain Israel Vogdes

[Fort Pickens] gave every advantage to the seceders. They are not required to give any notice of abrogation and may attack the fort without a moment's notice.

Even as Lincoln read Vogdes's letter, his aides were putting together plans of operations for the Navy and Army. Lieutenant David Porter, who would become one of the heroes of the coming war, was ordered to get himself to New York as quickly as possible, take command of a warship, sail it to Pensacola, and keep an eye on Fort Pickens. He was to halt any troop transport from Southern forces that was heading toward the fort. A transport of US troops would follow Porter by a few days. If Porter was fired upon, he was told by the president:

Abraham Lincoln

You will defend yourself and your expedition at whatever hazard, and if needful for such defense, inflict upon the assailants all the damage in your power within the range of your guns.

Many Southerners contended that Lincoln had no Constitutional power to raise an Army or enhance a Navy or prepare or conduct any war operations. He was overstepping the bounds of the Presidency. Lincoln, though, remained adamant about resupplying Sumter. Some called him a dictator.

Thomas Hall Jr., Editor, *The South*

There have been occasions in the history of this country when it was believed to be necessary to place at the disposal of the Executive Magistrate, means to defend its honor, and shield it from a foreign invasion, but never, until this calamitous period, has anyone been audacious enough to propose or advise the bestowal on the President such gigantic powers as Lincoln asks may be conferred on himself. . . . Daniel Webster openly declared in the Senate Chamber that sooner than make such a grant of power to the president he would prefer that the walls of the capitol should be battered down by the cannons of the enemy.

Hall's views were shared by many, and contributed to the confusion over Forts Sumter and now Pickens in New York. The people depended upon to outfit ships refused to do so. William Aspinwall, a shipbuilder, had agreed to lease the government his ship, the Baltic, *to carry troops to Charleston. A Captain Marshall was going to provide provisions for the several hundred soldiers. Now they both refused. Gustavus Fox reported from the docks there that these suppliers wished to dictate policy.*

Gustavus Fox

From being for a long time most earnest in this matter, they [the suppliers] are now astonished at the idea of the government attempting it, declaring that the time is past and that the people are reconciled to leaving this position and making the stand on Pickens &c.

The next day the suppliers balked again, arguing that news of the Sumter expedition would ruin a loan the government was going to float. Then Captain Marshall backed out of the deal altogether, asking Fox, incredibly, not if Lincoln had approved it, but if Seward had.

Gustavus Fox

This is serious, as he was expected to obtain all the provisions in what is called the desiccated form. These [provisions] would occupy only half the space of others, could all be carried in bags, in the boats, facilitating the landing and giving the garrison, as always, fresh provisions.

Fox told Montgomery Blair that he suspected the secretive hand of Seward behind the opposition to the plan.

Gustavus Fox

[It is] all political. Captain Marshall has been in Washington for two weeks and wishes to know if Mr. Seward goes for it. [I am] heart sick over the delays, obstacles and brief time allowed for a vital measure that should have had months [of preparation].

Lincoln knew of the opposition to his plan—although he hadn't told Blair that he knew. Aspinwall had written to Lincoln about why he was pulling out.

William Aspinwall

I did so under the conviction that were it even suspected that you contemplated re-inforcing Fort Sumter . . . the bids for the loan on Tuesday, if they reached the amount offered, would be at rates at which Gov. Chase would hesitate to accept.

There are other considerations which prompted me to regret that the attempt to re-inforce Fort Sumter should now be made, against the odds which have been allowed to accumulate since the early part of February.

What would be the influence on the money? The public mind is fully made to the evacuation of Fort Sumter. The relief of Fort Pickens and other feasible efforts to hold what is tenable would in my opinion strengthen the administration and strengthen and give courage to the Union men of the South.

Lincoln, though, remained adamant about resupplying Sumter. He told Fox to find other shippers and suppliers—and find them right away.

After the war, Montgomery Blair recalled the Sumter decision.

Montgomery Blair

Alone in the Cabinet, I resisted the surrender of Forts Sumter and Pickens and the dissolution of the Union which that surrender signified.

TWENTY

Pensacola, Florida
Fort Pickens: The Messy Thorn in Everybody's Side

The plans to resupply Forts Sumter and Pickens proceeded, but no one in Washington cared much about Fort Pickens. It was in the harbor of a small town in Florida—Pensacola—and far, far away. The press also ignored it. Pickens was just like all those dozens of federal forts that Lincoln, and Buchanan before him, had considered giving away. While Sumter came to represent the North–South dilemma, Pickens never did.

On March 31, Easter Sunday, planning had started for the resupply of Fort Pickens, but this ended in confusion, too. Erasmus Keyes, an aide to General Scott, told him of the difficulties involved in resupplying Pickens with food and troops. He told friends later that he had assumed Scott knew all of this, but the general did not. General Scott pulled a map of Florida off a shelf and handed it to Keyes.

General Winfield Scott
Take this map to Mr. Seward and repeat to him exactly what you have just said to me about the difficulty of re-supplying Fort Pickens.

Keyes, unlike Scott, did not think that anyone in the Lincoln government would actually vote to resupply Pickens. He took his time walking to Seward's home. The Secretary of State was surprised to see him. He told him to find Captain Meigs, get more maps, talk to General Scott again, and then meet him at the White House. But there turned out to be no time to see General Scott again, so Keyes and Meigs went to the White House.

They outlined their plans and neither Seward nor Lincoln knew what they were talking about because their conversation was all military jargon. Lincoln asked them to start over again and speak plainly. Frustrated, they did so. The president then told them what they planned was all right with him, and told them to go back to General Scott and fill him in on their conversation. They did not reach Scott until 6 , while he was having dinner. He nodded and approved the plan.

Was there an imminent threat that Confederate forces in the Florida area, under newly appointed Confederate General Braxton Bragg, would launch a sneak attack on Pickens? Probably not.

Reporter, *New York Tribune*

Notwithstanding the belligerent bulletin from Fort Pickens, no apprehension is entertained in official circles of an attack by General Bragg's force. . . . Jefferson Davis has ordered a large force to Pensacola, but probably with no more expectation of assailing it than Governor Pickens has of attacking Fort Sumter.

But Fort Pickens, added to Sumter, was growing into a problem that worried many people.

Ohio Republican

The evacuation of Fort Sumter is a bitter pill, it is all we can do to bear up against it. . . . but the evacuation of Fort Pickens . . . My God! . . . it would truly demoralize the government.

There was a plan to protect Fort Pickens, but, like the Sumter plan, it ran into snags as soon as it began to unfold. First, there was no money for the Sumter or Pickens expeditions. Somehow, Congress had not appropriated any money to the president for such purposes. Lincoln had to convince

Seward to take $10,000 out of emergency State Department funds to support the expeditions.

That confusion was followed by more confusion as the military departments battled with each other. Seward, Lincoln, Porter, Keyes, and Meigs all agreed that the ship Powhatan *in New York, a large vessel, was best suited for the long ocean voyage. Lincoln ordered it to sail. Others convinced Lincoln, though, that Secretary of the Navy Welles's department was full of spies and they did not want those men to get wind of the top-secret expedition. So they sent the* Powhatan, *a U.S. Navy ship, off to Florida without telling the head of the Navy.*

Welles had, in fact, taken the Powhatan *out of service because it was a run-down ship that had seen considerable service recently. It was put it back into service without his knowledge. A day later, Lincoln's secretary, John Nicolay, found Welles and gave him copies of the orders. The Secretary of the Navy was flabbergasted. They had gone over his head. The documents also showed an understanding of the ships and Navy that Welles knew Lincoln, a lawyer from the Midwest, could not have had. The people who wrote the documents had to be his own Navy people, who deliberately kept him in the dark.*

Furious, Welles went to the White House and found Lincoln. The president, seeing the anger in Welles's face, seemed perplexed.

Abraham Lincoln
What have I done wrong?

Welles exploded. Lincoln told him honestly that a group of Navy men had drafted the orders that he signed. He never read the orders, though. Welles asked if Seward had a hand in this. Lincoln admitted that he did. Welles exploded again.

Gideon Welles
These papers he had signed, many of them without reading—for he had not time, and if he could not trust the Secretary of State, he knew not

whom he could trust. I asked who were associated with Mr. Seward. "No one," said the President "but these young men were here as clerks to write down his plans and orders." I then asked if he knew the young men. He said one was Captain Meigs and the other was a Naval officer named Porter. . . . [H]e seemed disinclined to disclose or dwell on the project, but assured me he never would have signed the paper had he been aware of its contents, much of which had no connection with Mr. Seward's scheme. The President re-iterated they were not his instructions and wished me distinctly to understand they were not, although his named was appended to them—said the paper was an improper one—that he wished me to give it no more consideration than I thought proper—treat it as canceled—as if it had never been written.

The confusion extended to the Brooklyn Navy Yard. The commander there, Captain Andrew Foote, was a fill-in for the regular commander, who was on leave. Foote, who had little knowledge of the yard's operations, was suddenly asked to get the Powhatan *ready for sea duty and also find its officers, who had been sent elsewhere by Welles when he decommissioned the ship. Foote, then, had two sets of orders: one from Lincoln and one from Welles. Gustavus Fox arrived on April 1 to supervise the refitting of the* Powhatan. *Foote refused to follow Lincoln's orders unless they were approved by Welles. Fox needed three hours to convince him that the president was Welles's and Foote's commander-in-chief.*

Fox was certain that Lincoln and Welles both had ordered just one ship, the Powhatan, *but, unknown to just about anybody, Keyes and Meigs had commissioned three ships to sail and were getting them ready—while Foote genuinely believed he was only to refit a single ship.*

Lincoln, the unwitting source of the huge mix-up, was apologetic.

Gustavus Fox

Mr. Seward got up this Pensacola expedition and the President signed the orders in ignorance and unknown to the department. The President offers every apology possible and will do so in writing.

While all this confusion was going on in Washington and at the New York docks, it seems everyone in America knew that a military expedition of some kind, to some place, was being readied; it was all people talked about. In fact, on April 6, the suggested secret start date of the naval expedition to Charleston, the editor of the Democratic New York Evening Day Book *wrote about the frenzy.*

Editor, *New York Evening Day Book*

There is a remarkable bustle going on, both in the army and the navy, by the orders of our Negro Republican Administration that looks as if some savage and slaughterous design were in the wind. The Washington correspondents for nearly all the papers agree in ascribing these warlike preparations to a determination on the part of Lincoln and his Cabinet to blockade the southern ports. Did we not consider the party in power a set of madmen, we should at once pronounce such rumors false. Blockading the ports would be an act of war and the Executive department of the government has no power to declare war—that has been wisely reserved to Congress alone. We believe the revolutionary abolitionists, who are now in possession of the government, capable of usurping any power that they could hope to maintain; but even they are not mad enough to suppose that the city of Washington would be in their possession six weeks after the people should understand that they have usurped authority for the purpose of making war upon the South. It is probable that the present movement is with the design of making a demonstration of the federal power at Fort Pickens. . . . It is designed for effect, to give the red-hot Republicans something to talk about.

Most of the newspapers believed some sort of invasion was being prepared and could not be stopped except by extreme measures.

Editor, *New York Herald*

Our only hope now against civil war of indefinite duration seems to lie in the overthrow of the demoralizing, disorganizing and destructive

Republican sectional party of which "Honest Abe" Lincoln is the pliant instrument.

At Fort Sumter, there was no joy as the expeditions headed there and to Fort Pickens.

Major Robert Anderson

I fear that its result cannot fail to be disastrous to all concerned.

Anderson's depression was growing and it alarmed his soldiers.

Major Robert Anderson

I frankly say that my heart is not in the war, which I see is to be commenced.

Even so, Anderson did all he could to fortify Sumter against the attack from all sides which he was certain was coming. His men worked very hard and, after so many months of indecision, seemed to enjoy it. The men, singly and in groups, sang as they worked on the ramparts and other spots in the fort.

On the same day ships were being outfitted for the expeditions to Pickens and Sumter—with a war inevitable—residents in Charleston still believed that Sumter would be evacuated, that Seward was on their side, and that Lincoln had no stomach for war. The prospects for the new Confederate States of Americas were good, too—the price of cotton was at an all-time high. Charleston socialite Mary Pinckney, of the prominent Pinckney family, wrote to her brother Charley with great enthusiasm.

Mary Pinckney

The danger has passed away or so I and most people believe.

Mary paid no attention to the constant, loud artillery practice firing in the harbor.

Mary Pinckney

We regard it as no more than so many sneezes.

The mood in Charleston changed daily, though. The next day, Mary Chestnut, after complaining about a hard rainstorm that had swept through the city, went into great detail about a sudden downward mood swing among the population.

Mary Chestnut

The mood in the city was less optimistic. All soldiers in town were told to gather their guns in hand if the bells of St. Michael's began to peal. There had been a few rumors of some discontent in some slave quarters, some worries that disgruntled servants might attempt arson. The Mayor ordered the city's fire companies to keep a sharp eye out. Churches were packed. Ministers, rabbis, priests asked Providence to continue to bless their fair city and all its worthy efforts. Some spoke of war and strove for the proper homilies.

The next day, spirits plunged even further. The Ashley and Cooper Rivers had nearly flooded from the rains. People began to put messages on bulletin boards with rumors of a Union fleet that had just sailed from New York City headed for Charleston. The morning newspapers had stories to that same effect, although they had no hard evidence that an invasion was coming. Mary Chestnut was very worried.

Mary Chestnut

News so warlike I quake.

At Fort Sumter, Major Anderson quaked too, because despite all the turmoil in Charleston and in Washington, he still had no instructions about what to do.

Major Robert Anderson

The remarks made to me by Colonel Lamon, taken in connection with the tenor of newspaper articles, have induced me, as stated in previous communications, to believe that orders would soon be issued for my abandoning this work. [I see] a force so superior that a collision would, in all probability, terminate in the destruction of our force before relief could reach us, with only a few days provisions on hand . . . in hourly expectation of receiving definite instructions. . . .

On April 6, confusion ended and the plans for the expedition to deliver supplies to Fort Sumter were underway, Lincoln decided to send a messenger to Governor Pickens in Charleston to alert him to the fact that the supply ships had lifted anchor in New York City and that he needed to be aware of a possible confrontation in the harbor. The president did not entrust any secretary in his Cabinet, an experienced envoy, a noted diplomat, or a high-ranking general to deliver this news. He chose Robert Chew, an ordinary State Department worker to tell Governor Pickens.

When he met Chew in the White House, Lincoln told him that he was to see Governor Pickens upon his arrival in Charleston only if the fort had not been attacked yet and the Stars and Stripes were still flying over it. Chew was to hand Lincoln's written message to Pickens and leave a copy with him, returning to Washington with the original. Chew was not to discuss anything, just deliver the message. He was to go alone.

The situation changed that afternoon. Ted Talbot, the diplomat, returned from Charleston with a note from Major Anderson, who had no idea what was going on in the War Department and was confused.

Now Lincoln had to get a note to Anderson. He decided to send Talbot back to Charleston with Chew to deliver a message to Anderson, if they could, to tell him that supplies and men were on the way and that he had to hold out until they arrived.

The next day a Virginian, John Minor Botts, a longtime political power broker, presented Lincoln with a wild scheme: Call a national convention of all the states which would authorize the seceded states to purchase Fort

Sumter at a fair price and leave the Union and Confederacy without a confrontation. They would, Botts assured the president, come running back within a year. Lincoln knew his ships were sailing to Sumter as they spoke. He rejected the idea.

Seward wanted a convention, too. His would include all the states, North and South, to add new amendments to the Constitution to placate Southern slaveowners. Stephen Douglas went even further. He wanted a whole collection of countries in a new Union to avoid secession. Under his plan, the United States, North and South, would join Canada and Mexico in a gigantic North American trade union.

Lincoln was not interested in any of these plans. He knew that a confrontation would be forced at Sumter and that he would need more troops—quickly. On April 8, he sent a telegram to Pennsylvania Governor Andrew Curtin telling him that. Lincoln had asked Curtin, during a previous visit to the White House, to get a militia from his state ready for action in case there was trouble. Now he told Curtin:

Abraham Lincoln

I think the necessity of being ready increases. Look to it.

That same day, unknown to Lincoln, Seward finally ended his communications with the three Peace Commissioners from the South, leaving them with just a formal public statement from Lincoln and the situation in Charleston. They had been deceived. They were furious.

The commissioners had been holding out for more than a month and were certain they would prevail. Back on March 15, John Forsyth had asked Jefferson Davis to hold on, fueled by their strategy of appeasement, which they were certain would succeed.

John Forsyth

Lincoln inclines to peace. . . . Since the 4th of March, two of the Republican illusions have exploded, first that it was very easy to re-inforce the fort, and second that they could collect the [port] revenues from floating custom houses at sea.

They, of course, were wrong. President Davis alerted General Beauregard.

Jefferson Davis
Our Commissioners at Washington have received a flat refusal.

An angry President Davis wrote the governors of the seven Southern seceded states for help, asking them to recruit 20,000 more troops.

Jefferson Davis
The discontinuance by the United States of negotiations with the Commissioners representing this government, leaves no doubt as to the policy we should pursue.

At the same time the Peace Commissioners alerted Davis that they had failed, General Beauregard in Charleston insisted that the time to strike was very near.

General P. G. T. Beauregard
[The expulsion of Anderson] ought now to be decided on in a few days, for this state of uncertainty might not last longer than is necessary. . . . [with] provisions to be sent to Fort Sumter. Preparations [must be] made to compel him to a surrender, should the United States government not be willing to withdraw him peaceably.

Beauregard was anxious to order his men to level the fort. He soon afterward wrote to Davis:

General P. G. T. Beauregard

Batteries here ready to open. What instructions?

Secretary of War L. P. Walker, speaking for Davis, told him to be at the ready for an attack and not to let any ruse, such as supplies, deceive him.

L. P. Walker

Under no circumstances are you to allow provisions to be sent to Fort Sumter.

At this point, at the start of the second week of April, President Davis had two options. He could hold back an attack, let the fort be resupplied, and hope further negotiations would permit the Southern states to secede without military interference not only in Charleston, but everywhere. Or his forces could shell the fort to force Major Anderson to give up. He knew the fort was no danger to the residents of the city because it was four miles out in the harbor and the shells from its guns could not reach town. Davis had, in fact, told Governor Pickens back in January that the fort posed no threat to Charleston.

Jefferson Davis

The little garrison in its present position presses on nothing but point of pride.

In Washington, Secretary of State William Seward still believed there would not be trouble in Charleston. He hosted British journalist William Russell, of the London Times, *at his home on April 8. Worried but hopeful, he said:*

William Seward

When the Southern states see that we mean them no wrong—that we intend no violence to persons, rights or things—that the Federal government seeks only to impose obligations imposed on it in respect to the national property, they will see their mistake and one after another they will come back into the Union.

Seward showed him a dispatch asking all foreign governments to ignore the troubles at Fort Sumter. Seward thought it was a friendly note, but Russell became very alarmed as he read it.

....

William Russell

Even war with us may not be out of the list of those means which would be available for returning the broken union into a mass once more.

As the two men talked in Washington, the mix-up in orders for the Sumter expedition, launched amid a flurry of rumors, caused chaos. The Powhatan, *with three hundred troops ready for action at Fort Sumter, did not sail for the fort in Charleston, but for Pensacola. No one was sailing to Sumter, but as Abraham Lincoln went to sleep that night, he did not know that.*

On that same day, April 8, the weather was absolutely miserable at Fort Sumter. Soldiers awoke to a chilly, overcast morning. The waters in the harbor were choppy. A slight wind blew through the Charleston region, rustling the trees. It rained most of the day and the city of Charleston looked very, very bleak. Many of the downtown streets were flooded.

The weather in Charleston had been good, then bad, then good throughout winter and early spring. It had rained a lot and cold snaps had been frequent. Nearby counties even got snow. When the weather was good, though, the city was a dazzling gem to behold. In an April 8 letter to his brother that was never delivered, Wylie Crawford described Charleston on a sunny day.

....

Wylie Crawford

It was a beautiful sight, I assure you.

A day later, on April 9, Anderson received instructions from Secretary of War Cameron, speaking for Lincoln, that were not instructions at all. It was, we could call it today, presidential mumbo jumbo.

Simon Cameron
It is not, however, the intention of the President to subject your command to any danger or hardship beyond what, in your judgment, would be usual in military life, and he has entire confidence that you will act as becomes a patriot and soldier, and under all circumstances.

Just what did that mean?

Back in Washington and in the North that first week of April, there was a storm of editorial demands for Lincoln to do something about Fort Sumter.

Wisconsin Newspaper
The North must get down on its knees and ask Jeff Davis for the privilege to breathe.

Pennsylvania Newspaper
Lincoln is vain, weak, hypocritical, puerile, the weakest man who has ever been elected, a cross between a sandhill crane and an Andalusian jackass.

No one knew Lincoln had already made up his mind. Most politicians still saw the new president a mystery.

John Nicolay and John Hay, Lincoln's private secretaries
Neither, on the other hand, did they know him. He recognized them as Governors, Senators, statesmen, while they yet looked upon him as a simple frontier lawyer at most, and a rival to whom chance had

transferred the honor they felt due to themselves. . . . Perhaps the first real question of the Lincoln Cabinet was, "Who is the greatest man?" It is pretty safe to assert that no one—not even he himself—believed it was Abraham Lincoln.

In New York, wild rumors were heard everywhere. A whole fleet of naval vessels with thousands of troops was headed to Fort Sumter. More were headed for Fort Pickens. They would be there in a matter of days. No, another rumor said, the shelling of Fort Sumter had already started. No, said another, the fort had capitulated.

That morning, Lincoln put out a statement to a press association that seemed to prepare people for something in Charleston.

Abraham Lincoln

Extensive as the military and naval preparations are, it is persistently stated in administration quarters that they are for defensive purposes only and that nothing is intended not strictly justified by the laws, which it is the duty of the President to enforce to the extent of his ability. If resistance be made to his efforts in this particular, and bloodshed be the result, the responsibility must fall on those who provoke hostilities, and the assurance of the Inaugural is repeated that the administration will not be the aggressor.

The editors of major newspapers agreed with the president about who would fire the first shot, if one was fired.

New York Times

If the rebels fire at an unarmed supply ship and make a perfectly proper act the pretext for shedding the blood of loyal citizens, on their head be the responsibility.

New York Post
At Charleston, tomorrow, the rebels will elect between peace and war. If they declare for war, and shed the blood of loyal men, it only remains for the President to take measures to put down rebellion.

Louisville Journal
The secession leaders are relying very heavily on the first shock of battle for the promotion of a general secession feeling in the Southern States. If the general government commit any wrong or outrage upon South Carolina or Florida, it will be condemned, but if a United States vessel shall be fired into and her men slain for a mere attempt to take food to the government's troops in the government's own forts, and if war shall grow out of the collision, no spirit of secession or rebellion will be created thereby this side of the cotton line.

Many government officials agreed—even those who were not privy to Lincoln's strategy.

Joseph Holt, Secretary of War
[If South Carolina fires on Fort Sumter] and this plunges our country into a civil war, then upon them and those they represent rests the responsibility.

Even as Chew and Talbot arrived in Charleston on April 8 to inform Governor Pickens that supply ships were sailing for Sumter, fear grew throughout Charleston and the neighboring region. A planter's wife, whose husband and two sons had left her alone to join the Confederate Army, trembled. She scribbled in her diary:

Plantation Mistress
There are 600 negroes, perhaps, prowling in our midst. [The men] have all left me in this house alone, not a sound heard. What if Lincoln gains

the advantage & with sword in hand, ravaging the land & destroying our firesides with ruthless revenge. It is too horrible to think of.

A neighbor worried about her, and all the other women and children in range of Sumter's guns and any bombardment by US warships.

Charleston resident
God only knows what will be the result. I am ready for the issue at any moment but would be more satisfied if the women and children were in a place of safety.

Business in Charleston had come to a halt.

Charleston merchant
All business at a stand. Our shop may as well be closed.

Many residents turned to Providence.

Charleston resident
The God of Battles shall decide who is in the right.

On April 7, Mary Chestnut had been at a social gathering, a somber one, when former Governor John Manning arrived and pulled her aside. He bowed politely and stunned her with his news.

John Manning
Madam, your country has been invaded.

She stepped back, frightened.

Mary Chestnut
What does he mean?

Bystander
He means this. There are six men-o-war outside the bar. Talbot and Chew have come to say that hostilities are about to begin. Governor Pickens and Beauregard are holding a council of war.

The idea of an invasion did not really surprise most Southerners by then.

Judah Benjamin
At neither [Sumter or Pickens] can it be long delayed.

As Charlestonians mumbled and grumbled on April 8, Robert Chew and Theodore Talbot arrived at Governor Pickens's downtown hotel office to deliver the president's message. Pickens read it and then called in General Beauregard, who read it again.

Chew's mission turned out to be useless. Jefferson Davis wired General Beauregard to listen to Chew and then make demands he knew would be rejected.

Lincoln's message to Pickens, hand delivered by Chew, was clear.

Robert Chew
I am directed by the President of the United States to notify you to expect an attempt will be made to supply Fort Sumter with provisions only and that, if such an attempt be not resisted, no efforts to throw in men, arms, ammunition will be made, without further notice or in case of an attack upon the fort.

Everyone waited to see what Jefferson Davis would do. Some of the South's leading newspapers begged him to be cautious.

Editor, *New Orleans Times-Picayune*

He has achieved his reputation as a soldier, and we are sure he feels no desire to augment a fame that might content any man by Civil War. He will have much to do to restrain the eagerness of the young soldier who is panting to flash his maiden sword upon his country's enemies. He will have something to do to restrain the rashness of the misguided enthusiast, who requires the hands of Southern union cemented in blood. Would a little patience be more hurtful to us than the reputation of having struck the first blow?

There were many, though, who thought striking the first blow was not only a good idea, but would set up a fine strategy. One was Senator Wigfall of Texas, who wrote to Davis on April 10.

Senator Louis Wigfall

No one doubts that Lincoln intends war. The delay on his part is only to complete his preparations. All here is ready on our side. Our delay therefore is to his advantage and our disadvantage. Let us take Fort Sumter before we have to fight the fleet and the fort. General Beauregard will not act without your order. Let me suggest to you to send the order to him to begin the attack as soon as he is ready. Virginia is excited by the preparations and a bold stroke on our side will complete her purposes. Policy and prudence are urged upon us to begin at once.

Everyone, North and South, wanted the large state of Virginia and its tens of thousands of men on their side. Even General Scott venerated the state and its officer corps.

General Winfield Scott

With Virginia officers and Yankee troops, I could conquer the world.

Some Southern newspapers did not think the rebels would gain foreign allies or be victorious in a war.

Editor, *North Carolina Standard*

The whole world outside the slaveholding states, with slight exceptions, is opposed to slavery, and the whole world with slave labor thus rendered insecure, and comparatively valueless, will take sides with the North against us. The end will be . . . *Abolition!*

At Fort Sumter, while he told his officers and men that negotiations would provide the solders with a peaceful resolution, Major Anderson was certain there would be a war. Confederate forces had intercepted one of his letters to the War Department in which he said so.

Major Robert Anderson

[I predict] the most disastrous results [of an attack by the federal Navy] . . . throughout the country. . . . [M]y heart is not in the war which I see is to be thus commenced.

On April 12, after several telegrams between Davis and Beauregard, the Confederate president told his general in Charleston to get an evacuation date from Anderson and, if none was given, to shell the fort.

Jefferson Davis

[If they] supply Fort Sumter by force, you will at once demand its evacuation and, if this is refused, proceed in such manner as you may determine to reduce it.

It was the decision many had been hoping for.

Senator Louis Wigfall, Texas
There was a sound of revelry by night.

But his wife voiced a worry that was on many minds.

Mrs. Wigfall
The slaveowners must expect a servile insurrection, of course.

Mary Chestnut
On any stir of confusion, my heart is apt to beat so painfully. Now the agony was so stifling—I could neither see or hear. The men went off almost immediately. And I crept silently to my room where I sat down to a good cry.

Her friend, Mrs. Wigfall, came to her room.

Mary Chestnut
We had it out on the subject of Civil War. We solaced ourselves with dwelling on all its known horrors, and then we added what we had a right to expect, with Yankees in front and Negroes in the rear.

We met Mrs. Allen Green in the passageway, with blanched cheeks and streaming eyes. Former Governor John Means rushed out of his room in his dressing gown and he begged us to be calm. Even in this desperate moment, he had time to ridicule Governor Pickens.

Governor John Means, South Carolina
Governor Pickens has ordered in the plentitude of his wisdom seven cannon to be fired as a signal to the Seventh Regiment. Anderson will hear as well as the Seventh Regiment. Now you go back and be quiet—fighting in the streets has not begun yet.

Mary Chestnut
No sleep for anybody last night. The streets were alive with soldiers, men shouting, marching, singing. Wigfall, the stormy petrel, is the only happy person I see.

The next day . . .

Mary Chestnut
Things seem to have settled down a little. One can but hope still. Lincoln and Seward have made such silly advances and then far sillier drawings back. There may be a chance for peace, after all.

Things are happening so fast. My husband has been made an aide to General Beauregard. Three hours ago, we were quietly packing to go home. Now he tells me the attack upon Fort Sumter may begin tonight. Depends upon Anderson and the fleet outside. The *Herald* says this show of war outside the bar is intended for Texas.

John Manning came in with his sword and red sash, pleased as a boy to be on Beauregard's staff while the row goes on. He has gone with Wigfall to Captain Hartstene with instructions.

Mary's friend Mrs. Haynes, the gossip, stopped by her room.

Mrs. Haynes
[I've] one feeling, pity, for those who are not here.

Mary Chestnut
Jack Preston, Willie Alston—the "take life easys"—as they are called, with John Green, "the big brave," have gone down to the island, volunteered as privates.

Seven hundred men were sent over. Ammunition wagons rumbling along the streets all night. Anderson burning blue lights—signs and signals for the fleet outside, I suppose.

Today at dinner . . . there was an undercurrent of intense excitement. There could not have been a more brilliant circle. In addition to our usual quartet [Judge Withers, Langdon Cheves, and Trescott] our two former Governors dined with us, Means and Manning. These men all talked delightfully. For once in my life, I listened.

Governor Means rummaged a sword and red sash from somewhere and brought it for Colonel Chestnut, who has gone to demand the surrender of Fort Sumter.

And now, patience. We must wait.

TWENTY-ONE

Fort Sumter
The Bombardment

Mrs. Chestnut did not have to wait long. All of Charleston was full of tension, as were the Confederate Army camps and the Fort Sumter garrison. They were waiting for Major Anderson to surrender. They were waiting for Jefferson Davis's next step. They were all waiting for history to happen.

Mary Chestnut
Anderson will not capitulate.

Then she continued her diary.

Mary Chestnut
Yesterday was the merriest, maddest dinner we have had yet. Men were more audaciously wise and witty. We had an unspoken foreboding it was to be our last pleasant meeting. Mrs. Henry King rushed in.

Mrs. Henry King
The news—I come for the latest news. All of the men of the King family are on the island.

Mary Chestnut

James Chestnut returned. He said Anderson had been "interesting" but not inclined to communicate. He has gone back to Fort Sumter, with additional instructions. That boat ride to visit Major Anderson would kick off America's Civil War.

When they were about to leave the wharf, A. H. Boykin sprang into the boat, in great excitement. Felt himself ill-used. A likelihood of fighting and to be left behind!

All was havoc at Fort Sumter. A schooner sailing down the Atlantic Coast headed for Savannah with a cargo of ice ran into dense fog outside of Charleston. Its captain, not aware of the tense drama unfolding there, turned landward for Charleston to sit out the fog but did not alert anybody.

Captain Abner Doubleday

Confederates on Morris Island assumed the ship was the first in the expected fleet of naval ships that the South was certain would try to supply the fort. They fired a warning shot across the bow of the schooner, R. H. Shannon. The bewildered captain then ran up the stars and stripes to let the soldiers know he had not been hit. They interpreted this to mean he was identifying himself so they would know that he was part of the invading force.

This was regarded as a direct defiance and a heavy cannonade was at once opened on the vessel. Very much puzzled to account for this activity, he lowered the flag and the firing ceased. A boat's crew now put off from the shore to ascertain his character and purpose in entering the harbor. While this was going on, we were formed at our guns in readiness to fire, but were not allowed to do so, although there was every probability that the vessel would be sunk before our eyes. It is true we could not have reached the particular battery that was doing the mischief but the other works of the enemy were all under our guns. Not expecting immediate action, [they] were in a measure unprepared.

Anderson, however, contented himself by sending Seymour and Snyder over in a boat with a white flag to ask for an explanation.

[Anderson] evidently feared that it might be considered as a betrayal of his trust and he was very sensitive to everything that affected his honor.

Or, sensing a colossal sailing blunder, Anderson may have wisely averted starting the Civil War that night.

The previous day, General Beauregard received a terse note from Jefferson Davis.

Jefferson Davis

The Government [at Montgomery] has at no time placed any reliance on assurances by the government at Washington in respect to the evacuation of Fort Sumter, or entertained any confidence of the latter to make any concession or yield any point to which it is not driven by absolute necessity and I desire that you govern yourself with strict reference to this as the key to the policy of the Confederate states.

You are especially instructed to remit in no degree your efforts to prevent the re-inforcement of Fort Sumter and to keep yourself in a state of the simplest preparation and most perfect readiness to repel invasion—save only in commencing assault or attack, except to repel an invading or re-inforcing force, precisely as if you were in the presence of any enemy contemplating to surprise you.

The delays and apparent vacillation of the Washington government make it imperative that the further concession of courtesies . . . to Major Anderson . . . in supplies from the city must cease.

Put yourself on a war footing, but do not strike yet except to repel an enemy expedition. Cut off Anderson's food purchases in Charleston. Be ready for additional orders whenever the news comes that the Confederate diplomats in Washington have terminated their mission. Their departure probably will be your signal to open fire.

Incredibly, right in the middle of all this tension came the annual graduation ball at Charleston's Citadel, one of America's premier military academies and home to the boys who had boldly opened fire on the Star of the West *supply ship when it had tried to sail to Fort Sumter in early January. Citadel officials insisted on holding the ball. It was a gala event. All the men looked their handsomest and the young women their most dazzling.*

Emma Holmes was the mother of Carrie Holmes, who danced the night away in her sea green gown with flowers in her hair. She wrote:

Emma Holmes

With very many of the girls it is their first ball, and what gay visions do these magic words conjure up.

Even as the orchestra played and the young men and women swirled around the wide floor and the smell of flowers drifted across the ballroom, others worried about more than their dance steps.

Mary Chestnut

Today they say an engagement is imminent.

Reporter, *New York Tribune*

Unless all signs fail, the siege of Fort Sumter . . . is about to commence.

Edwin Ruffin, a staunch Confederate, had traveled all the way from Virginia to watch the beginning of the Civil War, if it did indeed come. He, like everyone else in Charleston, expected fireworks, and soon.

Edwin Ruffin

The troops & the citizens are becoming feverishly impatient for the reduction of Fort Sumter & the end of the present necessity of retaining the besieging forces.

Residents of Charleston did not know what or who to believe. Tensions had mounted in the city, fueled by a wild assessment of the Sumter dispute by a Southern journalist, James E. Harvey, working in Washington, whom people believed was part of the administration's decision-making apparatus. He was not.

James Harvey

It was positively determined not to withdraw Anderson. Supplies go immediately, supported by naval force.

That caused an uproar, so later in the day Harvey issued another statement. But this did nothing except confuse everyone.

James Harvey

Order issued for withdrawal of Anderson's command.

He then issued several more statements that seemed to say there might be an evacuation but it would fail. All were confused.

Similarly confusing messages and dispatches came out of Washington. There, Peace Commissioner Martin Crawford sided with the those favoring evacuation, but befuddled all with a dispatch that told Anderson there would be no withdrawal, but no resupply either. In fact, Crawford's note said, Lincoln was leaving everything up to the Sumter commander. The Union major was unhappy.

Major Robert Anderson

I cannot think that the government would abandon, without instructions and without advice, a command which has tried to do all its duty to our country. . . . After thirty-odd years of service, I do not wish it to be said that I had treasonably abandoned a post and turned over to unauthorized persons public property entrusted to my charge. I am entitled to this act of justice at the hands of my Government, and I feel confident that I shall not be disappointed.

Jefferson Davis, too, was perplexed by the mixed messages coming out of Washington.

Jefferson Davis

This is not the course of good will and does not tend to preserve the peace.

Davis's Secretary of War, L. P. Walker, did not want to be fooled by Lincoln and Seward. He wrote General Beauregard:

L. P. Walker

Give little credit to rumors of an amicable adjustment.

There certainly would not be an amicable adjustment. As Walker sent that message, Lincoln replied to a note from the Virginia Convention, which was still trying to decide whether or not to remain in the Union. In it, the president made it abundantly clear that he would stand by Fort Sumter, no matter the cost. The note, and others he sent right after the attack on Sumter, show his growing sense of power and his comfort in wielding it. Looking back on that time later, he wrote:

Abraham Lincoln

Having, at the beginning of my official term, expressed my intended policy as plainly as I was able, It is with deep regret and some mortification that I now learn that there is great and injurious uncertainty in the public mind, as to what that policy is, and what course I intend to pursue. Not having, as yet, seen occasion to change, it is now my purpose to pursue the course marked out in the Inaugural address. I command a careful consideration of the whole document as the best expression I can give of my purpose.

I repeat:

The power confided to me will be used to hold, occupy and possess the property and places belonging to the government and to collect the duties and imposts but, beyond what is necessary for these objects—there will be no invasion, no using of force against or among the people anywhere.

But if, as now appears to be true, in pursuit of a purpose to drive the United States authority from these places, an unprovoked assault has been made upon Fort Sumter, I shall hold myself at liberty to repossess, if I can, like places which had been seized before the government was devolved upon me.

And in every event, I shall, to the extent of my ability, repel force by force.

I consider the military posts and property situated within the states, which claim to have seceded, as yet belonging to the government of the United States, as much as they did before the supposed secession.

Davis hastily convened a Cabinet meeting that day, April 8, to discuss Governor Pickens's notification that the supply ships were on their way. His Cabinet secretaries were furious at what they believed to be an attack and angry that they had, they felt, been duped by Seward into thinking there would not be an assault.

In Washington in early April, Judge Campbell had demanded to see Seward and was lied to once more.

Judge Campbell
Does the President design to supply Sumter?

Seward looked right at him and said:

William Seward
I think not. It is a very irksome thing to him to evacuate it. His ears are open to everyone and they fill his head with schemes for its supply. I do not think that he will adopt any of them. There is no design to re-inforce it.

Furious when informed of Seward's lies and what appeared to be Lincoln's duplicitous policy, Jefferson Davis wanted his troops in Charleston under General Beauregard to bombard the fort immediately. He had Secretary of War L. P. Walker get in touch with Beauregard.

L. P. Walker
The status which you must at once re-establish and rigidly enforce is that of hostile forces in the presence of each other.

Robert Toombs, Confederate Secretary of State
[Bombardment will] be suicide. That is unnecessary. It puts us in the wrong. It is fatal.

Right at this time, James Chestnut and other aides to Beauregard were taking a boat to Sumter to hand Anderson an ultimatum from General Beauregard.

General P. G. T. Beauregard
I am ordered by the government of the Confederate States to demand the evacuation of Fort Sumter. . . . All proper facilities will be afforded

for the removal of yourself and command, together with company arms and property, and all private property, to any post in the United States which you may select. The flag which you have upheld so long and with so much fortitude, under the most trying circumstances, may be saluted by you on taking it down.

Major Robert Anderson
It is a demand with which I regret that my sense of honor, and my obligations to my government, prevent my compliance. . . .

He handed Chestnut the note.

Major Robert Anderson
Gentlemen, if you do not batter us to pieces, we shall be starved out in few days.

After midnight, Colonel Chestnut and Captain Stephen Lee sailed to Sumter with a final demand by Beauregard that asked them to surrender to avoid "a useless effusion of blood."

Major Robert Anderson
Cordially uniting with you in the desire to avoid the useless effusion of blood, I will, if provided with the proper and necessary means of transportation, evacuate Fort Sumter by noon on the fifteenth instant and I will not, in the meantime, open my fire on your forces unless compelled to do so by some hostile act against the fort of the flag of my government. . . .

It was 3:20 on April 12.

Colonel James Chestnut

By authority of Brigadier General, commanding the provisional forces of the Confederate States, we have the honor to notify you that we will open the fire of his batteries on Fort Sumter in one hour from this time.

James Chestnut, Stephen Lee, and several others sailed off into the night and the clock began to tick.

◆

While her husband was conferring with General Beauregard, Mary Chestnut seemed to know of the 4 deadline and she could not rest.

Mary Chestnut

I do not pretend to go to sleep. How can I? If Anderson does not accept terms at four, the orders are he shall be fired upon. I count four. St. Michaels' bells chime out and I begin to hope. At half past four, the heavy booming of a cannon. I sprang out of bed and on my knees, prostrate, I prayed as I never prayed before.

Davis then sent the order to Beauregard to bombard the fort.

Jefferson Davis

Let us take Fort Sumter.

At 4:20 there was a single loud burst of shot from a cannon located on Cummings Point. The cannon fire, set off by Virginia's Edmund Ruffin, was a signal to all the Confederate batteries that practically surrounded Fort Sumter to open fire. They did. Ruffin's cannonball, well aimed, struck the wall just a few feet from Doubleday's head and startled him. What followed, and continued into the early hours of the morning, was a dazzling and awesome show of fire and smoke around and over the fort.

Captain Abner Doubleday

In a moment, the firing burst forth in one continuous roar, and large patches of both the interior and exterior masonry began to rumble and fall in all directions. The place where I was had been used for the manufacture of cartridges. A shell soon struck near the ventilator and a puff of dense smoke entered the room, giving me a strong impression that there would be an immediate explosion. Fortunately, no sparks had penetrated inside.

Nineteen batteries were now hammering at us and the balls and shells from the ten inch Columbiads, accompanied by shells from the thirteen inch mortars which constantly bombarded us, made us feel as if the war had commenced in earnest.

The men at Sumter stayed safe throughout the night and had a hearty breakfast in the morning, even as the bombardment continued. The men were almost "merry," according to Doubleday.

There was one exception. Anderson had told all his civilian laborers and waitstaff go except for one lone African American. He was not feeling heroic; he was terrified.

Captain Abner Doubleday

He was a spruce looking mulatto from Charleston, very active and efficient on ordinary occasion, but now completely demoralized by the thunder of the guns and crushing of the shot around us. He leaned back against the wall . . . with fear. His eyes closed and his whole expression one of perfect despair.

Doubleday wrote later in his diary that this was the only apprehensive African American he had met in his years in the service and told friends that African American troops he met later in the war were extremely courageous. He wrote that they had fought well in Texas and throughout the South.

After breakfast, the Union Army at Fort Sumter started their half of the war.

Captain Abner Doubleday

I took the first detachment and marched them out to the casements, which looked out upon the powerful iron-clad battery at Cummings Point.

In aiming the first gun fired against the rebellion, I had no feeling of self-reproach, for I fully believed that the contest was inevitable and was not of our seeking. The United States was called upon not only to defend its sovereignty, but its right to exist as a nation. The only alternative was to submit to a powerful oligarchy who were determined to make freedom forever subordinate to slavery. To me, it was a contest, politically speaking, as to [whether] virtue or vice would rule.

The Union's first efforts bore little fruit. Doubleday's shot, while well-aimed, did no damage to the enemy's battery, and neither did most of the other cannonballs.

Captain Abner Doubleday

It seemed useless to attempt to silence the guns there.

The battle became intense immediately.

Captain Abner Doubleday

The enemy had ventured out from their entrenchments to watch the effect of their fire, but I sent them flying back to their shelter by the aid of a forty-two-pounder ball, which appeared to strike right in among them.

All the Union soldiers scrambled to defend themselves. Even Wylie Crawford, the fort's surgeon, joined the fray. Crawford had no sick or wounded in his office, so he raced to Doubleday for instructions on how to help.

Captain Abner Doubleday

He and Lieutenant Davis were detailed at the same time with me; and I soon heard their guns on the opposite side of the fort, echoing my own. They attacked Fort Moultrie with great vigor.

By that time, the battle had fully commenced.

Captain Abner Doubleday

The firing now became regular and was answered by the rebel guns which encircled us on the four points of the pentagon upon which the fort was built. . . . Showers of balls from ten inch Columbiads and forty two pounder and shells from thirteen inch mortars poured into the fort in one incessant stream causing great flakes of masonry to fall in all directions. When the immense mortar shells, after sailing high in the air, came down in a vertical direction and buried themselves in the parade ground their explosion shook the fort like an earthquake.

The Union troops at Fort Sumter soon realized that the Southern cannons were superior to their own and that when construction of the fort began years before, its walls were designed for defense against small-bore guns, not the huge guns in use in 1861.

Captain Abner Doubleday

The balls from a new Blakely gun on Cummings Point, however, had force enough to go entirely through the wall which sheltered us, and some of the fragments of brick which were knocked out wounded several of my detachment.

The cannon fire was intense.

Captain Abner Doubleday

After three hours of firing, my men became exhausted and Captain Seymour came with a fresh detachment to relieve us. He has a great deal of humor in his composition and said, jocosely "Doubleday, what in the world is the matter here and what is all this uproar about?"

I replied, "There is a trifling difference of opinion between us and our neighbors opposite and we are trying to settle it."

The men had no assistance from the naval fleet that had recently arrived and was anchored at sea within sight of the fort.

Captain Abner Doubleday

It would have had considerable difficulty in finding the channel, as the marks and buoys had all been taken up.

The Navy was criticized later for not aiding the fort by dropping off its three hundred men and engaging Beauregard in a sea battle. Doubleday disagreed.

Captain Abner Doubleday

This course would probably have resulted in the sinking of every vessel.

In addition to that, mass confusion resulted in the ships of the squadron arriving on different days, so a planned attack by thirty small launches from one ship, covered by fire from the others, became impossible. There was no naval attack. The Powhatan, *in fact, never arrived. One ship arrived two days late and another had to put in to shore when it sailed into a storm.*

Captain Abner Doubleday

The expedition was thus an utter failure.

As the men turned their eyes back from the ships at anchor, helpless, they realized that the marksmen aiming the guns in the Confederate batteries were not very good.

Captain Abner Doubleday

A great many shots were aimed at our flagstaff but nearly all of them passed above the fort and struck in the water beyond. I think we succeeded in silencing several guns in Fort Moultrie, and one or more in the Stevens battery.

Several hours later, Doubleday, Anderson, and their men became frustrated by their lack of firepower.

Abner Doubleday

As our balls bounded off the sloping iron rails like peas upon a trencher, utterly failing to make any impression, and as the shot from the Blakely gun came clear through our walls, Anderson directed that the men should cease firing at that particular place.

I regretted very much that the upper tier of guns had been abandoned, as they were all loaded and pointed and were of very heavy caliber. A wild Irish soldier, however, named John Carmody, slipped up upon the parapet and, without orders, fired the pieces there, one after another, on his own account. One of the ten inch balls so aimed made quite an impression on the Cummings Point battery; and if the fire could have been kept up it might possibly have knocked the ironwork to pieces.

Doubleday, like many officers, thought of his clothes and supplies in his room, fearful that they would be lost.

Captain Abner Doubleday

Finding one of my chests had been left in the officers' quarters, and that it would probably be knocked to pieces by the shells, I asked the mulatto, who still sat back against the wall, apparently asleep, to bear a hand and help me bring it out. He opened his eyes, shook his head dolefully and said "the major, he say I must not expose myself."

The chests were never moved.

Captain Abner Doubleday

Our own guns were very defective, as they had no breech-sights. In place of these, Seymour and myself were obliged to devise notched sticks, which answered the purpose, but were necessarily very imperfect.

The battle roared around the Union soldiers.

Captain Abner Doubleday

The firing continued all day, without any special incident and without our making much impression on the enemy's works. They had a great advantage over us as their fire was concentrated on the fort which was in the center of the circle, while ours was diffused over the circumference. Their missiles were exceedingly destructive to the upper exposed portion of the work but no essential injury was done to the lower casemates which sheltered us.

Some of these shells, however, set the officers' quarters on fire three times; but the flames were promptly extinguished once or twice through the exertion of Peter Hart, whose activity and gallantry were very conspicuous.

There were fires everywhere outside and inside the fort.

Captain Abner Doubleday

The officers' quarters were ignited by one of the shells, or by shot heated in the furnace at Fort Moultrie. The fire was put out, but at 10 A.M. a mortar shell passed through the roof and lodged in the flooring of the second story where it hung and started the flames afresh. This, too, was extinguished but the hot shots soon followed each other so rapidly that it was impossible for us to contend with them any longer. It became evident that the entire block, being built with wooden partitions, floor and roofing, must be consumed and that the magazine, containing three hundred barrels of powder would be endangered for, even after closing the metallic door, sparks might penetrate through the ventilator. The floor was covered with loose powder where a detail of men had been at work manufacturing cartridge bags out of old shirts, woolen blankets, etc.

The labor [in the fort] was accelerated by the shells which were bursting around us for [Confederates] had redoubled [their] activity at the first sign of a conflagration. We only succeeded in getting out some ninety-six barrels of powder and then we were obliged to close the massive copper door.

The fires intensified as the morning went on.

Captain Abner Doubleday

By 11 A.M. on April 14, the conflagration was terrible and disastrous. One-fifth the fort was on fire and the wind drove the smoke in dense masses into the angle where we had all taken refuge. It seemed impossible to escape suffocation. Some lay down close to the ground with handkerchiefs over their mouths and others posted themselves near the embrasures where the smoke was somewhat lessened by the draught of air. Everyone suffered severely.

The resupply expedition? It never got there. Fox and his ships were a few miles away, plodding through a torrential rainstorm and difficult seas that had soaked the Charleston area on the previous evening. There was no help on the way. By early afternoon, the situation seemed both dangerous and hopeless to Anderson.

Major Anderson surrendered Fort Sumter at 2:30

◆

All day on April 11, Lincoln had been busy getting ready for war. He even asked Sam Houston, the governor of Texas and a former military hero, to take command of all US forces in the state on behalf of the federal government. Houston refused. At a Cabinet meeting that day, Attorney General Edmund Bates ruminated about what might happen.

Edmund Bates

If Major Anderson holds out . . . one of two things will happen—either the fort will be well provisioned, the Southrons forbearing to assail the boats, or the fierce contest will ensue, the result of which could not be foreseen.

No, it could not.

When Lincoln heard Sumter had been bombarded, he took quick and decisive action.

Abraham Lincoln

Now, therefore, I, Abraham Lincoln, President of the United States, by virtue of the power in me vested by the Constitution and the laws, have thought to call forth, and do call forth, the militia of the several states of the Union, to the aggregate number of 75,000 in order to suppress said combinations and to cause the laws to be duly executed.

But military veterans had no faith in the green troops of volunteers that marched to Washington.

William Tecumseh Sherman

Volunteers and militia never were and never will be fit for invasion, and when tried it will be defeated and dropt by Lincoln like a hot potato. . . . The time will come in this country when professional knowledge will be appreciated, when men that can be trusted will be wanted. I cannot and will not mix myself in this present call.

Some Northerners understood the South's position and supported it. One was the editor of the Bangor (Maine) Democrat. *Right after the troop call-up he wrote:*

Editor, *Bangor Democrat*

If I were a Southerner, as I am a northerner, while a foreign troop was landed in my country, I would never lay down my arms—never, never, NEVER.

In the days that followed the Fort Sumter shelling, the United States made one last plea to Colonel Robert E. Lee of Virginia to take charge of its forces. Lincoln had asked him to do so a week or so earlier and Lee had put him off, telling him that if Virginia seceded, he would have to fight with Virginia. His home state did not secede until April 17. A day or so before that, Lee was called to the office of Francis Blair Sr. and given a message from President Lincoln.

Francis Blair Sr.

I told him what President Lincoln wanted him to do, he wanted him to take command of the army. . . . He said he could not, under any circumstances, consent to supersede his old commander [General Scott]. He asked me if I supposed the President would consider that proper. I said yes. . . . The matter was talked over by President Lincoln and myself for some hours on two or three different occasions. The President and Secretary Cameron expressed themselves as anxious to give the command of our army to Robert E. Lee.

Then Virginia seceded and Lee left his mansion in Arlington, which overlooked the Potomac and Washington, D.C., and joined the Confederate Army. (Lee's estate became what today is Arlington National Cemetery.)

During those same few days, the president told his private secretary, John Hay, that force had to be used to hold the nation together. There was no question of it.

Abraham Lincoln

For my own part, I consider that the first necessity upon us is that proving that popular government is not an absurdity. We must settle this question now—whether in a free government the minority have the right to break it up whenever they choose. If we fail, it will go far to prove the incapability of the people to govern themselves.

At the same time that members of Lincoln's government were picking up the pieces of the Fort Sumter shelling, calling up troops and trying to reorganize the executive branch, many in the South were calling for an invasion of the North and the capture of the capital.

Editor, *Richmond Examiner*

There is one wild shout of fierce resolve to capture Washington City at all and every human hazard. The filthy cage of unclean birds must and will be purified by fire. . . . Our people can take it and Scott, the arch-traitor, and Lincoln, the Beast, combined cannot prevent it. The just indignation of an outraged and deeply injured people will teach the Illinois Ape to retrace his journey across the borders of the free Negro states still more rapidly than he came.

There was chaos in Washington, D.C. Congressman John Sherman wrote his brother, William Tecumseh Sherman, a letter chronicling the apprehensions in the nation's capital and gave him remarkably good advice—and made an amazingly accurate prediction for his brother's future.

Representative John Sherman, Ohio

The military excitement here is intense. Since my arrival, I have seen all the heads of departments except Blair, several officers and many citizens. There is a fixed determination now to preserve the Union and enforce the laws at all hazards. Civil War is actually upon us and, strange to say, it brings a feeling of relief; the suspense is over. I have spent much of the day in talking about you. There is an earnest desire that you go into the war department, but I said that this was impossible. Chase is especially desirous that you accept, saying that you would be virtually Secretary of War and easily step into any military position that offers.

It is well for you to seriously consider your conclusion, although my opinion is that you ought not to accept. You ought to hold yourself in reserve. If troops are called for, as they surely will be in a few days, organize a regiment or brigade either in St. Louis or Ohio, and you will then get into the army in such a way as to secure promotion. By all means, take advantage of the present disturbances to get into the army, where you will at once put yourself in a high position for life. I know that promotion and every facility for advancement will be cordially extended by the authorities. You are a favorite in the army and have great strength in political circles. I urge you to avail yourself of these favorable circumstances to assure your position for life, for, after all, your present employment is of uncertain tenure in these stirring times.

Let me record a prediction. Whatever you may think of the signs of the times, the government will rise from this strife greater, stronger and more prosperous than ever. It will display energy and military power. The men who have confidence in it and do their full duty by it may reap whatever there is of honor and profit in public life while those who look on merely as spectators in the storm will fail to discharge the highest duty of a citizen, and suffer accordingly in public estimation. . . .

I write this in a great hurry, with numbers around me and exciting and important intelligence constantly repeated, even at this hour; but I am none the less in earnest. I hope to hear that you are on the high road to "the General" within thirty days.

In the end, Major Anderson was pleased about the way Sumter was handled, he told Secretary of War John Holt six days after the shelling.

John Holt

He [Anderson] was satisfied all that had occurred was providential—that the course pursued had been the means of fixing the eyes of the nation on Sumter, and awakening to the last degree its anxieties for its fate; so that when it fell, its fall proved the instrument of arousing the national enthusiasm and loyalty, as we now see them displayed in the eager rush to maintain the honor of the flag.

Lincoln saw a cannon-battered silver lining in the fall of Fort Sumter.

Abraham Lincoln

They attacked Sumter. It fell—and thus did more service than it otherwise could.

John Sherman's final thoughts on the nation and his brother:

Representative John Sherman, Ohio

We are on the eve of a terrible war. Every man will have to choose his position. You fortunately have the military education, prominence and character that will enable you to play a high part in the tragedy. You can't avoid taking such a part. Neutrality and indifference are impossible. If the government is to be maintained, it must be by military power, and that immediately. You can choose your own place. Some of your best friends here want you in the war department; Taylor, Shiras and a number of others talk to me so. If you want that place, with a sure prospect of promotion, you can have it, but you are not compelled to take it, but it seems to me you will be compelled to take some position, and that speedily.

Can't you come to Ohio and at once raise a regiment? It will immediately be in service. The administration intends to stand or fall by the Union, the entire Union, and the enforcement of the laws. I look for preliminary defeats. For the rebels have arms, organization, unity, but this advantage will not last long. The government will maintain itself or our Northern people are the veriest poltroons that ever disgraced humanity.

For me, I am for a war that will establish or overthrow the government and will purify the atmosphere of political life.

We need such a war and we have it now.

TWENTY-TWO

Columbus, Ohio

April 12, 1861

Glory to God!

In Ohio, news of the fort's bombardment on April 12 was brought into the state legislative chamber by a panting state senator who had run as fast as he could from a nearby telegraph office.

State Senator, Yelling to the Chamber
The telegraph announces the secessionists are bombarding Fort Sumter.

The legislators were stunned by the news and few could even speak. Then a longtime fiery abolitionist preacher, Abby Kelley Foster, stood and raised her arms up to the heavens and shouted at the top of her lungs.

Abby Kelley Foster
Glory to God!

Sources

The following are among the books used to obtain the oral histories for this work.

Beale, Howard. *Diary of Gideon Welles, Secretary of the Navy Under Lincoln and Johnson.* Volume 1. New York: W. W. Norton and Co., 1960.

Burton, Milby E. *The Siege of Charleston: 1861–1865.* Columbia: University of South Carolina Press, 1970.

Chestnut, Mary Boykin. *A Diary from Dixie.* Boston: Houghton-Mifflin Company, 1949.

Clinton, Catherine. *Mrs. Lincoln: A Life.* New York: HarperCollins, 2009.

Current, Richard. *Lincoln and the First Shot.* Philadelphia: J. B. Lippincott Co., 1963.

Davis, William C. *Jefferson Davis: The Man and His Hour.* New York: HarperCollins, 1991.

Detzer, David. *Allegiance: Fort Sumter, Charleston and the Beginning of the Civil War.* New York: Harcourt, 2001.

Dickey, Christopher. *Our Man in Charleston: Britain's Secret Agent in the Civil War South.* New York: Crown Publishers, 2015.

Frederickson, George. *The Inner Civil War: Northern Intellectuals and the Crisis of the Union.* New York: Harper and Row, 1965.

Goodheart, Adam. *1861: The Civil War Awakening.* New York: Alfred Knopf, Jr., 2011.

Goodwin, Doris Kearns. *Team of Rivals: The Political Genius of Abraham Lincoln*, New York: Simon and Schuster, 2005.

Klein, Maury. *Days of Defiance: Sumter, Secession and the Coming of the Civil War.* New York: Alfred Knopf, 1997.

Long, E. B., and Barbara Long. *The Civil War: Day by Day. An Almanac, 1861–1865.* New York: DeCapo Paperback, 1985.

Miller, William. *Lincoln's Virtues: An Ethical Biography.* New York: Alfred Knopf, 2012.

Mitgang, Herbert. *Abraham Lincoln: A Press Portrait.* New York, Fordham University Press, 2000.

Murray, Jennifer M. *The Civil War Begins.* Washington, D.C.: Center of Military History, 2012.

Nevins, Allan. *The War for the Union.* New York: Charles Scribner's Sons, 1959.

Nicolay, Helen. *Personal Portraits of Abraham Lincoln*. New York: The Century Co., 1913.

Oates, Stephen. *With Malice Towards None: The Life of Abraham Lincoln*. New York: Harper and Row, 1977.

Shaw, Albert. *Abraham Lincoln: The Year of His Election*. New York: The Review of Reviews Corporation, 1929.

Simpson, Brooks, Stephen Sears, and Aaron Sheehan-Dean. *The Civil War: The First Year: Told by Those Who Lived it*. New York: Library of America, 2011.

Smith, George Winston, and Charles Judah. *Life in the North during the Civil War: A Source History*. Albuquerque: N.M.: University of New Mexico Press, 1966.

Stahr, Walter, *Seward: Lincoln's Indispensable Man*. New York: Simon & Schuster, 2012.

Starobin, Paul. *Madness Rules the Hour: Charleston, 1860 and the Mania for War*. New York: Public Affairs Press, 2017.

Van Deusen, Glyndon. *William Henry Seward: Lincoln's Secretary of State, the Negotiator of the Alaska Purchase*. New York: Oxford University Press, 1967.

The War of the Rebellion: Compilation of the Official Records of the Union and Confederate Armies. Series 1, Volume 28, Part Two—*Correspondence*. U.S. Government Printing Office, 1890.

The War of the Rebellion: Compilation of the Official Records of the Union and Confederate Armies. Series 1, Volume 72. U.S. Government Printing Office, 1889.

Ward, Evelyn. *The Children of Bladensfield*. New York: Sand Dune Press, 1978.

Wiley, Bell. *Johnny Reb: The Common Soldier of the Confederacy*. Baton Rouge: Louisiana State University Press, 1943.

Williams, T. Harry, Ed. *P. G. T. Beauregard: Napoleon in Gray*. Baton Rouge: Louisiana State University Press, 1954.

Woodward, C. Vann, and Elisabeth Mullenfeld. *The Private Mary Chestnut: The Unpublished Civil War Diaries*. New York: Oxford University Press, 1984.

Index